P9-CFE-286

Pleasures and Perils

THE RUTGERS SERIES IN CHILDHOOD STUDIES

The Rutgers Series in Childhood Studies is dedicated to increasing our understanding of children and childhoods, past and present, throughout the world. Children's voices and experiences are central. Authors come from a variety of fields, including anthropology, criminal justice, history, literature, psychology, religion, and sociology. The books in this series are intended for students, scholars, practitioners, and those who formulate policies that affect children's everyday lives and futures.

Edited by Myra Bluebond-Langner, Distinguished Professor of Anthropology, Rutgers University, Camden, and founding director of the Rutgers University Center for Children and Childhood Studies

Advisory Board
 Joan Jacobs Brumberg, Cornell University
 Perri Klass, New York University
 Jill Korbin, Case Western Reserve University
 Bambi Schiefflin, New York University
 Enid Schildkraut, American Museum of Natural History
  and Museum for African Art

Pleasures and Perils

GIRLS' SEXUALITY IN A CARIBBEAN CONSUMER CULTURE

DEBRA CURTIS

RUTGERS UNIVERSITY PRESS
New Brunswick, New Jersey, and London

LIBRARY OF CONGRESS CATALOGING-IN-PUBLICATION DATA

Curtis, Debra, 1963–
    Pleasures and perils : girls' sexuality in a Caribbean consumer culture/Debra
Curtis.
       p. cm.—(The Rutgers series in childhood studies)
    Includes bibliographical references and index.
    ISBN 978-0-8135-4429-8 (hardcover : alk. paper)
    ISBN 978-0-8135-4430-4 (pbk. : alk. paper)
    1. Girls—Sexual behavior—Nevis. 2. Sex—Social aspects—Nevis. 3. Sex in
popular culture—Nevis. 4. Girls—Attitudes—Nevis. I. Title.
    HQ27.5.C87 2009
    306.7082'0972973—dc22

                       2008013958

A British Cataloging-in-Publication record for this book is available
from the British Library.

Copyright © 2009 by Debra Curtis

All rights reserved

No part of this book may be reproduced or utilized in any form or by any means,
electronic or mechanical, or by any information storage and retrieval system, without
written permission from the publisher. Please contact Rutgers University Press, 100
Joyce Kilmer Avenue, Piscataway, NJ 08854–8099. The only exception to this prohibition
is "fair use" as defined by U.S. copyright law.

Lyrics from "Go Down" © Sylvester "King Socrates" Hodge. Used by permission.

Lyrics from "How Many Licks." Words and Music by Mario Winans, Kimberly Jones, and
Mark Andrews. © 2000 Urban Warfare Music, Mr. Yeah, Butter Jinx Music, Yellow Man
Music, M. Winans, Undeas Music, and Notorious K.I.M. Music. All rights for Urban
Warfare Music and Mr. Yeah controlled and administered by EMI April Music Inc. All
rights for Undeas Music and Notorious K.I.M. Music controlled and administered by
Warner-Tamerlane Publishing Corp. International Copyright secured. Used by permis-
sion of Alfred Publishing Co., Inc., Hal Leonard Corporation, and Dallas Austin
Recording Projects.

Visit our Web site: http://rutgerspress.rutgers.edu

Manufactured in the United States of America

To my Parents
Eula and Tom
and to Steve, Emma, and Zoe

Contents

ACKNOWLEDGMENTS

I BEGAN GRADUATE SCHOOL in 1994, earned a Ph.D. in 2006, and finished this book in the summer of 2007; so needless to say, my debts are long and deep. I have been fortunate to receive assistance, support, and guidance from many wonderful people in my life—all of whom made this work possible, including my professors at Rutgers University, my generous and good-spirited colleagues and students at Salve Regina University in Newport, Rhode Island, old and new friends, and my cherished family. I begin by acknowledging my dear Nevisian friends. I would like to give special thanks to Ruthie, Eleanor, and Felicia. While these certainly are not their real names, I am hoping somehow that these women will recognize themselves in these narratives and know how much their stories contributed to my understanding of Nevisian life. Ruthie and Eleanor shared their lives with me and continue to do so. Felicia, who is, as readers will see, mature beyond her years, took time out of her busy school schedule to meet with me and to share her experiences and thoughts about what it means to be a girl on Nevis and after I left Nevis, Felicia, who is now in college, corresponded with me at length via e-mail, helping to clarify particular issues and ideas. In order to protect my friends on Nevis, I cannot thank them by using their real names. Nevertheless, I remain deeply indebted to them. I would like to thank a number of public officials and as well, community members on Nevis who went out of their way to assist my research efforts. These kindhearted people include Larry Richards, Vince Hubbard, Dr. Singh, Dr. Dias, Dr. Jacobs, Ermine Leader, Charmaine Howell, Andrea Nisbett, Mrs. Jones, Mrs. Morton, Mrs. Hodge, Mr. Liburd, Allison Hill, Joan Robinson, and the Yearwood family. While living on Nevis, I had the opportunity to meet the Sinclair family, especially Tori, whose companionship and generous hospitality made a difference in the quality of my research efforts. I must also thank Dr. Adly Meguid. In 2002, we sat down to a meal at his beautiful Mount Nevis hotel. It was during our long conversation that I knew for certain that I would return to Nevis to conduct my fieldwork.

My friends from graduate school, Becca Etz, Andy Bickford, Sabrina Chase, Sean Hoffman, and in particular, Edgar Rivera Colon and Paige West, both of whom read parts, if not all of the manuscript, are owed an immense amount of gratitude. An award from the National Science Foundation supported my fieldwork, but without the assistance and guidance from Teresa M. Delcorso at Rutgers I would not have been successful in obtaining funding. Constance Sutton and R. T. Smith both offered incredibly useful feedback on the nature of the project. I also want to thank Alan and Nancy Rushton for their friendship and guidance. Two professors from my graduate program at Rutgers, Michael Moffatt and Marc Manganaro, have my respect and gratitude. I learned a great deal from both individuals as a graduate student. I am also immensely grateful to my students at Salve Regina, who have listened enthusiastically to my stories about Nevis, all the while offering me useful suggestions. I want to thank Justine Axelsson, Stephanie Barrante, Bianca Brunelli, Sophie Hemmerdinger, Matilda Mutanguha, Caitlin McCurn, Michelle Quinn, Jason Robinson, Bridget Sheerin, Jamie Socci, Michelle Styger, Ian Kerr, Romana Manzoor, Hector Sevillano, and Ellen Stracensky.

In 1981, as a college student, I met Fred Errington, who quite frankly changed my life and inspired me to become an anthropologist. Over the years, Fred and Deborah Gewertz, both of whom have become dear and constant friends, have offered me an endless amount of support. When I was in graduate school, they read my research proposals, parts of my dissertation, the letters I sent to editors, a book prospectus, and eventually the manuscript for this book. Each time I reached out to them with yet another request, another favor, they never refused me, often getting back to me within days if not hours. Without them, this book would not have been published. It is as simple and as honest as that.

While at Rutgers I worked closely with Louisa Schein, Fran Mascia-Lees, Peter Guarnaccia, and Bruce Robbins. I have great respect for their commitment to scholarship, their professionalism, and their intellectual gifts. Fran Mascia-Lees offered penetrating and detailed remarks that refined my argument. She knew exactly what it was that I was trying to convey and helped me to express it. Peter Guarnaccia taught me what it means to be a compassionate intellectual. While conducting fieldwork and during the writing phase, I tried to model myself after Dr. Guarnaccia. I was very lucky to have had the opportunity to take graduate classes with Bruce Robbins who exposed me to a broad range of theoretical perspectives. In his seminars, Professor Robbins cultivated a challenging and exciting classroom environment, where I could not help but want to be a better student. And then, there is Louisa Schein, my former adviser whose brilliance is extraordinary. I have benefited tremendously from her talent and craft.

It gives me great pleasure to thank Adi Hovav, Myra Bluebond-Langner, and three reviewers for their rich critiques and generosity. Adi and Myra have been wonderfully supportive from the start. In many ways, they were the first to recognize the significance of this research on Nevisian girls and sexuality.

I was thrilled to learn the identities of two of the reviewers—Don Kulick and Richard Parker, both of whom have shaped my intellectual commitment to sexuality studies over the past thirteen years. I also have a long list of other anthropologists and scholars who I would like to recognize whose work has influenced me over the years. For inspiration I turn to the works of Roger Lancaster, Sidney Mintz, Gayle Rubin, Carol Vance, Fernando Coronil, Philippe Bourgois, Lila Abu-Lughod, Paul Farmer, Asad Talal, Clifford Geertz, Henrietta Moore, David Harvey, Nancy Scheper-Hughes, and Arthur Kleinman.

I very much appreciate the contribution that the Administration of Salve Regina has made to my research. I was able to take time off from Salve Regina for my fieldwork and was welcomed back with open arms and was able to resume my teaching as if I had never left. Special thanks to Sisters Therese Antone and Leona Misto, Stephen Trainor, and Dean de la Motte. The librarians at Salve Regina have been nothing short of wonderful. I appreciate and have benefited from the expertise of Christine Bagley, Joe Foley, and Cathy Rowe. Brian McDonnell and Dan Titus have always been willing to drop everything that they are doing to offer me technical support. I also want to thank my friends and colleagues at Salve Regina especially, Allen Antone, George Antone, Camille Allen, Paula Bolduc, Jane Bethune, Barbara Coleman, Jim Garman, Art Frankel, Steve Jeffrey, Barbara Kathe, Khalil Habib, Jim Hersh, Robin Hoffman, Tim Neary, Sheila Quinn, Mary Sokolowski, Tony Walsh, and Catherine Zipf—all of whom have helped me through this process in immeasurable ways, providing not only intellectual companionship but the kind of honest friendship that kept me going through the writing process. Jim Garman, Mary Sokolowski and Art Frankel deserve special recognition. Jim's fine sense of humor and critical engagement were always timely and helped move this project along. At each critical juncture throughout this process, Jim offered sound advice and guidance. Mary Sokolowski meticulously edited many versions of this project. I greatly admire her finely-honed writing abilities. I owe a great deal to Art Frankel, who was my key interlocutor. I am grateful for the long hours we spent discussing this project. Some of the most interesting parts of this book, assuming that there may be, are the result of his creative and intellectual insights. Art edited the entire manuscript in its final stages and his recommendations were enormously beneficial.

A special thanks is reserved for Leila de Bruyne or Big Leila, as she is affectionately called, who in the summer of 2007, weeks before my final deadline, read the entire manuscript and offered invaluable critiques. To her daughter, also named Leila de Bruyne, I am indebted as well. Leila, who is one of my former students, ended up teaching me more than I could ever have anticipated. She came into my life and into the lives of my family members and shared with us with her unbounded generosity and spirit. The work she does in Kenya with children is nothing short of inspirational.

I acknowledge my friends Stacey Alzaibak, Jane Bensal, Nancy Blodgett, Dawn Hale, Paige Goulart, Tanya Sergey, Candy Frankel, Erin McCormick, Roy King, Tom Perrotti, Whitney Peckham, Trish Sheehan, Kristin Poselli, Beth Ethier, Michael Murray, Sharon Dyer, and Gail Thorpe-Yates as well as my sisters Ellen Estrella, Tish Behan, and Jeanne Murray, and my nephew Dan Murray for their ongoing encouragement and support. My mother, Eulalia Curtis and my father, Thomas Curtis provided me with a foundation that sustains me today.

My beloved twin daughters Emma and Zoe were four when they moved to Nevis and were nine when I finally finished this project. Twenty years ago, I thought I wanted to be an anthropologist because I was convinced that it would make me become a better person, a more tolerant and more compassionate person with a sense of purpose. One day Emma and Zoe will understand how their presence in my life keeps me focused on that vision. Lastly, my greatest appreciation is reserved for my husband Steve, whose generous spirit and strength have never failed me. I borrowed his courage and he has kept me safe, happy, and healthy. This project is for him, my loving parents, and my amazingly divine daughters, Emma and Zoe.

Pleasures and Perils

CHAPTER 1

Introduction

THIS BOOK is about sex, sexuality, and teenage girls living on Nevis, a small English-speaking island in the Eastern Caribbean. It could be said that this work began when my interests in the field of public health gave way to a theoretical curiosity about specific cultural practices, such as the way public policy regulates intimate pleasures and how consumer culture might compete with the state's efforts to regulate sexuality. Fascinated by questions that explore the conjunction of the public and private spheres of sexuality, I began graduate study in anthropology. I was certain then that it was the only discipline that could help me thoroughly investigate the production of sexuality.

As for the Caribbean, I was first drawn there by my father. I had always known that he traveled to the Caribbean as a boat captain or as a tourist. But in the late eighties, I discovered that he had also been an amateur ethnographer as well when I came upon an audiotape he had made recording his observations of cultural life on one of the smaller Leeward islands. His interest in Caribbean societies sparked my own.

Later, after having begun my graduate work in anthropology, I had two memorable conversations that eventually pointed me in the direction of Nevis. The first was with a pediatrician who spoke to me at length one snowy winter night over dinner about his experiences on Nevis. He painted a picture much like my father's description of a neighboring island, namely, one of a vibrant society caught up in rapid changes as the result of globalization. The second conversation took place with an eminent Caribbeanist anthropologist about whether the study of sexuality in the West Indies was worthwhile; he tried to persuade me that while the contemporary fascination with the study of sexualities was fashionable, general interest in the subject would wane. Likening it to fashion, he explained that studies of sex would simply go out of style. I somehow felt as if a challenge had been issued. And so, in the winter of 2003, I traveled to Nevis and began my fieldwork.

I arrived in January. Soon after my arrival, I was scheduled to meet with a group of older girls in the public school in Charlestown. My daughters' preschool was closed for the day, so I decided to bring them with me into the secondary schools. Leaving our small village and turning onto the newly paved road that led to town, I was forced to drive slowly behind a herd of goats crossing a narrow road. After the last few stragglers managed to join the herd in the pasture, I sped up only to be delayed again by another driver, who had stopped in the middle of the road to speak with a schoolgirl. After what seemed like several minutes, the schoolgirl opened the passenger door and slid into the car.

We arrived at the school just after morning assembly had started. Most of the student body was gathered inside the large open-air auditorium; my daughters and I stood outside on the lawn watching the assembly with some of the female teachers and a guidance counselor. There were five male teachers standing apart from the students on the grass; their heads were bowed and their hands were clasped behind their backs as they assumed a relaxed "military" position. Two young girls stood directly in front of me, holding hands. They looked to be about thirteen years old. Dressed neatly in their blue jumpers and white shirts and wearing pretty blue ribbons in their hair, the girls focused their attention on the Methodist minister leading the student body in a regular Friday morning devotional. The girls' hands, loosely laced together, fell apart as one of the girls reached into her backpack and pulled out a pocket-size Bible. The minister instructed the students to open their Bibles. As if rehearsed, the student body, almost in perfect unison, recited a passage from the book of Luke.

After the morning assembly, the guidance counselor led me to a classroom with my daughters in tow. When we entered the classroom, she informed six girls that they would be taking a survey. The boys in the class gathered in a circle near the open windows. Some of the desks were turned upside down. With the exception of one poster promoting safe sex practices, the walls were bare and sounds of the students' voices reverberated off the concrete interior. I set the twins up with their crayons and Barbie dolls and proceeded to address the girls. Five of the girls were neatly dressed and sitting upright at their desks. But one of the older girls caught my attention. She stared at me blankly. Her skirt was on backward and unzipped and her white shirttails hung over her skirt covering what otherwise would have been her exposed belly. She sat with her legs spread open. Her pleated skirt, which draped between her legs, prevented her panties from being fully exposed. She sat silently and refused to fill out the survey. This girl stood out because her posture and body language, which signaled disobedience and defiance, was so unlike other girls her age whom I had met. Meanwhile, one of the boys asked for a copy of the survey, which I handed to him. He was a big boy, whose shirttails had come out, and he was wearing a chunky gold necklace around his forehead like a crown. I watched as he flipped through the pages of the survey and then proceeded to read some of the questions aloud. Rather than asking me for clarification, one of the girls walked past me to the group of boys. Bending over the boy who had been handed the survey, she quietly asked him a question about the survey. Within minutes the boy called me over and reported that "De girl was lyin' on de survey." He pointed to the girl and to the boy on his right and said, "See dat girl; she suckin' dis guy's dick just last night. He her boyfriend." The grinning boyfriend looked up and said, "Dat right, yeaaah." By then all the boys were laughing. Another boy yelled something about a "pre-cum" stain on his friend's pants. After collecting the surveys, a girl, who appeared to be about sixteen, asked if a boy could be allergic to condoms. Although I had only been on Nevis for a few weeks at the time, two other girls had brought this issue to my attention, namely, that their boyfriends refused to use condoms because they were supposedly allergic. Addressing my comments to the girls, I explained that some condoms are manufactured out of latex and while latex allergies do exist, they are not common and that perhaps the boy had other reasons for not wanting to use condoms. Overhearing my explanation, the boys near the windows howled with laughter.

By now, my daughters had grown restless, and I realized that the handful of girls who were willing to fill out the survey, had finished. The girl with the unzipped skirt had left her desk and gone over to an open window and was speaking to another girl with whom I had spent time, fifteen-year-old Jasmine. When Jasmine saw me, she shouted out my name and held out her arms. The other girl appeared surprised and for the first time I heard her speak. "Jasmine, how you know dis white lady? How you know her?" I waved to Jasmine and then eavesdropped as she explained to her suspicious schoolmate that I was writing a book about girls on Nevis. In that moment, I could not help but wonder if I had gained some credibility with the girl based on my association with Jasmine.

A few minutes later as my daughters and I were preparing to leave the school grounds, I noticed a huge, new SUV drive up the hill and approach the gate to the schoolyard. As it slowed down, I recognized the driver—a well-dressed, handsome man who appeared to be in his early forties, someone with whom I met socially, albeit briefly, at a friend's house. When the passenger door opened, a tall attractive teenage girl, who looked to be about sixteen years old, stepped out. I was unaware that the driver, the man whom I had met, had a teenage daughter. As she walked past a group of girls at a small picnic table, they began to whisper and snicker. I assumed that the girl was the target of jealousy and gossip because she was attractive and came from a wealthy family. Weeks later, I learned that the driver of the SUV was not the girl's father, but rather her wealthy, and married, boyfriend.

The very next morning, after I dropped my daughters off at school, I met with a representative from the local credit union to gather data on consumer loans and then headed over to the government office to collect statistics and information on housing and road construction. Before long, I was involved in a lengthy discussion concerning my research project with one of the inspectors, a woman in her late twenties. Gina leaned over to offer advice saying, "It's the boys and the men you should be studying. There's the problem. The men take advantage of the girls sexually. They promise them jewelry and things. . . . You've heard the saying, 'Twelve is lunchtime'?" As I reached across the desk to grab a pen and slip of paper, Gina tugged at my wrist preventing me from writing. "Don't worry," she said, "You'll hear it soon enough." I pressed her for details. "What does it mean?" I inquired. "You know, when a girl turns twelve she's fair game." I understood Gina's explanation. I explained to her that a comparative expression used by American youth is, "When there's grass on the field, play ball." Gina looked at me in earnest and said, "There's something else you should know; fathers think that they have to *have* their daughters first."

WHAT THIS BOOK IS ABOUT

My conversation with Gina and the scenes I witnessed at the school and on the way to the school raised a number of questions, and it is these questions that form the central focus of inquiry in this book. How, for instance, does a society that appears to be highly religious and pious, tolerate sexual permissiveness and the type of sexual unruliness displayed in a typical secondary-school classroom? How do public health messages about condom use and safe sex challenge the established Nevisian sexual norms? What is the nature of the relationships that girls experience with older men? Are these relationships inherently exploitative and detrimental? Are these teenage girls helpless victims, coming-of-age in a society where girls are sexualized and pursued by powerful older men? Do these schoolgirls have any control over their lives and are there ever moments when the girls are acting "freely," making their own decisions about sex? What is the connection between the teenage girls' sexual practices and economic development on Nevis? Why, in other words, would I, as an anthropologist, need to collect data on housing, construction, and consumer loans? Is sexuality tied to economics? Are the girls' sexual desires and practices influenced by consumer culture? Are girls trading sexual favors for jewelry and for other expensive goods? What about the issue of incest? Is it common? Is sexual coercion an aspect of the girls' coming-of-age experiences that requires consideration?

This ethnography will address these questions in order to examine adolescent sexualities among a group of girls living on Nevis. Such a study of adolescent sexualities is of utmost importance in a globalizing world because it is the site of two important conjunctions: between the local and the global, on the one hand, and the family and society, on the other hand. Like Margaret Mead, who, in *Coming of Age in Samoa* (1967), focused on the lives of girls on a small island society, I had similarly decided to focus almost exclusively on the girls living on Nevis. Mead rejected the assumption that adolescence is solely shaped by biological influences and thus universally experienced as a time of rebellion and strife. Following in Mead's intellectual footsteps, I also understand adolescence as culturally determined. However, while Mead rejected the notion of a universal adolescent experience, I am willing to entertain the possibility that, given the impact of globalization, there might be commonalities among youth around the world. Mead was not writing at a time of widespread use of, and desire for, cable television via satellite, the Internet, music videos, and international teen magazines. This is not to say that teens everywhere have equal access to these services and goods, but rather that globally mediated images, sexual scripts, and commodities may incite new shared subjectivities.

To tell the story of how these global influences are reshaping Nevisian girls' sexual subjectivities in a local cultural context, I also pay attention to what goes on in private. It is critical to question how some of the seemingly most intimate aspects of the coming-of-age process, namely, sexual practices and desires, are expressions of the distribution of power. In the pages that follow, I analyze how sexuality is a social and economic product capable of changing and varying within a culture and across a subject's lifetime, demonstrating its fluidity and malleability. I also examine sexual agency by paying attention to what girls actually do, and thus how girls themselves reproduce or influence sexual norms and practices. Finally, in order to understand the links between consumer culture and the production of sexualities, I investigate the practices of sexual-economic exchange through which girls trade sex, consciously or not, for access to goods and services. In short, I look at the ways sexuality is a domain of multiple contradictions: a locus of both power and powerlessness, of self-determination and cultural control.

Constructing Sexualities, Inventing Sexual Practices

There is a long history of anthropological literature on adolescent sexuality.[1] Fundamental contributions were made at the turn of the twentieth century by Bronislaw Malinowski and Margaret Mead whose early research not only provides cross-cultural ethnographic data on childhood and adolescent sexuality, but also contributes to the contemporary understanding of sexuality as culturally constructed and as learned within specific historical contexts.[2] But if ideas and beliefs about sex and sexuality are invented or manufactured, does this mean that sexual desires are also socially manufactured? Does this mean that what people find erotic is culturally produced? Put simply, yes. What appears to be sexually taboo or off-limits in one society or at one point in time may be permissible in another society or at another point in time. For example, on Nevis, when some older women recalled their early sexual experiences they often explained that performing fellatio was unimaginable. It was not that fellatio was considered repulsive or unpleasant, but rather that performing oral sex was simply not within their frame of reference nor was it expected of them. By contrast, on Nevis today, performing fellatio appeared to be a popular sexual practice among Nevisian girls.

Over the past decade girls on Nevis have *learned* about fellatio much in the same way girls learn about other cultural practices. In some instances, they learned about fellatio as a sex act from their girlfriends, older siblings, boyfriends, or parents. Girls were also exposed to references about fellatio from song lyrics or music videos. Some girls consumed imported pornography videos that depict images of fellatio; others viewed pornography on the Internet. The proliferation of these images and the cultural references to fellatio encouraged girls to consider it to be a common and socially acceptable sexual activity. However, while the cultural references to fellatio have increased and as it appeared to have gained popularity as a sex act, some of the younger girls I interviewed expressed some hesitancy about performing oral sex. While working in small groups with the girls, I was frequently asked questions that exposed the girls' ambivalence: "Is oral sex bad?" and "Can you get sick from swallowing cum?"

To suggest that sex and sexual practices are learned implies that there are rules about who is eligible to be a sexual partner and which sex acts are permissible and which are taboo. But even more fascinating to me is the possibility that the culturally constructed nature of sexuality also indicates that we learn the meaning of internal states as well, for instance, what we find pleasurable and what we experience as erotic. To make this argument, many anthropologists point to cross-cultural examples of the erotic, such as Chinese foot binding. For some men living in China, in past centuries, unwrapping a bound foot and the accompanying sights and smells were sexually exciting. This visceral response that men experienced, however erotic, is a learned response. I prefer, however, to look at a more contemporary example of erotic sensibilities and one that is closer to home.

In *Times Square Red, Times Square Blue* (1999), the social critic Samuel Delany describes just such an instance of learned sexual response at the level of an entire culture. Describing the advent of commercial porn theaters in New York in the 1970s, Delany writes, "Without intending to be, these movies represented a tremendous sexual education for their working-class audience— in the case of New York City, mostly Hispanic, black, and Catholic white" (78). Delany explains in great detail that during the first two years the theaters were open, the audience would "break out laughing" at pornographic scenes that depicted fellatio or cunnilingus. He recounts how audience members verbalized their disgust, making sounds like "Uhggggg," whenever oral sex was portrayed. However, times and cultural preferences changed, as Delany notes, and by the early eighties, whenever fellatio or cunnilingus were depicted, the noises, laughter, and displays of revulsion in the movie theaters ceased. Delany argues, "under pressure of those films many guys simply found themselves changing what turned them on" (78). In other words, as the cultural meaning of oral sex changed, men learned to view it or recognize it as an erotic experience. My point is not that people in New York City or in the rest of the United States were not engaging in forms of oral sex prior to the influence of the commercial porn industry, but rather that fellatio and cunnilingus became a part of the dominant and accepted sexual repertoire in large part because of the widespread consumption of pornography.

This perspective on sexuality, namely, that sexuality is culturally learned, makes it possible to study the social structures and cultural processes that influence a Nevisian girl's sexual practices and desires. In addition, this framework allows us to investigate how girls reproduce and/or change sexual cultures. Viewing sexuality as contingent upon, and produced within, a particular historical setting raises a host of questions about the production of sexuality and how it is shaped by cultural formations: How, for example, are girls' intimate practices and sexual experiences structured by Nevisian culture? What are the rules and practices that produce girls' sexualities on Nevis? How do the social and economic structures that shape sexual systems and norms become internalized by girls?[3]

This line of questioning brings into focus my understanding of *sexual subjectivity*, a term used to capture the dynamic interaction between culture and the individual. Anthropologists who research sexuality need to pay attention to the way individuals attempt to craft their sexual lives within particular social structures (Curtis 2004, 96). Therefore, it is necessary that we view what some anthropologists refer to as "agency," the ability to intentionally or unintentionally craft one's life, within the context of cultural constraints and opportunities. Anthropology has never reconciled the slippage between the use of concepts and phrases like "agency," "self-constitution," or what Stuart Hall (1996) refers to as the way individuals deliberately practice self-production (13). I use these concepts interchangeably throughout the text to refer to the way girls act in a deliberative manner to produce certain outcomes, whether or not they are conscious of the social constraints that have determined those outcomes.[4] The idea that individuals have agency or that they constitute their lives does not mean that there is an absence of social influences; but rather, anthropologists use the concept of "agency" to talk about the way, to borrow a phrase from Sherry Ortner (2006), "people (try to) act upon the world even as they are acted upon" (110).[5]

In my attempt to ethnographically research girls' sexual subjectivities on Nevis, I use another important concept—discourse—that allows me to think about how the way the girls' daily lives are shaped by larger cultural processes. In the past, anthropologists just like sociologists, used concepts such as "social norms" or "customs" as a means of referring to social rules and expectations; however, the concept of "social norms" and "customs," at least historically, did not invoke a dimension of power. While social norms were thought of as a way of shaping behavior and thus were considered a means of social control and constraint, the concept of discourse, however, allows us to examine how power saturates relationships on an everyday basis.[6]

For French intellectual Michel Foucault (1982), "discourse" refers to a collection of statements about a given subject—statements that are produced by experts or by individuals in power. These statements, in turn, comprise a body of knowledge about a given subject. Relative to sexuality, a body of knowledge, as conceptualized by Foucault, can be thought of as *that which can be spoken at any given moment*. In order to understand the impact of these statements, we need to consider the way these statements or, more precisely, *discourses* on sexuality act not only prescriptively, defining how sexuality is talked about, but also proscriptively, structuring intimate practices and experiences. In other words, discourses on sexuality control what is allowed and what is not allowed to be said about sex and furthermore, assign value or significance to sexual practices. For example, within Nevisian society the local discourse on sexuality does not promote female sexual pleasure. Certain sexual practices that maximize male pleasure are more highly regarded than those that might offer the possibility for female pleasure. Discourses such as this reflect a sort of collective understanding of sexuality, defining what is even considered to be "sex," deeming which sexual acts are allowed and which are desirable, and setting forth the rules and expectations associated with sexual behavior. When we use the concept of discourse to understand sexuality, we realize that all sexual practices, even the most passionate and spontaneous sexual encounters, are learned and highly scripted.

Taken together, this theoretical understanding of sexuality involves exploring the complex relationship between sexual practices (what people do); the effects of sexual discourse (how people recognize a repertoire of sexual acts, as well as a set of rules and expectations surrounding those acts); and social and economic structures (what kind of world they inhabit).[7] These practices, discourses, and structures are dynamic, particularly in a global world where agents with different scripts engage one another and where structures with different degrees of power collide and conjoin, making the global context of sexuality an important component of analysis.

GLOBALIZATION AND SEXUALITIES

So what exactly is the global context of Nevisian girls' sexualities? In order to get at this question, which considers the relationship between the girls' sexualities and the global cultural economy, it makes sense to first look briefly at how the Nevisian economy has been impacted by globalization in the past two decades.

The economy of Nevis is determined by both its present position within the international economic order as well as past historical circumstances (Kairi 2001, 167). From its colonial history up until the 1990s there were limited opportunities for employment on Nevis. In the past fifteen years, the island's economy has improved through increasing dependence upon tourism and the offshore banking industry. In addition to the growing number of jobs in the tourism sector, the construction industry has also grown with the construction of new hotels and tourist sites. The gross domestic product (GDP) has increased from U.S. $48 million in 1980 to U.S. $339 million in 2003.[8] For my purposes, the GDP of Nevis is an indicator of its economic growth over the past twenty-three years and less of an indicator of the standard of living on Nevis. In other words, the GDP is a measure of the size of the economy, not an indicator of the quality of life on Nevis. In part, the GDP is an expression of both private (consumer) and public (government) consumption. In terms of private consumption, the GDP factors in consumer expenditures is related to food, clothes, household products, and services. Government consumption includes expenditures on goods and services as well as on the salaries of public servants and funds allocated for law enforcement, health care, and education. Yet, despite this overall improvement in the Nevisian economy, the standard of living for individual Nevisians still remains low, and high poverty levels persist. Furthermore, despite growth in some sectors, the Nevisian economy remains unstable. Nevis has an overwhelming foreign debt payment— 170 percent of the current GDP—which negatively impacts domestic expenditures, including that which is spent on health and education programs.[9] Due to its dependence on tourism, the Nevisian economy has also experienced setbacks resulting from three major hurricanes in the 1990s as well as from the global decline in tourism subsequent to 9/11.

So, what is the connection between Nevisian girls' sexual practices and the Nevisian economy? The dynamic relationship between sexualities and economies has been taken up by a number of anthropologists.[10] What we learn from their work is to consider sexualities as embedded in economic systems, rather than as strictly determined by the economy. Of even greater significance, however, is that while sexuality is indeed embedded in economic systems, it has influences of its own, impacting economies as well as the activities of global markets. For example, it would be too simplistic to assert that even though many Nevisian girls still live in impoverished conditions, financial necessity has pushed them into sexual relationships with older men. The notion that sexuality and economics are mutually constitutive requires a more nuanced analysis. For instance, if there is an increase in consumer spending, as indicated by the growth of Nevis' GDP over time, then it would seem that factors related to consumption—the meaning of goods and services and the role that consumption plays in the production of lifestyles—would play a greater role in the everyday lives of Nevisians, impacting Nevisian society and social relationships, including the nature of sexual relationships.[11] As the result of a global youth culture, Nevisian teenagers are convinced that they are entitled to certain goods. Such expectations, fueled by popular media, incite consumer desires. But even more interestingly, these consumer desires interact with sexual desires, remaking the very nature of sexual relationships among Nevisians. Within Nevisian society, consumer culture has become a part of the social context in which sexuality and economics constitute each other.[12]

What else can be said about the relationship between sexuality, globalization, and consumer culture? The notion that all societies establish norms, discourses and expectations regarding sexual behavior is widely accepted among anthropologists and human sexuality experts alike. In the past fifteen years, as a result of the increased effects of globalization, anthropologists have begun to focus on the idea that while all societies have dominant sexual norms and discourses, competing sexual subcultures can coexist simultaneously.[13] In today's world, sexual forms, practices and desires, while geographically and historically diverse, are never completely disengaged from global influences.[14]

Many scholars are turning their attention to the way contemporary global influences interact with local cultures.[15] Some of the newer studies suggest the need to consider how global products, such as mass media, represent significant sites for understanding how sexuality and sexual meanings are produced. In other words, anthropologists have now started to explore how representations and images of sexuality in the media, such as pornographic films or music videos, are influencing the way individuals act sexually.[16] However, despite these theoretical interventions, which encourage dynamic viewpoints from which to conceive globalization and sexuality studies, I would argue that the majority of ethnographies of sexuality continue to come up short in terms of interrogating the interaction between globalization, consumer culture, and sexuality. I plan to argue that in order to understand Nevisian girls' lives in all of their complexity, the focus must remain on the very confluence of commodities, commodity desire, and mass media scripts, and the means by which these global flows interact with each other to shape sexual practices and desires.[17]

COMMODITY EROTICS

Intrigued by the relationship between commodity desires and sexual practices, I ask: "How might the desire produced by the market be intricately linked to the formation and negotiation of sexual subjectivity?" (Curtis 2004, 95)[18] Thus, one objective of this project is to explore the relationship between sexuality and economics by focusing on the pattern of sexual-economic exchange in which the girls on Nevis are engaged.[19] I am particularly interested in the exchange of sex for goods and services. Are there instances when economics (goods, services, and capital) compel sexuality (practices, desires and pleasures) and, conversely, are there instances when sexuality compels economics? The phrase "commodity erotics," allows me to explore both sides of the sexual-economic exchange equation.[20] In order to develop more fully the meaning of "commodity erotics," I turn my attention first to the more familiar and recognizable concepts of fetishism and commodity fetish; illuminating their differences helps to expose the relationship of sexuality to economy.

Fetishism has long been an idea that was used in order to understand the relationship between desires and material objects. It has been viewed as a perversion and a component of primitive religions (Apter 1993, 1). Sigmund Freud uses fetish in *The Three Essays* (2000) to explain sexual practices that deviate from what were considered normative sexual practices. In general terms, fetishism involves an item becoming associated with sexual arousal through a process of disavowal, specifically a young boy's refusal to acknowledge his mother's "castration." The Freudian conception of fetishism suggests that sexual arousal or desire is intricately tied to a *particular* object. This view forecloses the possibility of the erotic as more diffused.

If Freud's sexual fetish overemphasizes the link between a specific object and arousal, Karl Marx's "commodity fetish" ignores sexualities, bodies, and pleasures. Marx uses "commodity fetish" to refer to the mysteries of commodity exchange, more specifically, the way people become attached to goods and the way this attachment elides the relations of production that produce the commodities. Just as the sexual fetish involves disavowal of the reality of the female body according to Freud, so Marx's commodity fetish disavows the social relations of production. Insofar as Marx suggests that commodities are seductive and magical, his use of sexuality is metaphoric and not to be understood as a literal seduction. What is literal for Marx is the way commodity exchange transforms social awareness to the extent that "things" (goods and services) instruct social relations. Although the use of commodity fetish has proven to be productive in understanding how the dynamics and logics of capitalism structure human subjectivity (cf. Pietz 1993; Taussig 1980), its usefulness for understanding how commodities might affect sexual subjectivity is limited. This is because Marx's concept of "commodity fetish" does not account for the mutually constitutive relationship between sexuality and economy.

How are we to understand the commingling of sexualities and economics? In other words, how might commodities compel individuals' desires, thus affecting sexuality? Wolfgang Haug's (1996) critique of capitalism comes close to addressing these queries by offering a classic treatment of commodity aesthetics in capitalism. According to Haug, advertising relies on sexuality to transform commodities for the purposes of increasing their appearance of use-value, thus creating greater mass appeal and a greater exchange value. Haug writes, "Commodities borrow their aesthetic language from human courtship; but then the relationship is reversed and people borrow their aesthetic expression from the world of the commodity" (19), that is, from advertising. Here Haug creates a theoretical space to explore how commodities shape sexual experiences and, conversely, how sexual practice and desire might affect commodity desire and consumption.

If Haug is focused on "commodity aesthetics," I focus on "commodity erotics," a term Louisa Schein (1999) introduced in her comparative analysis of Cargo cults and Chinese consumerism. Schein (2003) revisited the concept in a study of masculinity, media, and transnationality within the Hmong diaspora to conceptualize the eroticization of commodities as a way of extending the erotic beyond the scope and limits of corporeal pleasures of genital activity (21). In the case between a Hmong/Miao woman and her Hmong man from America, the domain of the erotic becomes diffused (21); thus the "accompanying erotics would incorporate the scope of the physical pleasures accessed through a liaison with a suitor from the West—delectable foods, accoutrements such as jewelry and clothing for beautifying the body, liberation from rural labor and a reveling in plush comforts such as carpeted hotel rooms or residences with running water" (21). This leads Schein to propose that "we think of such corporeal pleasures as within the scope of erotics, not as other pleasures acquired by trading in one's sexual body" (21).

Similarly, writing about the proliferation of transnational commodities and media scripts with a particular focus on advertising in India, Purnima Mankekar (2004) theorizes the "conjunction between erotic desire and the desire to consume" (408). Here she identifies what she calls "commodity affect" (408), defining it as "a range of emotions evoked and constructed by the desire for commodities, some of which are suffused with erotics" (408). In other words, Mankekar is trying to understand the attraction to material goods by demonstrating how goods become infused with erotic significance and how the desire for commodities can itself be an erotic experience.[21]

These original formulations of commodity erotics are critical for understanding the production of sexuality among Nevisian girls. However, I want to push the meaning and usefulness of the concept further. For instance, how might a commodity compel a girl's desires, thus affecting not only her willingness to engage in sex, but also the internal meaning of what she finds erotic? It is not difficult to imagine how a girl engages in a sex act with a man in exchange for a commodity, like a cell phone, but is it possible, for example, to imagine that a girl's sexual pleasure or the eroticism she comes to associate with her sexuality might be enhanced by the promise of a shiny new cell phone? Is the promise of a commodity or a service, like a ride in a car, suffused with erotics? I am reminded of a comment Tobaa, my Nevisian neighbor, made one evening as we leaned against his sleek black Toyota Camry parked on the village road in front of my house. With a glimmer in his eye Tobaa explained, "Debra, it might surprise you to see how excited a girl gets when she sees the dashboard light up in my car." I assumed here that Tobaa was recalling occasions when green and red lights indicating instruments and gauges had titillating effects on Nevisian girls.[22]

Commodity erotics represents the commingling of erotic pleasures and sexual practices with commodity desires. Commodity erotics is complex, embedded in sexual-economic exchanges that represent a constellation of interactions between desiring subjects and desirable commodities. It is further complicated by the increasingly global influences of mass media on Nevis. By considering these globalized images and scripts, I explore a range of questions to interrogate commodity erotics, including these: What drives commodity desire among Nevisian girls? How do girls become attached to certain commodities? What do commodities signify to Nevisian girls? Do certain commodities signify sexual attractiveness? And if so, might that affect a girl's desirability and/or desirousness? How might the desire to consume commodities shape a girl's sexual desires and practices? And conversely, how might a girl's sexuality shape her desire for certain goods and services? This set of questions and others relate back to the complex relationship between that of culture and the individual. This coming-of-age story makes explicit the social forces, which both restrict and incite Nevisian girls' agency, by asking: How might the context of poverty combined with the influences of consumer culture shape a girl's sexual desires and practices?

This ethnography adds to the growing field of sexuality studies and seeks to remedy gaps in the anthropological literature. Yet it also seeks to remedy the gaps in the Caribbean literature on sexuality, which is a sparse and limited field. It is to this literature that I want to turn my attention in order to situate my work in the domain of Caribbean anthropology.

UNDERSTANDING SEXUALITIES IN THE CARIBBEAN: A LOOK AT THE LITERATURE

When anthropologists turn their attention in one direction to focus on a given subject, other important topics will inevitably be neglected. This is what has happened in the field of Caribbean studies, specifically as it relates to the treatment of sex and sexuality. Until recently, most of the ethnographic data on sexuality has been buried in important studies specific to Caribbean family systems, gender relations, or female labor issues (Curtis 2002; Kempadoo 2004).[23] Even among feminist scholars in the eighties there was a tendency to neglect sexuality and as a result, it has only recently become an object of analysis in its own right.

The image that students of Caribbean studies are left with is one in which single female-headed households dominate the region and female sexuality is cemented to economics. In other words, studies provide a very instrumental understanding of sexuality by suggesting that Caribbean women's sexual practices and desires are driven *purely* by economic interests, namely, that women trade sexual favors with men for access to cash, food, services and goods in order to provide for themselves and their children. The prevailing framework is one that links Caribbean women's sexuality more or less exclusively to economics and heterosexuality, thus ignoring the possibility that sexual pleasure or the erotic might be mediating factors.[24] Women's interest in sex for pleasure has not been considered to any great extent among Caribbean anthropologists with one recent notable exception; Gloria Wekker's *Politics of Passion* (2006) explores same-sex practices among women in Suriname. It is important to note that in my critique of this body of literature I am not dismissing the very real ways that Caribbean women's sexuality has been embedded in economics. In certain places in the Caribbean, prior to the social-economic changes brought about by tourism and by the offshore manufacturing industries, women had limited access to employment opportunities and were financially dependent on men. Maintaining relationships with multiple men, primarily the fathers of their children, provided women with the possibility of financial security. The problem with the way in which this has been formulated in the literature is that it is premised on the idea that women are not interested in sexual pleasure or sexual practices that are not associated with childrearing or procreation.[25]

My work is different from existing ethnographies on the Caribbean in that it focuses on the complex dynamism between sexuality and economics. I argue that we need to focus our attention on sexual pleasure and on the domain of the erotic for a more in-depth understanding of Nevisian sexualities. However, that is just one way that this ethnography is different. If we consider Caribbean women's sexuality as being obscured and thus misrepresented, then what can be said about the treatment of teenage girls' sexuality, namely, girls' sexual practices, desires, and notions of the erotic? Until recently, very little has been written about teenage girls and sexuality in the Caribbean. Needless to say, it has the potential to be a controversial subject, which is due at least in part to the fact that Nevisian girls, like girls in many places in the developing world, occupy an intensely marginalized social and economic position.

Within Nevisian society girls engage in sexual activity at a young age, sometimes by the age of eleven. It is also common for teenage girls to become sexually involved with men who are sometimes ten to fifteen years older. In some instances these men are their boyfriends; in others, they are simply men with whom they have sex in exchange for cash and goods. In a society where girls have little access to economic resources and many live in impoverished conditions, we need to consider the exploitative features that structure these relationships. In addition to this economic marginalization, I came across repeated stories of rampant sexual violence, in which girls feared their mother's boyfriends and in which pastures and secluded village roads lined with mango and breadfruit trees were potentially dangerous sexual sites. I also encountered rumors of mothers who send their daughters out to be sexually "serviced" by older men in exchange for cash. Given these considerations, how do you pay attention to sexual pleasure and still do justice to a cultural context of pervasive exploitation, danger, and violence?

This ethnography paints a complicated picture of the coming-of-age process on Nevis. It is filled with stories about how girls living in impoverished conditions are seduced by and seduce men who drive fancy imported cars and who have access to goods and cash. It describes stories of girls being forced into having sexual relations, and how within Nevisian society sexual coercion has become the norm, blurring the line between coercion and consent. It describes how girls dress provocatively to capture men's attentions and how girls forsake ideal religious values for sexual pleasures and for the desires of consumer culture. It also reveals what it is like to come-of-age in a society that because of its external debts and financial priorities cannot afford to pay enough attention to sexual education and reproductive health despite the fact that 20 percent of the annual births are born to girls under the age of eighteen and that the Caribbean is seeing an increase in the incidence and prevalence of HIV. In view of the fact that this is the cultural system in which the girls come-of-age and particularly given the social and economic disparities between the girls and men, it begs the question: Are the girls always exploited and are thus victims? Such a view, by emphasizing the conditions of sexual exploitation and, by downplaying girls' sexual pleasure, runs the risk of ignoring the manner in which girls craft their own sexual subjectivities. By contrast, my research shows that there are instances when some of the girls manipulate the cultural rules in order to better suit their interests.[26] But it is a fine line between exploitation and pleasure. Thus, this ethnography does not celebrate sexuality inasmuch as it frames the girls' sexualities within the twin processes of violence and pleasure and attends to both the pleasures and perils of coming-of-age on Nevis.[27]

RACE AND SEX

A similar relationship between violence and pleasure also exists between race and sex. Since this book is primarily concerned with the sexual subjectivity of girls living in a postcolonial society, an examination of racialized-sexualized discourses about black sexuality is in order. Contemporary discourses on race and sex is often explored through the lens of colonial prejudices about black sexuality. Since the Middle Ages, colonial authorities have portrayed blacks as having an abnormal insatiable sex drive. By the eighteenth century, black men and women were depicted as sexually deviant; moreover, in "scientific" discourse, the black woman was represented as possessing an animal-like sexual appetite (Gilman 1985; 81–83).[28] The legacy of colonial discourse continues to drive sex tourism in the Caribbean. The reputation of the dark-skinned woman or the mulatto figure, viewed as both exotic and sexually permissive, attracts European and American men to places such as Cuba and the Dominican Republic (Brennan 2004; Kempadoo and Doezema 1998).

Although the issue of transnational sex work is beyond the scope of this project, we nevertheless need to ask: What is the significance of racialized-sexualized discourses among Nevisian girls today? The view that Caribbean women seek out sex in exchange for access to goods and services evokes an image of Caribbean women as sexually manipulative. This study consciously seeks to avoid misinterpreting the Nevisian girls who exchange sex for commodities and money by separating their stories from the women portrayed in earlier studies. Already, it seems that within the popular imagination black girls are unfairly portrayed as promiscuous, as having as too much "agency." Their reputation for promiscuity encourages the impression that they are at risk of becoming pregnant at an early age or contracting sexually transmitted diseases, including HIV, thus becoming a drain on the state's financial resources. We find threads of this theme within the public health and international family-planning literature that focuses on changing the "lifestyles" of girls from developing countries in order to reduce the incidence of teen pregnancy and the transmission of HIV. This view has now become institutionalized. And the underlying assumption that young girls are fully in control of their lives and the choices they make, including the choices they make about their sexual practices, is inaccurate. Within academic circles there are still other debates about sexuality, agency, and Third World women and girls. At least within the literature on transactional sex, women and girls from developing countries are portrayed as victims who are completely powerless. This approach dominates the literature on prostitution and human trafficking. There are, however, a handful of scholars writing about prostitution who argue that the idea that Third World/non-Western women and girls are powerless is demeaning and represents a form of neocolonialism (Kempadoo and Doezema 1998). To complicate matters further, other scholars writing about sexuality, global poverty, and health maintain that there are dangers in overestimating agency (Farmer et al. 1996).[29] How do these issues relate to Nevisian girls and how do contemporary racialized and sexualized stereotypes shape Nevisian girls' sexuality? This ethnographic study attempts to bring together a number of these key themes around agency, power, and girls by positioning Nevisian girls' sexual practices within a broad historical, social, and economic framework as well as within a broad racial context. This becomes most evident in the analysis of contemporary hip-hop music and its impact on Nevisian girls as well as through an analysis of present-day sexual-economic patterns in which the girls participate.

FIELDWORK: RESEARCHING SEX AND SEXUALITY

About five months into my fieldwork on Nevis, I had convinced myself that anyone who has known love's promises or its tricks should understand why Nevisian girls, even young girls, have sex. The problem with my formulation is obvious: while romantic on some level, it fails to consider the fact that some Nevisian girls are forced into having sex, and that some girls have sex simply for its pleasure, for money, or for both. Perhaps my initial misreading of Nevisian girls' desires for sex simply exposes my own cultural bias, based on a Western tendency to conflate sex with love (de Zalduondo and Bernard 1995). But the girls themselves seemed to encourage such misdirection—the narratives they created about their first sexual experiences were love stories. However, at the same time that the girls spoke of love and intimacy in their own experiences, they also freely critiqued their girlfriends' and classmates' sexual lives as being manipulative, driven by a desire for consumer goods. The theme of this pattern was simple: *my* experiences, many of the girls seemed to be saying, are about real love, real intimacy; *your* experiences make you a whore because you get things for sex.

This became apparent to me one day while I was hanging out with three fifteen-year-old schoolgirls. I had asked them if they thought Nevisian girls preferred older men. Jasmine, the more outspoken of the girls, explained, "Yeah. It's because de girls want to be in fashion. So de want de older man who has de money. De girls get all turned on by de lines, just like what de rap star say, 'You so sexy. . . .'" I interrupted Jasmine and asked, "So you're telling me that the girls are not attracted to these men." Jasmine laughed and assumed an almost condescending tone, as if she was tired of always having to explain things to me. "Dey do it because dey need the stuff from de older men. If dey don't have sex wit dem, dey ain't going to get de money dat dey need to buy what dey want."

But there is something more at work in the scenario I am sketching than the machinations of how girls trade sex for consumer goods. Because in the numerous conversations that I had with them, the girls also spoke of sexual desires—both their own and that of their peers. In that very same conversation in which Jasmine commented upon the way her peers seduced men in order to acquire things, Rosa, a girl who was usually very quiet, chimed in. I had waited for a long time after Jasmine had stopped talking before I asked another question. Finally, I wondered out loud: "Why else do girls have sex?" Rosa spoke up, "For pleasure, for pleasure."

It is my job as the anthropologist to interpret these stories and bits of conversation, combining them with my own observations so that I might develop an understanding of both the girls' sexual experiences and beliefs, as well an increased understanding of the cultural context for their sexual behaviors. I use the girls' stories to sketch larger cultural scripts for a fuller appreciation of how Nevisian cultural logic unfolds in the everyday lives of teenage girls. There were many moments of cultural confusion on my part and thus, these conversations with the girls illustrate some of the methodological difficulties that I faced in my attempt to map the Nevisian sexual landscape.

The point I am trying to stress is that researching sexuality, like other sensitive topics, presents particular methodological challenges. I realized early on that girls would not always readily confide in me and that many times they would withhold stories and personal histories that were difficult or shameful to talk about. Yet despite the apparent sensitivity of the topic, my experience on Nevis also proved that there was a distinct range of sexual topics that were considered acceptable for everyday conversation. This book addresses the methodological challenges of sex research by examining Nevisian girls' sexualities through a variety of quantitative and qualitative measures. By using a quantitative survey with a number of qualitative approaches, particularly participant observation and repeated in-depth interviews, I hoped to capture the day-to-day realities of sex and girls on the island.

Beginning in January 2003 and extending through to July 2003, I engaged in participant observation, administered surveys, initiated focus groups, conducted in-depth interviews, and performed content analyses of various globally and locally generated media images and texts. There are approximately 953 girls between the ages of ten and nineteen living on Nevis. I administered surveys to 153 girls and conducted in-depth interviews with 12. In addition, I conducted nine focus groups with approximately 70 girls overall.

I began my research with a period of participant observation during which time people on Nevis had the opportunity to become accustomed to my presence and, I, in turn, had the opportunity to get to know the community. During this time, I became acquainted with a wide range of people, including several girls whose ages ranged from twelve to seventeen, community leaders, neighbors, shepherds, and a number of women in their thirties with whom I had weekly, if not daily, discussions. My intention in the first few weeks was to speak informally with as many people as I could about life on Nevis and to build personal contacts. With the girls, I wanted to begin to get a sense of how they talked about boys, sex, television, and consumer culture. During this initial period of participant observation, I also spent time at several offices connected with the Ministry of Health and with the community health centers in order to learn more about how health workers viewed girls' sexuality on Nevis.[30]

Since Nevis is small compared with other islands in the region, locals recognize newcomers, particularly if the newcomer is white and engaged in daily activities in which residents take part, such as setting up utilities and going grocery shopping. It was not uncommon by the end of my first month on Nevis to meet people for the first time and have them say, "Oh, you're the American writing a book about Nevis." The fact that people recognized me demonstrates how quickly word travels on the island. Case in point: early one January morning I was meeting with Shirley Wilkes, a health educator, trying to set up meetings with high school guidance counselors to initiate focus groups. Immediately following the meeting with Wilkes, I drove six miles or so out to the countryside to see a seamstress who was to make my daughters' school uniforms. With the newly paved roads, it took me fewer than twenty minutes to travel south of Zetlands village. After arriving at the shop, the seamstress casually asked, "How was your meeting with Shirley?" I learned quickly that the "island culture" in which everyone knows everyone else's business would prove to be a double-edged sword in terms of my research practices. It became apparent early on that if I arranged to meet with individuals, community leaders, and schoolgirls alike, then within hours after our interviews, others in the community would know about it.

During the initial stages of fieldwork I also gained tremendous insight from talking with my neighbors, shop clerks, and shepherds, who, for example, frequently offered unsolicited but helpful research advice. Time and again I heard, "Just the girls? Why aren't you studying the boys? Talk to the busmen [local bus drivers]; they're the problem." Early on, I learned that most of the individuals with whom I engaged on a regular basis (by that I mean everyday or at least every other day) had strong opinions about the subject of girls and sexuality. For instance, on my second day in the field, I met a man in my village named Miles who locals affectionately called "The Horse Whisperer" because of his unique ability to train horses. Miles tended to two horses, Crazy Horse and Cream-Boy, in the pasture abutting the house I lived in with my daughters. The first time we met, I was sweeping my front porch and beating my rugs, having just moved in the day before. Miles was in the pasture some twenty feet away. When I told him about the nature of my stay on Nevis, he smartly inquired, "You be studyin' de girls from dat porch?" In that moment I couldn't help but reflect back on the experience of Bronislaw Malinowski, the father of British anthropology. In a well-known film about Malinowski's life and contribution to anthropology, the film's narrator explains how the anthropologist made a conscious effort to "come down from the veranda" and to live among the people with whom he studied. In 1914, Malinowski was the first anthropologist to conduct participant observation, living among his subjects for an extended period of time, learning their language, and making a concerted effort to grasp the natives' point of view. Anthropologists who came before Malinowski are regarded as "armchair" anthropologists: it has become commonplace to imagine these early scholars conducting their research in libraries or conducting structured interviews but living apart from the people whom they studied and spending their evenings in the homes of colonial officers or missionaries. The poetry of Miles' remarks resonates with Malinowski's greatest contribution to anthropology, his stepping off the veranda and into the lives of his subjects.

During that initial visit with Miles, he shared with me an observation that occupied my mind throughout my fieldwork. Miles maintained that the girls on Nevis were maturing at a faster rate than girls of previous generations as the result of the increase in the consumption of processed foods. As Miles observed, "Dey come to you like dey big women and den you see dat dey just children. . . . De hormones in de chicken, dis makin' dem sick." I, myself, made this mistake a number of times. At the beach I would be talking to girls who I assumed were at least eighteen given their developed breasts, their height, and their full hips, only to be informed that I was mistaken. On one occasion I mistook a twelve-year-old for a woman in her early twenties.

Given the size and population of Nevis, it was not uncommon to interact with a wide range of individuals in the course of one day. I could, for example, have an in-depth interview with a schoolgirl in the morning, spend time in the field with a village shepherd in the mid-morning, meet wealthy North American tourists for coffee, and then have dinner with Nevis' prominent citizens. This was how day-to-day fieldwork on Nevis progressed. My contacts and daily interactions with people, including Nevisians, expatriates, and tourists alike, proved to be more cosmopolitan in nature than an average day in New Brunswick, New Jersey, the site of Rutgers University or Newport, Rhode Island, where I currently teach anthropology at Salve Regina University.

Throughout my fieldwork, participant observation was a critical method for eliciting ideas about sexuality and probing how these ideas were reproduced and/or challenged. By socializing with Nevisians, I gained a clearer understanding of how they made sense of sexual discourses and practices including those mediated by family, church, TV, peers, and health sources. I also interviewed officials, health care workers, clergy, and parents. I engaged young men, usually bus drivers, construction workers, shop keepers, and shepherds. Let me offer an example of how productive participant observation proved to be for eliciting data on sexuality.

One of my fondest memories on Nevis involves a night when I had arranged to meet a former Miss Culturama, the winner of the island's annual beauty contest.[31] I was supposed to meet the former beauty queen on the steps of the public library one evening in May, but she never showed. In the evenings, the square in Charlestown becomes a place where young men meet and hang out. Most of the shops close, but a few street venders selling hot chicken and beers are open for business. I was sitting on the library steps and talking with Thomas, a British photographer and returning national, and

Dolores, a teacher from the secondary school. We talked about new sexual trends on Nevis. Thomas maintained that oral sex (females performing on males) had been imported from the United States, and stressed the fact that female tourists had introduced it to the beachboys.[32] Dolores recounted that oral sex, performed by either men or women, was not part of the sexual repertoire on Nevis when she was growing up in the 1980s. Later that week I spoke with one of the local boat captains, a man I visited with at a beach bar at least three or four times a week. When I told him what Thomas had said about female tourists introducing oral sex to the island, he insisted that the photographer was wrong. "White women didn't bring it to the island. HBO did."

During one of our many talks about sexuality, Eleanor, a close friend and informant who grew up in the eighties, also asserted that oral sex was a relatively new practice. Eleanor explains, "We never heard of blow jobs [during] my time growin up—or suckin, I say, 'Momma, Peti wants me to suck. Is suckin'-nasty?'" At that point in our interaction, Eleanor read the look of skepticism on my face—a look that she interpreted correctly as, "You talk to your mom about giving head?" Eleanor responded to my look by explaining, "You gotta understand Debra; Momma and me are sisters; she got me when she was sixteen. We grew up together." That sexual customs and desires are imported as the result of global flows, like traveling bodies and television images, which in turn shape intimate practices and spaces, will be taken up in subsequent chapters. At this point I use these examples to demonstrate how my daily interactions helped me to learn how global and local processes interact to form a complex social and economic context in which Nevisian sexuality is constructed.[33]

AT SCHOOL WITH THE GIRLS

I relied on focus groups to develop an understanding of what matters most to Nevisian girls and the significant social categories from which they view their world.[34] Between February and March 2003, I organized nine focus groups with the approval of the head of the Education Department and with the help of the guidance counselors at two of the public schools, Gingerland Secondary (GSS) and Charlestown Secondary (CSS), and the assistant principal at Lynn Jeffers, a private secondary school in Charlestown. The age-stratified groups (12–13-year-olds, 14–15-year-olds, and 16–17-year-olds) were recruited from health education and family life classes.

To begin to understand the dominant cultural norms and practices related to sexuality as conceptualized by girls, I used a free-listing exercise. In this case I gave each girl a slip of paper and a pencil and asked them to list all of the sexual practices girls might engage in. I explicitly said, "Not sexual practices that girls *should* be doing, but all the practices you think they *might* be participating in." I then collected the lists and asked the girls to clarify terms with which

I was unfamiliar, such as *pulling tongue, ride for a ride*, and *back-shots*. All of the girls in each of the nine groups were familiar with the local expression "pulling tongue," which is the equivalent to the American slang "French kissing" or "making out." But in each of the three groups comprised of twelve-to-thirteen-year-olds, certain sexual expressions—such as "ride for a ride," which connotes an exchange of a sexual favor for a ride in a car, or "back-shot," which refers to the position in which a female is on her knees while her partner enters her vagina from behind—required further explanation. It was often the case that one brave girl, in response to my inquiry, would explain what the unfamiliar terms meant, thus clarifying the term for me as well as for others in the room. These moments elicited cries and roars of laughter from the girls, peppered with commentary such as "Yucky!" or "Freaky!" In each of the groups, after I had collected the lists and clarified the terms, I then asked a number of general questions related to sexuality such as: What does "having sex" mean? Are Nevisian girls having sex? What causes girls to have sex? Why do girls have sex?

Consistently, and not surprisingly, the younger girls between the ages of twelve and fourteen at all three schools were the most animated and energetic. They were also well-mannered and for the most part, took their roles and responsibilities seriously. I experienced the most resistance with the sixteen-to-seventeen-year-olds. It may have been that they were suspicious of a white woman asking them questions about sex, even couched in general terms. It's not that the girls were insolent, at least not in the focus groups. It's that they lacked the enthusiasm expressed by the younger girls. It may have even been that my status as an adult intimidated them. I suspect, however, that it may have been that there was more at stake for the older girls in that if they talked even in general terms about matters related to sexuality, their peers in the room might interpret their comments as admissions and testimonies. Given what I know about Nevisian culture, the experience of sitting down with an adult and talking openly about sexuality was in all probability a new experience for the majority of the girls.[35]

TALKING WITH GIRLS, HANGING OUT

At the end of each focus group, I announced that I would be interviewing girls one-on-one and encouraged willing participants to give me their names and telephone numbers. Because the Nevisian girls were in school most of the day, I sometimes met with girls after school, but mostly I met with them on the weekends. During the entire month of April, when schools were on break, there was greater flexibility to meet with girls during the week. I usually arranged to meet with a girl on a Saturday or a Sunday after I had spoken with the girl's parent or grandparent and secured consent from both a parent and the teen. We typically met in Charlestown and drove to a beach restaurant for lunch, which was very popular with the girls who, rarely if ever had the opportunity to eat out. Sometimes we sat in my car on the side of the road; other times, I interviewed the girls in their homes, on the beach, and if it wasn't too windy or populated, at a local café.[36]

During these interviews, which I taped with the girl's and her parent's permission, I collected life histories, thus acquiring information about a girl's childhood, family life, education, leisure activities, travel experience, and religious and civic activities; exposure to, and perception of, safe sex and family-planning education; and beliefs and attitudes about sexuality. A sexual history, including contraceptive experience, if any, was obtained. I elicited information from each informant about individual TV-viewing habits and patterns. I collected information about shopping habits and consumption desires.

Originally, I had intended to collect life histories and sexual narratives from only girls between the ages of twelve and seventeen. However, during my first month on Nevis, I became acquainted with fifteen other women, some of whom were in their twenties, others in their thirties, and all of whom proved to be valuable resources. These interviews unfolded rather spontaneously at first until I realized how fruitful the data were. Born in the late 1970s or early 1980s, these women were able to articulate with greater clarity than the younger girls both the changes in Nevisian society over the past two decades as well as the practices that remained unchanged. They were also more reflective and insightful regarding the cultural and economic dimensions of adolescence. Put simply, their narratives proved to be rich venues for understanding social change on Nevis and what it was like to come-of-age during a time of cultural transformation. I use their coming-of-age stories to understand how much Nevisian society has changed over the last two decades. In doing so, I was more fully able to chart the cultural continuities and discontinuities experienced by adolescent girls on the island.

A word or two about how I present the girls' and other Nevisians' stories seem to be in order. Throughout this book, I preserve the integrity of the Nevisian dialect. By using the language that was originally expressed, one gains a clear understanding of the relationship between language and sexuality. As well, I have aimed at accuracy of language in order to assure readers that they are reading the Nevisian girls' stories, and not my own. While many anthropologists translate from another language into English, I am of the opinion that preserving the local dialect, in this instance, helps to maintain the integrity of the project as a whole and it allows the reader to make his or her own conclusions about the discursive nature of sexuality. Changing the language risks distorting the Nevisian voices and alters the character of the ethnography. I might also add that despite the impression some might have that the use of the local dialect reproduces a sense of the exotic other, I argue that changing the dialect so that it is more accessible is a projection of colonial prejudices.

THE POLITICS OF WRITING ABOUT SEXUALITY

As I immersed myself more deeply in Nevisian culture, I often thought of the eminent Caribbeanist anthropologist whose challenge helped propel me even more eagerly into my project. Would studies of sex and sexuality go out of style, as he predicted? Although I understand how the popularity of certain academic subjects rises and falls, I came to believe more firmly that the study of sexuality transcends any simplistic notion of academic chic. Jeffery Weeks (1986) observes that "sexuality has become the focus of fierce ethical and political divisions" (1). As Weeks suggests, such contestations arise because, simply put, sex matters. Sex matters because questions of sex and sexuality lie at the core of a number of important social issues, such as the nature and role of "family life," HIV prevention, family planning, and teenage pregnancy. Sex and sexuality are also political concerns in the sense that bodies, lifestyles, and public health policy become the grounds on which these social issues are contested. And finally, sex and sexuality are economic concerns because they involve the allocation and distribution of state, federal, and international moneys. The politics of AIDS, for instance, illustrates ethical and political divisions, particularly as it relates to the contestation of the allocation of resources and the increase in what Dennis Altman (2001) refers to as behavioral surveillance by the state in the effort to prevent HIV. Altman emphasizes the fact that this increased surveillance cannot be disassociated from moral discourse.

Despite the perception that academic studies of sex are fashionable, the title of a recent article in the *New York Times*, "Long after Kinsey, Only the Brave Study Sex" (Carey 2004) speaks to how scholars may actually risk academic marginalization, which implies that these researchers are likely to face financial consequences for pursuing their research interests. While these issues are not addressed in the article, this may be because some academics in a position to make decisions impacting a junior scholar's career may view sexuality studies as superfluous to "real" economic and political issues. But for others, a contemporary sexuality scholar who investigates sexual practices and norms may play an important role in normalizing sexual difference. Such normalization may have profound and deeply political consequences. In the current politically conservative atmosphere, the stakes are high for anyone suggesting that sexual difference is an expected, indeed "normal," facet of human society. If certain sexual forms and practices, such as same-sex unions, become normalized, conservatives may feel that the very future of society is at stake. Thus, despite the perception espoused by my esteemed colleague that sex research is merely a passing and inconsequential academic fancy, I argue to the contrary that the study of sex makes all the difference in the world because it has the potential to remake the world, that is, who we are and who we may become.

The Politics of Representation:
A Grounded Perspective

If one assumes as I do that constructions of sexualities can be reproduced on many levels, including representational projects such as this one, then it is critical to attend to the politics of representation embedded in this ethnography on Nevisian girls and sexualities. If, as James Clifford (1986) asserts, all ethnographies are enmeshed in and structured by power inequalities (9), then what are the politics and ethics at stake in this project? What is being conveyed here through the ethnographic lens? What sort of discourse on Nevisian sexualities is being produced? I will begin to frame my answers to these questions by relating two stories, one involving an informant named Ruthie Collins, a hardworking mother of three, and the other, Vance Amory, the nation's premier and one of the most powerful men on Nevis.

During one of my last visits with Ruthie, I could tell from the look on her face that she wanted to ask me something of a serious nature. She was a woman in her thirties, born and raised on Nevis, a mother of three and someone with whom I spent a substantial amount of time. Ruthie was someone I considered to be a key informant. Even though my research focused primarily on girls, Ruthie's insights and explanations about Nevisian cultural practices, including sexual customs and norms, proved to be invaluable. As Russell Barnard (2002) describes, individuals like Ruthie are people who are, "for whatever reasons of their own, ready and willing to walk you through their culture and show you the ropes" (187). At this particular moment, Ruthie's usually wide brown eyes narrowed as she asked, "Debra, de stories we tell you, de stories me tell you, nobody will know right?" Ruthie posed this question to me the day before I was supposed to leave Nevis to return to New England. Ruthie was raising important questions—questions of informants taking me into their confidence about the most intimate of matters and questions of my own positioning as a privileged white woman interrogating sex practices in a black, postcolonial culture. Her parting query was shared by others involved in this ethnography as well.

About three months before, in May 2003, I was required to go to the government administration offices in Charlestown and obtain an extension for my family's stay on Nevis. This involved notifying government officials of my place of residence, registering at the police office, and paying a fee. While waiting for the paperwork to be completed, I talked at length with a middle-aged female government employee who displayed great interest in, and enthusiasm for, my research project. She offered her insights into youth culture, as well as the names and telephone numbers of community leaders, including her pastor, whom she thought I should interview. At one point during our discussion she encouraged me to meet the premier. I was pleased with the opportunity but felt that I was ill-prepared that particular morning. Quite candidly,

I explained that it was not only because I felt unprepared mentally to meet him, but also that I was not dressed for the occasion. Looking down at my plain dark-colored cotton sundress, which by Nevisian standards looked more like a housedress, the administrative assistant assured me that I looked fine. With that she picked up the phone and called the premier, whose office was down the corridor. Within minutes I was ushered down the hall. Before knocking, the administrative assistant tucked in the back flap of my poorly sewn dress, smoothed out the fabric on my shoulders, glanced at my unruly hairstyle, and then tapped on the door. The premier was seated at a large stately desk, talking on the phone. From what I could discern, a friend had been hospitalized and he was just being notified. After I was introduced, I briefly explained the nature and scope of my project on girls and sexuality, describing how I had been working closely with the members of the Ministry of Health and the Department of Education. I further explained that I hoped that my research findings would have practical significance and might be helpful for informing government policy makers in their effort to work with adolescents to prevent the spread of STDs and reduce the rate of teen pregnancies. The entire time I spoke, the premier stared blankly at me. He never once asked me a question and when I was finished, there was an awkward silence between us. While seated in the brown leather chair, I remember thinking—either quite naively or vainly, "Why isn't this man shaking my hand and praising my efforts to help his country?"

My encounter with the national AIDS coordinator, Andrea Nisbett, may provide some answers. I met Andrea early during my fieldwork. She was an intelligent and iconoclastic thinker. She was also one of the more progressive individuals I had met on Nevis; her commitment to AIDS education and issues related to gender equality were seemingly uncompromising. Andrea and I were fond of each other and often our conversations strayed from the topic of public health and sexuality to more personal subjects—our children or career aspirations. Andrea had a wonderful sense of humor, in part because she was so outspoken and perceptive. Like Ruthie, Andrea was someone I could count on to explain the rules of Nevisian culture. A few days after my encounter with the premier, Andrea and I were sitting in one of the government offices and I told her about my impressions of the impromptu meeting. I commented to her, "Maybe he wasn't really listening to my explanation; maybe he was distracted by the news he had received on the telephone about a sick friend moments before I entered the office." Andrea looked at me long and hard and said, "Or maybe he was thinking, 'Who's this white woman telling our stories—portraying Nevis in a disparaging way to the rest of the world?'"

I describe these two incidents at length—Ruthie's gentle but earnest query and Andrea's bold assessment of the premier's behavior—to elucidate the politics and ethics of representing my informants' sexual lives. By turning my ethnographic gaze toward their private, intimate worlds, I hope to understand the context in which girls' sexual subjectivities are produced and the cultural norms that shape them. However, in doing so, I run the risk of committing a multitude of injuries, not the least of which is exploiting my informants' confidences and portraying Nevis and Nevisians negatively, and stereotypically. Both Ruthie's and Andrea's questions are addressed by, Clifford (1986) who reminds us to consider the following: What happens when individuals, in this case Nevisians, who have historically been economically and politically marginalized people, enter the ethnographic space of the Western imagination, particularly when the focus of the subject is sexuality (5)?

To understand the possible implications of this question I turn to Franz Fanon's (1967) description of what black sexuality signifies in the white colonial imagination. The following comments represent a racist colonial discourse—a discourse Fanon analyzes in order to understand and resist the effects of racism. Fanon writes: "In relation to the Negro, everything takes place on the genital level. . . . As for the Negroes, they have tremendous sexual powers. What do you expect, with all the freedom they have in their jungles! They copulate at all times and in all places. They are really genital. They have so many children that they cannot even count them" (157).

The consequences of my work are important, given this context, and it is critical that this project not participate in the proliferation of sexual stereotyping that was one of the very underpinnings of colonial ideology. So how do I write about "black sex" on Nevis without reproducing the colonial imagination so painfully described by Fanon?

In taking on such a challenge, I turned to the work of previous scholars. There have been a number of studies that either implicitly or explicitly draw attention to the subject of black sexuality in the Caribbean. The dominant social science research in this area of the world includes studies of polygamy, serial monogamy, promiscuity, and/or concubinage that seek to better understand and explain family structures. Edith Clarke's study, *My Mother Who Fathered Me*, published in 1957, is an example of this genre. Following what was considered an unsuccessful campaign launched in 1944–1945 by the Jamaican governor's wife—a campaign designed to discipline and change the social and moral effects of promiscuity—the Social Science Research Council in Britain sponsored Clarke in her study of the "problems of promiscuity," "marital instability," and "high illegitimacy" rates. Two decades later, Mariam Slater, a graduate student from Columbia University, wrote her dissertation on the "Negro family" in Martinique. Unlike Clarke, Slater attempts to distance herself from the pathologizing discourses of the Negro family in analyzing the effects of miscegenation during slavery. Throughout Slater's ethnography, however, competing images of black women's sexuality emerge, and it becomes difficult to disentangle the ethnographic data, the anthropologist's interpretations, and the legacy of colonial racial ideology. For example, Slater writes: "The attitude of the whites toward the behaviorally black is that they are all promiscuous, that they 'make love like cats,' that they go off to the cane fields at puberty and never come out. This is partially substantiated by the fact that any white can have any black woman willingly" (151–152).

There are striking similarities between Fanon's reading of the white imagination and Slater's text. Both expose the problems of writing about black sexuality. But how can I avoid pathologizing black sexuality? Will my ethnography become another example of what Evelynn Hammonds (1997) describes as the colonization of black women's bodies? In other words, is this portrayal of Nevisian sexualities another form of symbolic domination? In "Toward a Genealogy of Black Female Sexuality," Hammonds calls upon black female scholars to break the silence surrounding the subject of black female sexuality. But where do I fit in as a white female?

My argument requires that I make explicit my subject position as a white, anti-racist ethnographer interrogating sexual subjectivities in a postcolonial context. I am keenly aware of the discourses that inform my ethnography, including those generated within anthropology, the legacy of racial ideologies, and the ethics and the politics of representing postcolonial subjectivities.

However, despite my subject position, I challenge Hammonds's epistemological assumption that only black women can write about black sexualities. Hammonds's comments are embedded in a type of essentialist identity politics that organizes itself around a single ontological category such as skin color. Implied in her work is the idea that an ethnographer, based solely on her experience as a black woman, would be better positioned to represent other black women's sexualities regardless of their cultural backgrounds and regardless of differences between the potential women in nationality, class or sexual orientation. The problem with this assumption is obvious: experience is never singular or unitary. Challenging the type of political-epistemological position represented by Hammonds generates new possibilities for potentially transformative scholarship that opposes re-inscribing racial stereotypes and instead promotes critical intellectual exchange that cuts across racial, cultural, and geographic boundaries.

This ethnography aims for such a crosscutting trajectory by investigating the hegemonic and subversive qualities of the Nevisian girls' experiences. The suffering that many girls face as the result of enduring cultural patterns and Nevis' specific historical and economic trajectory haunts my own narrative. Some of these harsh and common realities include the fact that girls suffer as a result of limited instruction related to reproductive health; that girls suffer from the health risks inherent in teen pregnancy; that they suffer from conditions of poverty that might ensue when one's education is interrupted by pregnancy; that girls are subjected to sexual coercion at the hands of older men who more than likely are their relatives or close family friends; and that Nevisian society condones multiple partners for men. Yet to look only at girls suffering represents only a partial understanding of the complexity of their sexualities and coming-of-age process on Nevis. *Pleasures and Perils* posits that girls' sexualities on Nevis are constituted along two axes: first, one that foregrounds the negative and constraining aspects of sexuality just noted and second, one that recognizes the creative and positive possibilities of sexuality despite the seemingly overwhelming obstacles that Nevisian girls face. This book highlights numerous moments when girls describe how they experience great affection, excitement, and emotional connection. The stories included in this ethnography suggest that the coming-of-age process on Nevis provides girls with the opportunities to experience new forms of pleasure, to resist traditional structures of power, and to challenge dominant ideologies about sexuality. I hope that the significance of this ethnography lies in its ability to represent the fullness and richness and all of the many contradictions of Nevisian girls' sexualities. It is by capturing this fullness—this multidimensional quality—of Nevisian girls' experiences that I hope to challenge the very structure and process of racial stereotyping and to provide a body of work that will contribute to an anthropological understanding of the range of human sexualities.

CHAPTER 2

Globalizing Nevis

RADICAL SHIFTS FROM SUBSISTENCE TO CONSUMERISM

RUTHIE RECOUNTS how as a girl growing up in the 1980s, she used to arrange to meet her paramour in a dark pasture or in an alley late in the evening long after her great-grandmother, with whom she lived, had gone to bed. This is not too dissimilar from what I learned from girls coming-of-age today. For instance, girls participating in the focus groups at various schools explained a number of ways that their peers secretly arranged to meet with their boyfriends. Vickie, a fifteen-year-old at Lynn Jeffers, leaned forward over the tape recorder, lowered her voice, and remarked, "Nevisian girls can be very sneaky." With the other girls listening, Vicki described how girls have a number of ways to "get what dey want." If a girl wanted to be alone with her boyfriend or with another man, for instance, she might climb into the backseat of his car and lie down on the floor so as not to be seen by family members or by other people from her village who might recognize her and inform her parents; this way her boyfriend could drive through town and through other smaller villages to get to some of the more secluded beaches so that the two might be alone. I also learned that it was not uncommon for a girl to turn her cell phone to a vibrating mode; that way, if her boyfriend wanted to contact her, no one, such as her parents or siblings, would be privy to the call, and she might speak to her boyfriend all night in her bedroom or arrange to meet him after everyone else in the house was asleep.

Apart from the fact that they have cell phones to depend on and access to cars for transportation, the girls' desires and Ruthie's appear similar, namely to steal a few precious moments alone with their boyfriends. The social continuities are the same—girls seeking out pleasurable moments with boys, away from the scrutiny of their parents or from other family members; however, the cultural and economic context in which girls of today negotiate their subjectivities has changed drastically from when Ruthie came of age in the 1980s. Assuming that the production of subjectivities can never be understood apart from the social and economic context in which they are embedded, the girls' lives need to be situated and understood within the changing and dynamic aspects of Nevisian social life. In this chapter, I provide a description of the changes in Nevisian society that have had the greatest impact on various aspects of the coming-of-age process. I focus on the last two decades because while Nevis, like other Caribbean islands, has always been affected by global influences, since the 1980s, the small island society has undergone radical changes as a result of the increased dependency on tourism and on other economic development opportunities, including the offshore financing industry.[1]

Over the past twenty years, with a greater economic base, the Nevisian government, as well as local businesses have been able to make a number of infrastructural changes affecting social life. For example, in the late 1980s, for the first time, Nevisians had access to network and non-network TV via satellite; waterlines providing water throughout villages to individual homes were laid; primary schools in Charlestown, which were once segregated according to sex, became coeducational; the telecommunication system offered phone services to all residents; the Voice of Nevis, a privately owned radio station, went on the air; the first self-serve grocery store was opened; and in 1991, the Four Seasons resort opened. All of these developments would prove to have profound effects on social and economic life on Nevis. Prior to the 1980s, Nevisians, including girls, were more tied to subsistence economy. As such, everyday activities were largely determined by chores that facilitated daily living needs; as a result, there were fewer opportunities for leisure activities associated with a consumer culture, such as watching television, shopping, listening to music, or surfing the Internet. Additionally, there were limited opportunities for exposure to multiple global influences, including mediated images and scripts presently available to Nevisians. In sum, subsistence living produced obvious constraints on leisure that restricted the girls' access to images and scripts within and outside Nevisian culture.[2] I would also argue that subsistence living limited both knowledge of, and opportunities for, sexual activities. For example, busy girls with little knowledge about sex were likely to follow a traditional discourse when it came to sexual practices. This is not to say that when growing up, Ruthie and/or women her age and older did not meet their boyfriends or enjoy rendezvous; rather, these opportunities were limited due to the restrictions placed on their time.

It is also important to stress how the size of Nevis, both in terms of geography and population, affects the daily lives of the girls, including, of course, their sexual activity. The island is relatively small, 36 square miles and it is populated by roughly 10,000 individuals. A Nevisian girl as young as thirteen recognized the significance of this when she told me, "It's tough; everybody sees; everybody knows." During a focus group at Lynn Jeffers, an older girl put it this way, when we were discussing whether or not girls felt comfortable buying condoms at the drugstore. "It takes a microscope to a look at a mustard seed, but on Nevis we can see it with a naked eye. A girl can't hide anything here on Nevis." I heard repeatedly how the sheer smallness of the island influenced the girls' lives. In general, it is not uncommon for girls to live with their mothers and their grandmothers and to have grown up in the villages in which their mothers were raised. This contributes to "everyone knowin' everythin' about everyone," as yet another girl noted. Despite the traditional features that seem to dominate village life on Nevis, not the least of which is the most obvious one, that everyone knows everyone else, Nevis has become increasingly influenced by transnational forces. The apparent absence of privacy does not appear to have mitigated the effects of transnational forces on sexual practices and desires. Some girls have learned to be sufficiently deceptive (as previously described) to produce the privacy typically required for sex and/or have discounted the importance of privacy in order to produce the type of sexualities that global forces incite. It is in documenting these changes that I hope to demonstrate how growing up on Nevis in 2003 was markedly different than growing up on Nevis as recently as the mid-1980s.

SOCIAL AND ECONOMIC SHIFTS: A CHANGING LANDSCAPE

From the 1840s up until about twenty years ago, employment opportunities on Nevis were limited.[3] During the 1980s the average annual salary for those employed in the few hotels or as laborers was approximately U.S.$375 per year. The 1980 census figures showed that approximately 54 percent of men and women were unemployed. This figure may not have included individuals and families who were earning a living within the informal economy, subsisting on trade and bartering, and engaging in small farming endeavors (Weisburd 1984). Many people migrated throughout the Caribbean region, as well as to England and the United States in search of employment.[4] In a survey conducted among school children in 1981, 46 percent reported having at least one parent abroad and 22 percent reported that both parents had migrated (1984). While current census figures on migration are unavailable at this time, there has been a noticeable shift in migration patterns with out-migration slowing down considerably. Nevis is also experiencing a high rate of nationals returning to take advantage of the growing economic opportunities on Nevis. Public servants in government jobs are paid approximately U.S.$100 per week. Entry-level schoolteachers with minimal training earn approximately U.S.$150 per week. Schoolteachers with university degrees earn U.S.$250 per week. Generally, wait staff and hotel employees earn anywhere from U.S.$100 to U.S.$200 per week depending on the restaurant and resort. Laborers employed as plumbers, electricians, masons, or in other related trades including construction work earn U.S.$35 per day.

Over the past twenty years, while there has been an overall increase in the standard of living and quality of life among Nevisians, a 2001 study commissioned by the Caribbean Development Bank estimated that 32 percent of Nevisians live in poverty. Poverty, according to the study, was defined as not having the money to meet the minimal monthly food costs and other basic requirements—in other words, households with an income of EC$328.41 (Eastern Caribbean or U.S.$124.00) or less per month were considered as living below the poverty line (Kairi 2001).

For those who are gainfully employed, 21 percent are employed in tourism, 13 percent earn a living working in construction, 13 percent in agriculture, and 22 percent work in the public sector (Kairi 2001, 30). Most of the current agricultural activity involves small-scale businesses, including animal husbandry, beekeeping, and vegetable farming. Fishing, while a long-standing tradition on Nevis and a popular livelihood, has declined as the result of overfishing. There is a commercial fishing industry whereby fishermen sell their catch at the open market and to some small restaurants as well. The offshore financial industry contributes 11 percent to the total government revenue on Nevis, but employs only a handful of locals, as non-nationals own most of the financial service providers. The few nationals who are employed in the financial service industry represent some of the highest paid professionals on Nevis (Kairi 2001).

The biggest hotel on Nevis, the Four Seasons, opened in 1991 and now directly employs 20 percent of the workforce on Nevis. (It is currently estimated that 4,000 individuals make up the Nevisian working population.) However, according to the Four Seasons' human resource director, the hotel's presence on the island influences as much as 40 percent of Nevisians indirectly; for example, taxi drivers, local restaurants owners, and shopkeepers all benefit financially from its presence. Women between the ages of twenty and forty years old make up 60 percent of the Four Seasons' employees. There are also other smaller hotels on the island employing Nevisians as waitpersons, chambermaids, kitchen-help, groundskeepers, bartenders, security guards, tour guides, drivers, and clerks. Including the 200 or so beds at the Four Seasons, there are approximately 400 hotel beds on the island.

Up until the late 1980s when employment opportunities were limited and many people relied on remittances from relatives living abroad, houses usually consisted of two to three rooms constructed out of wood. A small number of affluent Nevisians built concrete homes. In terms of utilities and services, 69 percent of households relied on wood or charcoal for cooking stoves. Most people cooked in an outdoor shed to reduce the amount and extent of damage in the event of a fire. Women and children, mostly girls, washed the household clothes in buckets, and then laid the clothes on large stones to scrub them and left them to dry in the hot sun. In the 1980s, 75 percent of Nevisian households used pit-toilets and over 53 percent did not have access to water pipes in their

yards or houses (Weisburd 1984). Women and children also collected water at
the village standpipe where there were frequent water restrictions. Many of
the women in their thirties whom I interviewed, when asked about their childhoods, recounted in great detail the number of chores that they had to perform
before and after school. Repeatedly I heard, "Girls today have too much time on
der hands; dats de problem." A woman in her late thirties recalled how everyday
she had chores that would take her a few hours to complete; this included finding feed for her pig, filling drums with water from the village standpipe, and
washing out the one blouse and uniform she had for school in preparation for
the next day. In 1988, the Nevis Water Department laid water lines, and for the
first time households began paying for water (Robinson 2000).

In the early 1980s, 55 percent of Nevisians lived without electricity. In the
mid-1980s there were only a small number of telephones on the island and
even fewer lines to connect with the Saint Kitts switchboard to facilitate international or regional calls. A hotel owner recalls that in the early eighties his
family would hire people to sit at the phone the entire day. Their sole purpose
was to attempt to get an outside line to connect with the switchboard on Saint
Kitts. Phone lines were buried and telephone service was made available to all
residents in 1986, which produced an increase in telephones from 450 to
4,500 island-wide (Robinson 2000).

Prior to the 1980s, most Nevisian households relied on home gardens and
reared small-scale livestock, including chickens, sheep, goats, and pigs, for
subsistence. Local shops stocked a limited amount of poor quality imported
foods such as frozen chicken parts (imported from the U.S.), tinned milk,
wheat, flour, rice, macaroni and cheese, sugar, and potatoes (Weisburd 1984).
Commonly consumed and inexpensive foods were rice and bread, which are
high in calories but relatively low in terms of vitamins and nutritional value.
Fruit from local trees, including mangoes, breadfruits, and bananas, were dietary
staples as was cassava bread, a flat cake similar to a pancake, which is made from
grated cassava and prepared on a heavy skillet. Salt-fish, yams, pumpkins, corn-
meal, and pigeon peas were also common foods (Weisburd 1984). However, not
all Nevisians had equal access to resources in order to buy imported or locally
produced foods. Eleanor, a close friend and informant and a woman in her thirties, recalls that when she was growing up, she went to school hungry almost
every day. "I draw water on lime leaf and add sugar for breakfast," she said
describing a variation of bush tea made from pouring hot water on lime leaves
or lemon grass. Ruthie added this, "Growing up, I only had milk once a week.
My only milk was coconut milk." Ruthie's great-grandmother would grind up
the coconut and squeeze the milk out and add it to her tea on Sundays.

In the late 1980s a number of small self-serve food stores selling imported
foods opened up in Charlestown, the capital of Nevis. Trevor Chapman, a local
entrepreneur, reportedly was the first on the island to sell frozen dinners,

namely, pizzas. The first self-serve grocery store, which opened in the late 1980s, offered an array of goods and foodstuffs. Rams grocery store, a large competitor, opened for business in 2001. Rams sells just about everything: fruits, vegetables, meats, bread, dairy products, frozen entrées, canned goods, cereal, soda, alcohol, candy, cleaning supplies, cigarettes, and pharmaceutical products, such as aspirin and anti-diarrhea medicines and first aid supplies. The layout of the store, marketing strategies, and customer service are very similar to large chain food stores in the United States. There are also two bakeries on the island and snackettes in most of the villages selling flour, canned goods, beer, soda, salt fish, and dry goods. In addition to the relatively new self-serve grocery stores, in the late nineties, a number of stores opened supplying various goods and services ranging from lumber (for new home construction) and home goods (including household appliances, such as washers, dryers, and televisions) to beauty services, cosmetic goods, audiovisual equipment, books, wholesale plants and flowers, lingerie, computers, and clothing.

To finance some of these goods, Nevisians turn to the Nevis Co-Operative Credit Union, which was established in 1972, providing consumer loans to Nevisians for new home construction and additions, education, travel, furniture and appliances, and funeral, motor vehicle, medical, wedding, and legal expenses. Its current membership is comprised of over 4,000 people. Funding is also available at the credit union for small businesses. In 1989 the credit union gave out 468 loans totaling EC$1.8 million (U.S.$711,537); by 2001, the Credit Union distributed 596 loans totaling EC$8.7 million (U.S.$3.3 million) (Nevis Co-Operative Credit Union Report and Statements of Accounts 1989, 2001). The rise in Nevisian consumerism, as evidenced by the increase in consumer lending, appears to be a direct result of the presence of the Four Seasons on Nevis. Recall that 20 percent of the Nevisian workforce is employed by the Four Seasons, which typically pays employees significantly greater wages than other jobs Nevisians might have. What I intend to explore throughout the rest of this project, are the ways in which the increase in consumerism, for example, new and larger stores and a greater availability of products along with greater access to money, affects the production of sexual subjectivities among Nevisians and particularly among girls.

Up until the 1980s, the one major road that circled the island was unevenly paved. The roads leading off the main road to the villages were dirt or made up of two concrete tracks. In the countryside men relied mostly on donkeys for transportation, and women and children walked. There were few cars and trucks. Children walked to and from school. Some older Nevisian women recall having to walk three to four miles to school and back. With the increase in tourism, roads have been upgraded. In 2003, there were at least twenty minibuses providing transportation between Charlestown and the smaller villages. The number of privately owned automobiles has increased drastically over the last ten years, primarily as the result of the expansion of employment opportunities in the tourism sector. It should be noted that automobiles also provide greater access to privacy and/or to secluded areas—as indicated by some of my informants. Furthermore, automobiles are typically marketed as indicators of status and therefore become important in social exchange, principally in terms of the sexual-economic exchange patterns in which Nevisian girls engage.

BRIEF OVERVIEW OF THE EDUCATION SYSTEM

Before 1975 children were not required to attend school.[5] In 1975, the government passed the Education Act mandating compulsory education for children and adolescents. In 1984, the Education Department desegregated primary schools based on gender, allowing primary-aged boys and girls to attend school together for the first time. The current Nevisian school system is modeled after the British system. There are a number of primary schools for students 5–11 years old and three secondary schools (one of which, as previously mentioned, is privately run) for students 12–16 years old. Within the secondary schools, six stratified Forms are used to designate grades. Within each of the six Forms there are levels, which further stratify the groups. Academic performance and test scores determine placement into specific levels. For example, Form 1-A would be the highest class for 12- to 13-year-olds; Form 2-A would be the highest class for 13- to 14-year-olds; Form 3-A would be the highest class for 14- to 15-year-olds, and so on. Schools are in session from September to July, and classes are held Monday through Friday.

There are a variety of postsecondary education and training programs offered within the Federation of St. Kitts and Nevis of which some graduates take advantage. The Clarence Fitzroy Bryant College located on St. Kitts offers courses affiliated with the University of West Indies in the arts, sciences, and humanities. In addition, there are a number of private institutions, although they are costly and consequently cater mostly to international students, including Ross University School of Veterinary Medicine on St. Kitts and the Medical University of the Americas on Nevis.

CONSUMER CULTURE

When older Nevisians reflect upon the changes in their society over the past ten years, especially the events and conditions that have had the greatest influence on their lives, they generally point to two events: first, the opening of the Four Seasons, and second, the availability and widespread consumption of cable television via satellite. In 1988, which was the year when a significant number of my informants were born, Cable TV of Nevis Ltd., began providing television programming on Nevis via satellite. I mention the age of my informants and the introduction of cable TV because many of the girls I worked with could not imagine their lives without television. Still, there were a significant number of girls who could recall that as small children they did not have access to television and of these girls, most could actually recall with great vividness the first time their families acquired a TV. In the 1980s, due to limited employment opportunities and a virtually nonexistent hotel industry (fewer than 200 beds on the island), the majority of people on Nevis could not afford to purchase televisions. If they did manage to purchase a set, it was a black-and-white set and it was brought in from St. Thomas or St. Martin. Up until 1988, Nevisians had access to one or two regional channels depending on where they lived on the island. Cable TV of Nevis Ltd now offers a variety of packages. The basic service rate per month is EC$50 (U.S.$19.00) which includes twelve channels. Subscribers have access to, among other channels, ESPN International, CNN, VH1 Music Videos, local programming, Nickelodeon, and the Disney channel. For EC$70 (U.S.$26.00), subscribers on Nevis can have a Tier package with forty-two channels that include Court TV, the Family Channel, Fox Network, the History Channel, Black Entertainment Television (BET), Lifetime TV and National Geographic. Four percent of subscribers have access to all of these channels, plus the option of HBO, Cinemax, the Movie channel, and/or Disney for an extra fee. The most popular package is the Tier package without the movie channels. Local broadcasting is offered with the basic service. Locally broadcast shows include local news shows, government-sponsored TV programs, educational, agricultural and health-related programs, spelling bees, beauty pageants, cultural events, and the locally produced *Get Real* program that spotlights Nevisian adolescents discussing popular topics.

In 1995, the first Internet service was provided to a private financial company. By 2001, a small coffee shop featuring Internet access had opened on Main Street and for a fee, customers could access the World Wide Web. The public library also has two computers, which allow free Internet access for up to fifteen minutes. In 2003, two new computer stores opened selling Gateways, Dells, and other imported computers and software. It is also possible to order and ship computers to Nevis from the United States, but customers are required to pay up to 80 percent in duty fees. Access to network and non-network programs and the Internet no doubt provides access to new sexual scripts. The connections between these changes in Nevisian society and changes in sexual scripts will be explored fully in chapter 4.

The rise in consumerism, then, is distinctively marked by globalization. This is not meant to overlook the fact that social life of Nevis has, for centuries, been affected by global economic, cultural, and political connections, but rather it is meant to acknowledge the new degree to which, and intensity with which, globalization has affected social life on Nevis. Obviously, the desire for, and access to, these various consumer goods and services vary among Nevisians. Consumer culture takes many forms in this small island society particularly in light of the fact that approximately 32 percent of the people live off of EC$328 a month (Kairi 2001).

In an effort to describe more fully the extent to which consumer goods are consumed and circulated on Nevis, it is useful to lay out some figures regarding the girls' access to, and use of, the most pertinent consumer goods and services—the meaning and implications of which will be explored in chapter 6. Of the 153 girls surveyed, 96 percent report owning a television set with 91 percent reportedly having access to cable. Six percent of the girls reported watching TV one hour per day, 28 percent 2–3 hours per day, 27 percent 4–5 hours per day, and 8 percent 6 or more hours per day. Of the 153 girls surveyed, 97 percent indicated having a computer in their homes and 18 percent of the girls reported owning cell phones.

TOURISM: SOCIAL AND ECONOMIC IMPACT

It is difficult if not impossible to tease apart the effects produced by these sources of global influences on Nevis. As discussed in the previous section, the rise in the consumption of consumer goods and services as well as infrastructural changes, such as water lines, the availability of electricity, and new road construction, are all linked to the increase of, and dependency on, tourism. The most obvious social effects of tourism is that it changed the economic climate of the entire island, not only by contributing to the government's revenue but also by providing a livelihood for close to 40 percent of the working population and by increasing the standard of living for many. For example, many women like Ruthie became financially independent as the result of working at the Four Seasons. Once employed by the resort, Ruthie was able to secure a EC$25,000 loan from the credit union in 1993 to build her two-bedroom concrete house. She eventually installed electricity and plumbing and was able to purchase a bed, a television, a stovetop, and a number of kitchen utensils.

As well as affecting the economic climate, many Nevisians maintain that the growth in the hotel industry and the presence of the Four Seasons in particular has produced a large number of, what locals are now calling, "latchkey" children and teens who arrive home from school and are left alone while their mothers or grandmothers work a late shift. Unsupervised, girls reported going out with boys at night, walking the streets, watching television, and/or surfing the internet. Latchkey children and teenagers no doubt have more freedom to engage in sexual practices given the increased opportunities for privacy and more unfettered access to friends and sexual partners.

Tourism also affects social life on Nevis because of the way goods and activities associated with tourism become desirable and thus encourage commodity consumption among Nevisians, particularly if there is prestige associated with the consumption of specific goods and services. Tourists signify glamour, excessive materialism, luxury and wealth. This is represented on Nevis, for example, by the tourists' ability to afford hotel rooms where the price of one night's stay might range from U.S.$400 to well over a U.S.$1,000, by the luxurious villas and cars they rent, by the expensive camera equipment they carry, and by the pricey imported liquor and extravagant foods that fill their grocery carts at the local supermarkets. Nevisians are also well aware of their island's reputation as an exclusive retreat for the international elite. Celebrities like Britney Spears, Kelly Ripa, Bobby Brown, Whitney Houston, Michael Douglas, and Mel Gibson are among the "superstars" who have spent holidays at the Four Seasons. Tourists' and celebrities' behaviors and consumption practices incite desire. These desires can be inflamed further by images viewed on television, on the Internet, and in Hollywood movies.

Commodity consumption serves as just one way in which tourism might be viewed as a site of desire. Not only can Nevisians acquire new desires from their observations of tourists, but we also need to consider the sexual interactions between tourists and Nevisians as a potential contributor to such desire. While Nevis is not a site for sex tourism like other Caribbean islands, such as Cuba or the Dominican Republic (Kempadoo 1999), male and female tourists do engage in sexual relationships with Nevisians creating situations that have the possibility of affecting the local sexual culture.[6] Recall Thomas's account of how oral sex (females performing this act on males) had been imported from the United States, and that in particular, female tourists had introduced it to the beachboys. This account suggests that the local sexual discourse is transformed when people with varying sexual ideologies intermingle.

Compared to the Nevisians who are employed by the hotels, the girls with whom I worked had little direct contact with tourists on a daily basis unless they worked part-time at the supermarket or at another family business in town where tourists might shop. However, it is important to stress that given the size of population on Nevis and the significant percentage of Nevisians who come in contact with tourists, it is not difficult to imagine girls being affected by the changes in the local sexual culture.

Tourism has produced social and demographic changes in other ways as well. In recent years, Nevis has been experiencing an influx of returning nationals as well as immigrants from Guyana and the Dominican Republic who arrive in order to work in the growing tourist industry, many of whom bring with them their young families. Additionally, at the time of my visit to Nevis, there were about 900 people who had moved to Nevis from England, the United States, and/or Canada, some of whom are working in tourism, and others, once tourists, had relocated permanently to Nevis. The way these various cultural groups, namely, wealthy tourists, expatriates, and recent immigrants, are treated within Nevisian society demonstrates how markers of social difference such as skin color, nationality, and class are significant aspects of social life. For instance, Dominican women are viewed by some Nevisians as contributing to the increasing rise of a "commercial sex" problem on Nevis, and thus are considered responsible for the spread of HIV. Guyanese immigrants, on the other hand, are blamed for taking away jobs from Nevisians. Both groups, Dominicans and Guyanese, face social marginalization as a result of these suspicions. For example, I was told by several teachers in the secondary schools to avoid the Guyanese girls because they were "liars." One informant of mine, a fifteen-year-old Guyanese girl who was performing at the top of her class and whose family had recently immigrated to Nevis, was concerned that she would miss out on taking the standardized test required to get into college. She and her mother were convinced that the teachers would purposely give her misinformation as to the time and date of the test schedule. Like some of their teachers, Nevisian girls were also known to discriminate against and reproduce stereotypes about their Guyanese classmates. For instance, a contestant for a talent show performed a song about an unfaithful and abusive boyfriend. While attempting to bring awareness to the issue of domestic violence, the girl reproduced negative stereotypes about immigrant populations. The song highlighted how a girl had been beaten by her partner and how he had "run around" with other women. At one point in the performance the contestant declares, "And when it wasn't a Jamaican, it was [pausing for an effect] . . . wha de one wid all dem gold teeth in she mouth come from again? [pausing again for a response for the audience] Yes Guyana!" Women from the Dominican Republic were also targeted in the performance as women who steal Nevisian men away from their partners. This is an instance in which the girls, like many Nevisians, in response to the influx of immigrants, are promulgating a sexual discourse that casts foreign women, including Guyanese and Dominican schoolgirls living on Nevis, as sexual others and as sexually promiscuous.

There are other ways in which skin color, nationality, and class work together, politically and socially, on Nevis.[7] First, it is important to point out that there does not appear to be sharp social classes delineated by skin color. A light-skinned upper social class does not currently monopolize resources such as land, wealth, and political power as it did at the turn of the twentieth century. However, the only secondary private school on Nevis caters to the children of the expatriate community as well as to the island's elite, namely, sons and daughters of government employees, doctors, and lawyers. These privileged students represent both "clear-skinned" and "dark-skinned" Nevisians. Given the relative newness of the private school and the small number of graduates, it is difficult to assess whether or not, for instance, these graduates secure higher-paying jobs or are more likely to gain entrance at universities. Still, a type of social status is attached to attending the only private secondary school on the island where one's parents are required to pay and the teachers are individuals who are primarily trained in either England or the United States. What is more, the students attending the school view themselves as socially and economically advantaged.

NEVISIAN CIVIL SOCIETY

The improvement in the local economy has elevated women's social and economic statuses and coincides with a growing civil society that is taking shape in the form of a number of non-governmental organizations (NGO) focused on the welfare of women and children. As we shall see, this increase in the status of women in Nevisian society has had an impact on the sexual culture, particularly as it relates to the subject of sexual violence, which has only recently become a public health matter.

Some of the new NGOs are affiliated with local churches, including a number of youth groups. Some are community action groups, grassroots in their orientation and focused on social change. Nevis has an active Girl Brigade and Girl Guides program, which are similar to the Girl Scouts of America, providing personal development activities for girls between the ages of seven and twenty. While the Girl Guides and the Girl Brigades are linked to, and are extensions of, long-standing religious movements on Nevis, the Change Center, organized around gender issues, is a new NGO in the community. The center, the first of its kind on Nevis, provides assistance and support for women and children who are victims of sexual and physical abuse. Its presence signifies a change in terms of women's status and the importance some Nevisians place on women's mental and physical well-being. The politics of the center mirror aspects of Nevisian cultural politics related to gender issues. For example, while the center receives a small amount of funding from the government, segments of the community view its mission as meddling in domestic affairs. Domestic violence, like sexuality, is viewed by Nevisians as a private matter. The center and its supporters view domestic violence as well as sexual violence as public health issues, a view that is not widespread among Nevisians.

As just noted, Nevis has experienced tremendous economic growth as well as a variety of social changes. The economic growth and social changes no doubt affect each other. Girls are no longer required to do chores that could take them up to two or three hours to complete before and after school, leaving them with more free time. Since there are now water lines, girls no longer carry drums to the standpipe to collect water. The availability of electricity, combined with more disposable income to purchase stovetops or ovens, means that girls no longer have to spend time collecting firewood. The newly paved roads, combined with varied modes of transportation to accommodate the increasing number of employed persons, results in the fact that girls no longer have to walk to and from school. Of course, other chores such as shopping in the supermarket or going downtown to stand in line to pay the cable or water bills, have supplanted the old chores, but these newer chores are less labor intensive and less time-consuming. With more money and more free time girls have more opportunities to consume imported commodities that reflect the mediated images and scripts they see on TV or in the fashion magazines that are readily available at the checkout counter in the relatively new grocery stores and pharmacies. Additionally, exposure to the wealthy tourists educates Nevisian girls about new lifestyles to which they were previously not exposed. In addition to the growing consumer culture and the rise of a civil society there have been significant educational reforms, not the least of which was to make education mandatory and to desegregate the schools based on gender, putting girls and boys in closer proximity, which makes the products, images, and behaviors related to sex more relevant. In other words, there is more incentive for paying attention to these new messages and scripts.

NARROWING THE FIELD: LIFE IN JESSUP

For a more contextualized understanding of the research setting and for a more detailed look at the conditions of my fieldwork, it is worthwhile to look closely at the rhythm of village life. From January to July 2003, I lived with my twin daughters in Jessup, a community of about 300 households and approximately 600 people. It was quite similar to other Nevisian villages and had not escaped the changing social and economic conditions just described. Living where I did, in an older and more established village, surrounded by Nevisians as opposed to living in a development that was comprised of lavish villas and new homes occupied by expatriates and the elite members of Nevisian society, I was able to participate in the life of the village and to know its people, particularly the girls, from an intimate distance rather than from afar. Experiencing the village-based rhythm of daily life helped me to see firsthand how the recent economic and social changes affected Nevisian society, and specifically, how these changes resulted in the globalization of girls' sexualities.

By 7:30 a.m. the village was bustling with activity, given the heat that would be coming later in the day. Construction workers had begun working on the houses in the village. The local bakery ran a delivery service, and its old white beat-up-Toyota made its way through the village slowing down in front of the houses of its regular customers, beeping the horn repeatedly to summon the occupants. At this time of day several people, mostly women and children, walked down the hill that leads out of the village toward the main road to catch a ride or a bus into Charlestown. However, there were always a few women carrying babies or toddlers walking up the hill to drop off their children at the new day care center. These women represented a growing population of mothers who worked and did not have a mother or grandmother to rely on for childcare. Family members were also likely to be working outside the home or perhaps had even migrated to look for work in the United States or England.

The concrete house we rented, with electricity and water, bordered two villages, Paradise Estates to the north and Jessup to the southeast. The houses in Paradise Estates were painted in pastels; some were various shades of yellow, blue, and pale pink. The residents of Paradise Estates were either returning nationals from England, local business owners, or prominent Nevisian families involved in state politics. Two families were non-nationals employed by the Four Seasons. A returning national whose father worked for the Nevisian government owned the house we rented.

Looking westward one could see the Caribbean Sea and St. Kitts and toward the east there was a view of Mount Nevis and the hills of Jessup village. The houses in Jessup were older and more modest than those in Paradise Estates. Some were concrete and some remain unfinished with second stories waiting to be built. In instances like this, one could see three-foot iron rods sticking out of the concrete that served as the roof of the house. Sometimes cement blocks were amassed in the corner of the yard, which indicated that money had run out and people were waiting to save more to resume construction. Small two-room wooden houses resting on concrete foundations were common in Jessup. While most people had gardens, yards were generally not as well-maintained as they were in Paradise Estates. Rusted car parts, old appliances, and trash littered the yards. Chickens and roosters scrambled about the yards, frequently stopping to peck and scratch at the dirt. By contrast, the houses in Paradise Estates were all concrete. Most were large, with three or four bedrooms and fences and elaborate iron gates designed to keep out the livestock, which grazed or passed nearby, which if given the opportunity would destroy a garden in a few hours.

Like clockwork, or rather, in step with the rhythm of the village life, every morning the children from Saint Thomas Primary School cut through the village pasture near our house on their way to school. The hills in the village were steep, and the road from the top is about two miles long so it was not uncommon to see primary schoolchildren dressed in their brown and yellow uniforms piled in the back of trucks, with some of the boys perched on the sides of the truck while it careened down the hill. By 8:00 a.m. on most weekdays I could hear children singing—their voices carried across Garretts' pasture, which separated my house from the schoolyard.

The afternoon presented its own quiet pace. Late in the day barefoot boys rode their bicycles through the village. Shepherds managed their herds of goats. Before sunset, Miles tended to two horses in the nearby pasture. Every night he appeared in his white jeep with two large buckets of water for his animals. Using a machete he cut back some of the shrubs. Tethered to ropes, Miles's two horses obediently followed behind as he moved them around the pasture for better grazing. This sight was in contrast to George's unmanageable goats. From what I learned, George was also a Rastafarian from a nearby village. Like Miles, he appeared nightly leading nine or ten goats on separate ropes to the upper grazing lands. George talked loudly to his animals as he worked through tangled lines and managed his disorderly herd.

The night's activities occurred with as much regularity as the rest of the day. In the late evening as I prepared my field notes from the day's work, I could hear the men's choir from the Anglican church; their voices carried with the wind just like the schoolchildren's morning songs. It was soothing but in some ways ironic that my days in the field would begin and end with the sounds of religious hymns. Religious discourse permeates all aspects of social life on Nevis. As I sat down each night after my daughters were fast asleep to review my field notes from the day just ended—stories about sexual escapades and fragments of girls' pleasures and desires—what impressed me the most was how two seemingly incongruent aspects of social life, namely, sexuality and religion, would be the most formative aspects of life on Nevis. In chapter 3, I turn to a discussion on this very subject—the tensions and contradictions between religious moral discourse on the one hand, and older more established sexual traditions on the other hand.

CHAPTER 3

Competing Discourses
and Moralities at Play

AALIYAH'S CD WAS playing in the laundromat. I could hear Eleanor and Ruthie arguing, their voices competing with Aaliyah's sexy lyrics. Eleanor insisted that she would never wear a sleeveless dress to church. The music stopped abruptly. "There goes the power again," reported Ruthie. Eleanor was bent on convincing Ruthie that she was right. Eleanor's sister had apparently worn a sleeveless dress to church service on Sunday and Eleanor saw it as a blatant sign of disrespect and indecency. The recent incident had dominated Eleanor's family conversations. Eleanor lives with her mother, stepfather, a sister, her sister's children, and her own children. That her sister had violated what Eleanor deemed to be acceptable standards of dress for church had visibly upset Eleanor. When she and Ruthie approached me outside in the yard she was still discussing the matter. Eleanor described in great detail how her sister wore a thin, form-fitting dress to church without a proper slip underneath, thus revealing her panty lines. "She do dis on purpose. . . . It show de shape of her booty." As Eleanor explained, Ruthie playfully gestured to her own buttocks and swung her hips. Eleanor looked at her with disgust. "I never wear a dress like dat to church," as she said this she pointed to my sleeveless purple cotton sundress. "We're supposed to wear hats to church. I don't anymore," Eleanor explained. I learned that Eleanor's sister was involved with a white expatriate who, according to Eleanor and Ruthie, buys her Victoria's Secret underpants that she likes to wear to church under her tight dresses, accentuating her figure. Eleanor continued, "When she come home from church yesterday, me momma asks, 'Where you comin' from dressin' like dat?'" In hearing her daughter's reply, Eleanor's mother reportedly admonished her daughter, instructing her, "Next time you wear a slip." Ruthie smiled and winked at me and said, "Eleanor's sister, she real sexy."

That conversation took place in early January sometime during the first few weeks of my fieldwork on Nevis. By late June, when the mangoes hung from the trees like Christmas ornaments, I had seen a much different side of

Eleanor. One summer morning while standing in the yard, Eleanor, on her first try, picked up a stone and hit an overripe mango so that it landed almost perfectly at her feet. Eleanor's perfect aim didn't surprise me. I had watched Eleanor knock down a shock-shock from a flamboyant tree on her first attempt. Now that surprised me. "Shock-shocks" as they are commonly referred to, are long, six- to twelve-inch brown pods about an inch wide that hang down from the trees. Knocking them down from the branches is a children's pastime in the West Indies. Sometime in May, Eleanor had stopped me in the yard instructing me to wait. As she bent over to find a stone, I thought I'd be there all afternoon. Eleanor was not the most athletic-looking woman at 5'3, weighing close to 160 pounds with "coke bottle" eyeglasses, I had a hard time imagining that her aim would be anything close to accurate. But her aim, a skill she must have developed as a child, was dead-on. Aiming up at the branches, Eleanor threw the small stone with such force that she managed to knock off the shock-shock. This was a little gift she wanted my daughters to have. When the pod shakes, the seeds inside make a rattling sound. After awhile nothing surprised me about Eleanor. As clichéd as it sounds, in many ways we had come to expect the unexpected from each other. On the warm morning in June after she had knocked a mango from the tree, we were standing at the sink in the laundromat and sharing pieces of the fruit, careful not to let its juices run onto our blouses. What follows was instructive in many ways as it highlights how a Nevisian woman like Eleanor could embody and perform in different social contexts the contradictions and the tensions that I so often observed and experienced firsthand throughout Nevisian culture between religious propriety on one hand, and sexual permissiveness on the other hand.

First, it is important to explain that Eleanor was a private person; although she loved to share her opinions, it took her awhile to warm up to me. She prided herself on being a homebody and told me that she preferred spending time with her sisters, mother, and children on weeknights and looked forward to keeping company with the father of her youngest child on the weekends. She attended church services on Sunday and devoured romance novels in her spare time. On this particular morning our conversation once again turned toward men and sexual pleasure. Wiping her hands on a towel to clean the mango's juices, Eleanor explained the best way to "take it up the ass," referring to what she considered to be the optimal conditions for anal penetration by a male partner. She bent over the counter with her legs spread apart, her back arched and her elbows supporting her weight; as she did this she lifted up her buttocks and skillfully rotated her hips. While still bent over the counter Eleanor debated with Ruthie the merits of using a condom and a lubricant. They both insisted on using a condom, but Ruthie tried to persuade us that "our natural [vaginal] juices, dey just as good." Ruthie and I watched with great amusement clapping our hands together as the pace of Eleanor's movements quickened. Just then, a male tourist peeked his head through the door apparently looking for service. Utterly embarrassed, Eleanor let out a shriek and ran into the next room, leaving Ruthie and me behind to collect ourselves and deal with him.

The juxtaposition of these two scenes elucidates what I see as the social discontinuities produced by seemingly contradictory and at times incompatible discourses, namely, religion and traditional discourses on sexuality, which appear to be two of the strongest determinants shaping subjectivities on Nevis.[1] I juxtapose the debate that took place between Eleanor and Ruthie about acceptable standards of dress for church with a story involving one of the many times that Eleanor offered sexual tutoring, in this instance on the practice of anal sex, to highlight the multidimensionality of Nevisian sexualities. In this chapter, I will examine the contemporary religious moral discourses as well as traditional discourses on sexuality, in order to argue that there are competing discourses producing normative practices among Nevisians and more importantly how these discourses interact, that is, the specifics of this competition. As we will see, while the traditional discourses on sexuality do not reflect ideal values and notions of sexuality, they are nevertheless producing normalized sexual practices, subject to specific codes and social regulations. Before proceeding with this course of action, I examine the historical roots of the contemporary religious discourse.

CULTURE OF RESPECTABILITY: COLONIAL AND RELIGIOUS MORALITIES

Contemporary Nevisian notions of sexual morality are embedded in religious discourse and need to be understood in the context from which they emerged, namely, the Methodist society. The permissive sexual system that grew out of the plantation complex on Nevis generated a social climate that was to be challenged by missionaries. In the 1780s, Methodists initiated a mission on Nevis and began promoting white European sensibilities and a new morality linked to respectability. Notions of respectability tied to sexual behavior and sexual propriety that emerged among the middle class in Europe were transported to Nevis via the Methodist society.[2] Methodists condemned much of Afro-Caribbean culture including the slaves' family systems that garnered most of the missionaries' attention and efforts. Sexual restraint and a sanctified sexuality were considered virtues that the Methodist society attempted to introduce through various religious and educational institutions (Olwig 1993). Methodists promoted a new morality in its schools. Attempting to make marriage normative, Methodists started officiating marriages among slaves. By the nineteenth century, marriage and a sanctified sexuality became the organizing principles for a new moral order prompted and institutionalized by the Methodist society on Nevis (Olwig 1993, 69–135). However, the

Anglican church by this time began to compete with the Methodists for the moral leadership on Nevis and as a result, in 1828, a marriage act was passed on Nevis making marriages performed by the Methodist church illegal and recognized only those performed by the Church of England or Ireland (82).

After emancipation in 1834, European churches continued promoting and teaching a "culture of respectability" in the church-run schools, focusing on manners, grooming, appearance, and sexual civility. The missionaries' vision of a moral order competed with the post-emancipation culture that had established itself on Nevis (Olwig 1993, 92–112). The English emphasis on respectability constituted itself against the popular culture developed by the Afro-Caribbean population, which in many ways continued to reinforce sexual behavior and relationships common to plantation life. For instance, within post-emancipation societies in the West Indies, a type of masculinity that was linked to fecundity was valorized within the Afro-Caribbean popular culture, which, in turn, structured gender relationships such that men often avoided legally sanctioned unions and women overlooked their partners' multiple sexual relations.[3] This, according to Diane Austin-Broos (1997), forced poorer women "as a matter of practical necessity" (197) to look for a series of male partners to support them and their children. Karen Olwig (1993) recounts an interesting set of stories when describing how a Methodist sense of morality often competed with the local norms and values on Nevis. She describes how a chapel keeper in 1861 was expelled from the society for impregnating two young women, one right after the other. In another incident, a woman was expelled from the church for renting out rooms to couples who were not legally married. The landlady had refused to adhere to the church's demands to evict the renters maintaining that it was an economic necessity for her to rent rooms to individuals regardless of their marital status. That visiting unions, concubinage, and co-residential unions were normative within the Afro-Caribbean culture after emancipation prompted the Anglican reverend Jones in 1887 to write in his diaries that marriage is "altogether an afterthought with these people" (106).

By the turn of the century, a light-skinned local elite had established itself on Nevis. This elite cultural group, according to Olwig, worked to uphold the European morality or at least to give the appearance that this was the case. Olwig also paints a picture of a small middle class that fostered and attempted to adhere to a "culture of respectability" with a focus on marriage and sexual propriety. But according to Olwig (1993), notions of respectability become localized. Olwig writes: "Despite this orientation towards the English culture of respectability, the middle class seems to have developed specifically local patterns as far as relations between the sexes were concerned. Whereas women were expected to spend most of their time in the home, men had considerably more leeway in their social relationships, including sexual ones, and it was quite common for a male of the middle class to have a number of 'outside' children as well as children with his wife" (119).

Certain aspects of respectability were beyond the economic means of poorer women, particularly marriage. "Marriage had become associated with a certain social standing" (Olwig 1993, 82), demonstrated by having the economic means to own one's house. A cultural requirement for marriage consequently was an unattainable goal for the majority of the Afro-Caribbean people living on Nevis, thereby denying many women of limited means the ability to live up to the English notions of respectability. It is not surprising then that when new denominations of Christianity, such as the Pilgrim Holiness Church, began their missionizing efforts on Nevis in 1910, they attracted some of the poorer residents of Nevis, many of whom were women. Olwig attributes this to a number of factors. First, the Pilgrim Holiness Church distributed secondhand clothing collected from the United States which provided people with decent church clothes that they otherwise would not have and discouraged them from joining other more established churches. Second, women were given church leadership roles and encouraged to become preachers. This new avenue for respectability and potential to increase their social status appealed to many women who otherwise, as a result of their limited economic means, had limited ways to gain social respect in the community (1993, 123–125). Olwig writes:

> The significance of this elevated spiritual position is apparent in the special clothing which was reserved for the church. Church attendance was particularly important for the women, for whom involvement in church affairs presented the main possibility of obtaining a position of respect in the local community. The necessity of their continued involvement in the hard physical labor connected with sharecrop farming clearly precluded any aspirations, on their part, to become well tended housewives. Furthermore, the close association of marriage with the establishment of a proper home meant that many women with children did not marry, or they only married at a relatively late age, when they were able to afford to establish themselves in a family house. For these women whose everyday life-style branded them as anything but respectable, the Church provided a means of seeking salvation from their earthly "sins." (125–126)

Church participation and attendance are still very much the means by which women and girls in particular gain access to social respectability within their community. The historical colonial moralities linked to religious movements like the Methodist church and then later to other Christian sects continue to influence present-day sexual moral codes and discourses on Nevis.

PRESENT-DAY RELIGIOUS MORALITIES

Catholicism, Seventh Day Adventism, Jehovah's Witnesses, Baptist, and Pentecostalism are among the religious practices represented on Nevis. Religious life is an important aspect of Nevisian social life, and intersects with multiple cultural domains, including politics, education, and family life, in order to exert social control. The prime minister opens and closes his political addresses with blessings, children pray and sing religious hymns in public schools, and discussions related to public health often are infused with religious themes. Religious programs on television and on the radio are popular. For example, it is not uncommon to walk into shops or homes and see religious programs on television or hear religious broadcasting on the radio. Some vans used for public transportation are named after books in the Old Testament, such as "Exodus"; other names have religious connotations, such as "Dignity." Most Nevisians are Christians and attend church services and Bible meetings regularly. A woman in her thirties recalled church-life as a child: "When I was little, Sunday was the day to go to church, as many churches as you could fit in. We dressed in our Sunday best. We had service in the morning, followed by Sunday school, and then we returned home for lunch. On Sunday nights if you lived pretty close to another church and there was a service, your mother sent you. She might not go but she sent you anyway, even if it wasn't your church. If they passed out treats at Sunday night service then you wanted to go back the next week, even if you weren't a member. It didn't make any difference, as long as there was a church we went."

What stands out in this woman's account is the impressive number of hours that were spent engaged in religious services, and while not every moment was involved in prayer, singing, and/or listening to sermons, most of the time was devoted to these activities—all of this suggests how religious discourse functions as one of the strongest determinants shaping social life on Nevis. It is not that we can assume that going to church makes one chaste; rather, what this woman's comments suggest is that religious activities structure the girls' experiences and how they come to understand themselves as young women within this social context.

Experiences such as the one just described were also related to me by the girls. They spoke of having a specific church affiliation, but then many girls described attending services on a regular basis with friends and extended family at churches where they were not formally members. Often, at least among the girls, church life was talked about more as a social venue than as an expression of their spiritual lives or religious subjectivities. As Yvonne, a thirteen-year-old, says: "I really, really into church. I really like it. It gives me a chance to get out of the house."

Most girls, when asked questions about their religious beliefs, responded by listing a number of social activities in which they participate, such as Bible study, youth group activities, or choirs. The girls apparently viewed their participation in church-related social activities as evidence of their religiosity. One mature sixteen-year-old named Felicia attempted to articulate the influence religion had on her life. Felicia explained:

I grew up in an Anglican church. I didn't really have a choice in the matter. I went to Sunday school and sang in the choir, and did little dance things when the church had concerts. When I became a teen, I joined the Anglican Young People's Association—that was really fun, because I was constantly with people my own age. At night we would attend meetings and have fund-raisers. I was very active in church and read the Bible and all that good stuff. So, it is safe to say that I am a Christian and because of that I guess I am supposed to be really strict with my views concerning moral behavior. The truth is I'm really not. I can totally respect someone's views and beliefs. For example, gays and lesbians, I think they are really fun people in general and I respect that they have made their own decision, but at the same time, that's not a lifestyle I would ever choose for myself, because in the eyes of God that type of behavior is a major sin. Most of the decisions I make hardly ever have anything to do with how God would see it, which is kind of sad, I guess. I know if I were to do things based on that I probably wouldn't be able to do anything. As a young person, there are times when I cuss, and disrespect my parents . . . all of this the Bible frowns on. So I'm pretty much at odds with the Bible's teaching, even though I know them so well. Some time ago, I got involved with a man who my mother just absolutely hated. She tried everything to make me see things her way. She even went as far as to have our church pastor sit and talk with me. That was the first time my church life directly crossed paths with my personal life. I was a bit embarrassed but at the same time, I was furious that he had the audacity to lecture me on my personal life. I did end up lying to the pastor about a few things, like had I had sex. . . . I felt guilty at the end of it all. I guess in some way I always feel like, "Hey I'm young; I'll have time to repent later when I'm old and gray."

Felicia was one of the more academically successful girls on Nevis. It is worth noting that when Felicia and I were together she rarely spoke in a Nevisian dialect and rarely used local idioms. She lives with her mother and younger siblings. She performed at the top of the class, had many close girl friends, and enjoyed modeling for a local company. When we met she was dating a man in his thirties. One of her most important goals in life was to move off-island and attend college in the United States. Felicia's comments highlight the tension between what Stuart Hall (1996) refers to as discursive regulation and the practices of subjective self-constitution (13). In terms of the production of subjectivity, her comments can be interpreted as evidence for both the affect of religious discourse, on the one hand, and her capacity for agency on the other hand. She recognizes herself, an integral process of subjectivity (12), in light of how she thinks she measures up to the teachings of the Bible. Felicia accounts for her behavior in relation to Christian teachings, referencing her

1. Saint Paul's Anglican Church, Charlestown.

relationship with her mother and her position toward gays and lesbians. However, while it is apparent that her notions of right and wrong are guided by Christian teachings, Felicia also disavows the impact of religious discourse in her life. This disavowal, among other practices, can be viewed as the process of self-constitution. Similarly, her account of her interaction with her pastor is also revealing. While she lied to her pastor in claiming that she was not sexually active and was angered by their encounter, "at the end of it all" Felicia still felt guilty. Felicia's assertion that she can "repent" when she is older suggests, at least at this time in her life, illustrates that she views herself as not living up to the moral standards imposed on her. Felicia's subjectivity is constituted as much by religious forces as by her resistance.

The social processes that produce Felicia's subjectivity are not always compatible, and as we shall see, contradictory discourses have the effect of subverting each other. For example, in chapter 4 Felicia describes how she wants to emulate the girls in music videos in order to be "sexy" and to attract boys. Felicia's desires to be like the girls in the videos represent what older Nevisians view as the threat of consumerism and television culture. The ideal religious moral discourse is undermined by the pleasures of the imported consumer culture. For many Nevisians, the foreign influences that are perceived to undermine Nevisian morality can be reduced if womens' and girls' sexualities are managed. This is evident in the contemporary moral discourse that focuses on teen sexualities. Before examining the moral discourse on sexuality, it is important to note that womens' and girls' sexualities have always been managed; however, sex was much less of a spectacle in the past and much less tied to conspicuous consumption than to paying rent and feeding a family. In chapter 5 I will examine closely how younger and older Nevisians draw the line regarding the propriety of sexual-economic exchange. Needless to say, the older generation's questioning of the morality of girls' sexual practices cannot be fully understood in the absence of such an analysis.

Against "Slouching towards Gomorrah"

The dominant Nevisian moral discourse on sex and sexuality does not have its roots in a secular moral philosophy; rather, it is intimately tied to fundamental Christian tradition. A significant percentage of the population practices and tries to adhere to the teachings of Christianity. What this means in terms of everyday life for Nevisians is that moral discussions about sexuality reflect back on what is commonly referred to in the Christian churches as "God's will." The moral discourse concerning sexuality on Nevis can be characterized as mirroring the teachings in the Bible. Many of the older Nevisians who commented on sexuality grounded their discussion of sexuality in terms of religious teachings and scripture. I found this to be true among practicing Catholics, Baptists, Methodists, and nondenominational Christian sects.

Like any other form of moral discourse on sex and sexuality, the moral discourse circulating on Nevis is intended to guide and control sexual behavior.

The moral discourse on Nevis targeted at young people, not surprisingly, espouses sexual virtue and chastity. The issue of "teenage pregnancy" is also the subject of moral discussions. It is estimated that one out of every five live births is born to a teenage mother (Statistical Report, Health Information Unit 2001). For girls, staying off the streets at night, abstaining from sexual activity, heading home after school and avoiding loitering in town, doing well in school, earning high scores on exams, avoiding the negative effects of U.S. culture, specifically BET and soap operas, avoiding boys and older men, and attending church and church-sponsored youth group activities are conditions and activities that make a girl virtuous in the eyes of the religious community. When focusing on youth, community leaders often use U.S. culture as a gauge by which to measure Nevisian morality. Interestingly, the more closely Nevisian youth appear to mirror the customs and lifestyles of U.S. youth, the greater the perceived threat that Nevisian youth pose to Nevisian morality. During an interview, Reverend Percival of Saint George's Anglican Church spoke directly to this in a discussion on girls and sexuality:

> Well, I will begin by saying to you that Robert Bork has written a book, *Slouching Towards Gomorrah* and in it he has described the pathetic way in which the American society has changed . . . and in it he has enumerated a number of situations that cause the pathetic situation as it stands in the United States vis-à-vis behavior, and he has likened that behavior . . . to the Sodom and Gomorrah situation . . . [concerning Nevis] because of television, because of the easy access to the American States . . . because of our economic situation and the arrival of Four Seasons coming to our shores and that which is beaming into us. . . . Nevis is slouching towards gomorrah (May 19, 2003).

Slouching Towards Gomorrah (1997) offers a critique of the rise of modern liberalism, popular culture, and academia in the United States. It represents a conservative explanation for what some view as a decline in American morality. Lamenting what he saw as the specific effects of American culture on Nevisian society, Reverend Percival continued:

> Here we have the situation where parents are at work all night, and the children are home by themselves. You find that instead of getting into books and researching on the Internet for information to enhance their education, they get into the Internet and get into areas [to] pick up . . . sex things. Then they can also put on the TV and they have these sets beaming into their bedroom, so here we go again. . . . We also have the situation where they show you [on television shows] how these young ladies are able to take their

boyfriends into their rooms and sleep with them, and so that is being done here as well, so that the boyfriends come over at night [while the parents are working] and then they leave in the morning. Parents come home in the morning. So these are the ills, which we are faced with and our girls, in spite of us saying to them, well, "this is not the right way," are doing it. You see, Debra, you have stages in life. You have morality. You do have the Christian life, which you have to give yourself to the Lord; [then] things will just fall in line and take progress. Your education is the first stage. When you have had that, then you look forward to getting married and living a decent life. For them [the girls] that is on the peripheral because of the fact that there is no money with it. . . . So the main thing here is money . . . money brings with it all the styles . . . but then your dress code is not commensurate with what is morally right, your whole makeup, et cetera, and these things are expensive, and so in order to fall in line with what is beaming into our bedrooms, what is beaming into our society, one has to get money . . . and those who don't have it are encouraged to go looking. They go locate [money]. . . . They go to the policeman. They go with the teachers and with some politicians [looking for money]. . . . You see how pathetic it is . . . a mess . . . that's where we are.

When Reverend Percival states that "in order to fall in line with what is beaming into our bedrooms, what is beaming into our society, one has to get money," he is speaking directly to the links between consumer culture and sexualities. He is gesturing to the power of commodity desire, commodity erotics, and the sexual-economic exchange system that is dominant within Nevisian society, all of which compete with the Christian lifestyle. According to the reverend, "to fall in line with what is beaming into our bedrooms," girls go in search of men with economic resources, men who hold steady jobs like policemen, teachers, and politicians. He sees this as a result of the influence of U.S. culture; he does not perceive, at least not in this instance anyway, that the practice of girls or women seeking men with whom they might exchange sex for access to goods or cash is a long-standing pattern on Nevis (which will be explored later in this chapter and more fully in the following chapters).

Many professionals, including youth leaders, teachers, and guidance counselors, expressed concern about what they perceived to be a decline in Nevisian morality. Francine Baker, a local attorney and leader of the Girl Brigade, a youth organization that has its roots in the Methodist society, reiterated Reverend Percival's sentiment about the moral health of the nation. In what follows, Francine Baker reflected upon what she viewed as the recent decline in Nevisian standards of morality:

You don't know how many times I have to tell the girls [to] stop slouching. "You shouldn't slouch," I tell them. "Sit up with your back straight and tall." What is lacking right now is the discipline. I think we've had a whole breakdown in society. The church has failed. The schools have failed. The parents have failed. Some of these structures that were in place need to be put back in place if we are going to have anything of a society forty years from now. [For instance], when I came back to Nevis in 1991, there weren't any loiterers on the street. You didn't find young men sitting on the street. In 1991, there weren't any guys sitting around the street aimlessly doing nothing—in the middle of the day, at night, any time of day. As a matter-of-fact when I came to Nevis, I first lived in Cotton Ground, and after 5:00 p.m. you couldn't get a bus. There was no bus traveling to Cotton Ground. You would have to walk, because there was nothing happening in Charlestown. There had been seven passenger buses on the island. Now there are at least twenty buses. And guys weren't sitting on the street, neither daytime nor evening time because they were working. They were all working. You were either working or in school. And if you were neither working or in school, you would be too ashamed to sit on the street. Now, it's a posing thing to be on the street and calling all the girls as they pass.

Baker begins with what she sees as a general lack of moral discipline that is reflected in the postures of girls, but she then links the girls' body postures to larger social and economic processes in her account of the "whole breakdown in society." With little effort, Baker's comments can be mined to understand aspects of the dominant moral discourse, but first the fragments of her story need to be pieced together. Baker is asserting that since 1991, which coincides with the opening of the Four Seasons, the social and economic climate on Nevis has changed. The fact that there are many buses that run back and forth from Charlestown to the smaller villages throughout the island, providing transportation at all hours and thus increasing the mobility of Nevisians, signals a lack of restriction for Baker. The greater opportunity for mobility represents greater freedom, and thus greater opportunity for people (specifically young men) to "hang out" away from their homes and away from the watchful eyes of family members and other villagers. What's missing from Baker's comments are a host of factors and explanations that might account for why there are more buses (to transport the increased number of workers to and from the local hotels) and why there appear to be more men "hanging out" (with the improvement of economic conditions, there has been a decrease in out-migration, particularly among younger men who now have more options to do shift work or seasonal labor).

What is striking about Baker's comments is that the "breakdown" in Nevisian morality is expressed by the bodies of youth—girls "slouch" and guys "hang out" and "pose." In both instances, the lack of apparent discipline is articulated by bodily freedom or "looseness." The lack of bodily discipline marks the decline in the status and influence of church, family, and schools, according to Baker. What can be surmised from her account is that the "moral" body is the disciplined body, the closely controlled and restricted body. Many Nevisians, including Baker, link the decline of Nevisian morality to the negative effects of certain global influences, namely, U.S. consumer culture, which thrives on the bodies of youth. Baker's observations about young bodies may be pointing to the links between bodies, new lifestyles, and new consumerist subjectivities (Giddens 1991)—a subject I return to in chapters 4 and 6.

I turn now to traditional discourses circulating on Nevis that often compete with religious moral discourses. Similar to the religious discourses that can be traced to colonial influences, these traditional discourses on sexuality also reflect and articulate long-standing cultural patterns.

PRESCRIPTIVE SEXUAL TRADITIONS

It is worthwhile to consider the multiple and often contradictory sexual discourses that coexist simultaneously with moral (religious) discourses on Nevis. It has become commonplace in anthropology to reject the idea that societies have a unified sexual culture.[4] I thought it is important to document the contradictions and tensions between the dominant (religious) morality on Nevis and what actually takes place in everyday life. The best way to convey these contradictions is to offer a number of disparate vignettes to reveal the contours and regular features that constitute sexualities on Nevis.

Story 1: Pastor Rogers, Her Father, and Girls like Tinnea

Pastor Rogers looked out the window across the field as she watched the children play. She was distracted, thinking about Tinnea and her siblings. Tinnea is eleven and regularly comes to school wearing a dirty jumper and shoes without socks: she rarely brings lunch. Having been sent home from school the previous Friday for not having her lunch, Tinnea broke into a house in the nearby village to get food. I had met Tinnea earlier that morning. She was sitting in the teachers' lounge, slouched over, picking at her fingers. There was dirt between her braids and her hemline was torn and frayed. Her nails were broken and her cuticles peeling and raw from her unrelenting picking. She spoke quietly and tearfully. I tried to distract her as she looked past me to the head teacher and police officer standing in the doorway who came from town to talk to her. Pastor Rogers, the guidance counselor at this particular primary school, returned to the lounge. She had a gentle demeanor. She pulled her chair close to Tinnea's and softly asked, "Do you want to go live someplace where you'll get breakfast, lunch, and dinner everyday?" Tinnea moved her small bony head back and forth whispering, "No, no, no." After awhile, the pastor let Tinnea go back to class and explained to me that Tinnea, a five-year-old brother, and a seven-year-old sister were neglected by their mother and seemed to have no one to care for them. "People are poor here on Nevis, but this kind of neglect is unusual. There's usually someone in the family to feed a hungry child—an aunty, a grandmother, someone like that. I know that the neighbors feed them sometimes. . . . Their mother takes the money that the church gives her and goes to Saint Kitts to see her boyfriend, leaving the children alone."

After young Tinnea left the lounge, Pastor Rogers and I discussed the nature of my research. I had met the pastor at a family life curriculum meeting that was attended by the primary and secondary school guidance counselors, a local health educator, and a UN representative specializing in health and family education. Pastor Rogers called me the following week to invite me to speak with her female students. She was particularly interested in the transition that girls experience when they leave primary school at the age of twelve to enter secondary school. She alluded to the fact that girls are under a lot of pressure from older boys at school and from men in the community. She told me a bit about her family and in particular how her mother never married her father. I soon realized that she was setting me up for a story, which she proceeded to tell with care. "One day when I was living in a dorm over on Saint Kitts attending nursing school, I heard some of the other students talking about a man, an older man who was going with a schoolgirl. I interrupted the girls and asked, 'What's the name of this man?' Then, they spoke my father's name. I heard my father's name." Pastor Rogers stood up at his point and asked if I wanted to meet some of the older girls at the school, the twelve-year-olds who would be graduating and attending secondary school. They all wore blue plaid jumpers and clean white blouses. Some wore matching ribbons and bows in their hair. The pastor told them that I was writing a book about girls and TV and they all started shouting out their favorite televisions shows: *Disney*, *Mary Kate and Ashley*, and "Dora the Explorer." It was after I had spent time with the girls, that I returned back to the lounge and found Pastor Rogers gazing out the window.

Several weeks later, in the middle of the day, while driving with Jasmine, a fifteen-year-old girl, I spotted a woman, barefoot and wearing a sheer nightgown and leaning against a new white SUV, a vehicle that looked larger than some of the small wooden houses in the village. "Who's that?" I asked. "Oh dat be Tinnea and dems momma." Prying, I asked, "Who is she speaking with?" Smiling, Jasmine responded, "Oh she, yeah, she know how to get things; she does." Later that day I visited a friend, Sally, a white expatriate who lives in the same village as Tinnea and her siblings. My friend had a puzzled look on her face as I told her that I made arrangements with the principal of the nearby school to fund Tinnea and her siblings' lunch program. Sally said, "Not the ones that run around in their mother's nightgown." I could not help but laugh. Sally's otherwise attractive face appeared contorted. I asked, "You mean because you think they are crazy or because they have nothing else to wear?" Sally rolled her blue eyes. "They are all crazy and they are all little thieves. I have to watch my purse when I give them rides to school because I see their little hands reaching in my bag. . . . And their mother, I know who she is. She's always talking to me about pussy. I don't know if she thinks I want some or if she's a lesbian. They're all crazy."

Story 2: Cataloging Sexual Unions and Other Problems
Related to Conjugal Taxonomies

I had spent the better part of this particular morning with the official government statistician, Larry Richards, a smart, soft-spoken individual. I had stopped by his office to ask a question about marriage trends. After about an hour we figured out that even if we could determine the rate of marriage per 1,000 persons for 2001 (broken down according to parishes) I would have nothing with which to compare it. For instance, 1980 and 1990 figures are not available. I was trying to determine whether the general improvements in economic conditions on the island might correlate with an increase in legal marriages. Traditionally, couples have visiting unions or common-law marriages and if they do marry legally, it's when they have the economic means to buy or build their own house. Given that incomes have increased significantly since 1990, I assumed that more couples would marry.

Visiting unions are common among Nevisians. For instance, the father of Eleanor's daughter came every weekend from Saint Kitts, taking the ferry to see Eleanor and their daughter and bringing food and money. Moreover, such arrangements are acknowledged on the form used for the national census in the section on marital/union status with an option to check off "visiting unions" as one type of partnership. In my survey of the girls, 39 percent of the 153 girls reported living with their fathers. Still, I have no way of determining if their fathers and mothers are legally married or in a "common-law marriage." Even if these children live with both parents, their parents may be living in common-law marriages and/or their fathers may have "outside" children. When men referred to their children on Nevis, it was not uncommon for them to say, for example, "two in" and "two out." This expression referred to the children a man had with his existing partner and other children he had fathered. Such an expression reminds me of the evening my husband and I visited with Mr. Bosworth, who reportedly had 47 siblings. My husband and Mr. Bosworth debated the merits of "keeping two women at the same time in different households." Mr. Bosworth tried to convince my husband that as long as a man could financially take care of both families then there was nothing wrong with keeping multiple wives. I learned from teachers and guidance counselors that it was not uncommon that when children entered high school, they met siblings they never knew they had as a result of their fathers having other families in different villages.

Story 3: Vanessa's Story

The first time Vanessa "stood me up" was a morning in May. I had arranged to pick her up at her house in Barnes Ghaut, a village just six miles north of Jessups where I lived. As I approached the house I saw Vanessa's grandmother sitting on the front steps of the small concrete house; behind her and to the right was the washing machine. I could barely understand the old woman as the machine made a loud grinding noise as if its motor was about to give out. "Dey all gone to Saint Kitts for de day. Me daughter is gettin' married." "Today?" I asked in disbelief. This surprised me because I spent time with Vanessa as well as Jasmine, Vanessa's cousin and the older woman's other granddaughter, over the weekend and no one mentioned the impending wedding. "Jean is getting married today over on Saint Kitts?" I asked. "Yep, dat's right and he won't even work. Jean has his two kids. She tell me dis mornin' while me still in bed and he won't even work. Used to be dat he work in engineerin' at de Four Seasons; now he won't even work." Vanessa, who stood me up, was the older woman's paternal granddaughter. When Vanessa and I finally did meet in private, days later, it was to conduct an in-depth interview. Vanessa was a twenty-year-old woman whom I met through her cousin Jasmine. Vanessa lived in a small concrete house with ten relatives, including her grandmother, an invalid uncle, another uncle, her aunt Jean, and Jean's five children—all of whom are younger than fifteen-years of age and one of whom is Jasmine. Two out of the five children have the same father. Vanessa's twenty-two-year-old cousin also lived in the house and both of his parents were living off the island. Vanessa's father lived on Saint Thomas and her mother lived in the Dominican Republic. Vanessa had a two-year-old son who lived with his father in another village on Nevis. She told me that her baby's "crying all de time wrecked it for everybody in de house" so the baby boy is being raised by his paternal grandmother. Her son was born on Saint Thomas where, according to Vanessa, he would have a better chance of gaining U.S. citizenship. When she returned to Nevis with her newborn son two years ago, she learned that his father was expecting another child. When I asked if she was still having sex with the father of her child, Vanessa laughed and shook her head from side to side, saying, "No, no, when me sees him in town we just talk." When I asked if she had a boyfriend, Vanessa explained that she did but that they were not speaking because she learned that he was married. As Vanessa says this she lets out a big laugh.

Vanessa met her new boyfriend through a mutual friend and soon after they met he invited her to a dance in town. After that occasion he began picking her up in front of her house and they would go to another house to have sex, a house Vanessa first assumed was his house. This occurred about ten times. "We used to go to a house me thinks is his but me never sleep by he de whole night, you see . . . anyway it his friend's house." At some point Vanessa's own friends began to tell her that her new boyfriend was married. She confronted him and he told her that he was married with two children. Vanessa told me that on their nights out they did not talk much about "private matters"; instead they had sex including sexual intercourse. They never used condoms and Vanessa says that her boyfriend "pulled out." According to Vanessa, her family does not know about her relationship with a married man. However, early on in the relationship Vanessa's ex-boyfriend (the father of her child) confronted her by saying, "You going 'round with a married man." At the time Vanessa denied this because she did not know that her new boyfriend was married. Vanessa explained that her boyfriend took her to dinner and had given her about EC $250 (U.S. $100) on at least four occasions. According to Vanessa, they often drove through Charlestown together with the tinted windows in his car rolled down. When she confronted him about being married he explained that he avoided telling her because he was sure if she knew then she would not have sex with him. Vanessa's boyfriend also told her it was her responsibility to "pick up" on the fact that he was married. Vanessa believed that she "did things" in bed for this man that his wife would not do for him, such as oral sex. The significance of this comment is that according to a number of informants, girls performing oral sex on men is a relatively new and novel sexual practice. Still, she said, "Even when I never used to really do dat he like me all de time, me thinks it de good sex . . . or I young; I no know." Vanessa reported that he was very romantic and often told her that she was beautiful. Vanessa shared the following story:

> When he wife went off island he took me by he real house and I see wedding picture. Yep, den he do me right there. I try and cut it off. I feel guilty, so me stop. . . . Me tell me one good friend. He a boy and me tell him about de married man. He say, "Please, please, please, don't get into dat. You could wait till somebody come your way." He tell me dat a married woman like him but he never get himself involve because it bring you down. . . . You think dat, Debra? You think it bring you bad luck? . . . I had to break off. Anyway, I no call him no more. Me have de cell number so me never care about de home number. Me miss him. He good at it. He good; he good; he good.

I assumed at this point when Vanessa repeatedly espoused her former boyfriend's qualities, "He good; he good; he good," that she was referring to his skills as a sexual partner. However, looking back, it may have been more than that. Vanessa may have been lamenting more than the loss of a lover.

It may be that Vanessa longed for his company, his displays of affection, his imported car, the cash he provided, and the various forms of entertainment he provided her.

Story 4: Multiple Partners in the Hotel Business

A white American female hotel owner narrated this story to me. In the course of our discussion, Diane, who had lived on Nevis for over five years, tried to summarize some of what she called "human resource problems" as they related to gender relations. Here is Diane:

> A former employee who worked in the kitchen had four children, two of whom she had with two different managers from my hotel. This created huge problems; I mean HR problems between two key employees, as it involved a manager from Food and Beverage and another manager from the front of the house. The front house manager, the individual in charge of waitstaff, bartenders, and hostesses, was by all counts a respectable man with a wife and kids. They had to work with each other you see—these two men and it caused a lot of problems. They couldn't communicate. The children were two to three years apart. She lost her job, not because of this but because she was a horrible employee. . . . I've been here for five years and I've attended maybe two weddings and there are at least six new babies born each year among my employees. . . . When I go to the states I spend . . . [two hundred dollars] on baby clothes to bring back for my new mothers. I've got one woman in the kitchen who's twenty-five years-old with five children—all five are from different men. She comes from the country. I've got another woman in housekeeping; she's in her twenties. She has kids and she's married and she's having a child with another man.

PUTTING THE PIECES TOGETHER:
WHAT STORIES REVEAL

These stories, when taken together, illustrate the dominant sexual patterns circulating on Nevis that compete with religious notions of morality that constitute girls' sexualities. At first glance, these stories may appear more like kinship patterns, but as we know, kinship affects, and is affected by, sexual life. What do these stories reveal about the range of tolerable sexual practices on Nevis? First, what becomes clear are the following: the dominance of the practice of having multiple sexual partners; the seeming absence of stigma associated with multiple partners by virtue of the commonness of the practice; the idea that sexual exclusivity may be an ideal for some, but is not practiced by most Nevisians; the appearance of sexual permissiveness; and finally, the sheer multiplicity in the types of sexual unions.

Furthermore, Nevisians link a man's sexual charisma to his "reproductive success." In other words, the more children a man has, the more he is sexually appealing to women. The type of masculinity expressed through fecundity that seemed to dictate historical sexual relations remains influential today and is expressed in the popular Nevisian saying, "No woman wants a man no woman wants." This form of masculinity is coupled with the idea that a man has a powerful sex drive and appetite, which is viewed as a part of his natural constitution. To rationalize this, Nevisian men and women often say, "Men do what men got to do." What men do not do, according to the dominant sexual discourse on Nevis, is to have sex with other men. Same-sex unions, particularly between homosexual males, are regarded as the antithesis of Nevisian masculinity; thus a man who is thought to have had sex with or desired another man is called an "anti-man." Same-sex relations between women are also regarded as taboo and socially unacceptable.

In terms of girls' sexualities, what these stories do not reveal concerns the way girls on Nevis, more specifically Sixth Form girls, come to epitomize the object of male sexual desire. Sixth Formers, who by the Nevisian educational model are first-year college students (or within the American system of education, high school seniors), are considered to be the most academically successful students on Nevis. Following the British model, Nevisian students are ranked early on in secondary schools. Those who earn the highest marks on exams taken in their fifth year are eligible to continue their education at local, regional, and international universities and colleges. I asked Jean Harris, the minister of health, why academic success is linked to sexual desirability, and she responded: "I think among people she represents the pinnacle of education and the future. . . . And among men, most of all, the thirty-year-old men and sometimes even older, are attracted to that newness with all the future ahead. I've noticed them . . . they [men] do everything to catch the girls' attention. I've actually seen men salivating over them. They see them with all the future ahead, all the possibilities. They have all the possibilities. The girls are popular. They are educated. They are ripe and ready to step off from their education and into the world."

While Sixth Form girls may epitomize the object of male sexual desire, they are not the only objects of desire. Schoolgirls in general are often the target of men's affections. In saying this, it is important to keep in mind that many girls actively seek out older boys and men for attention, affection, and sexual relations.

That men actively seek out schoolgirls as sexual partners appears to challenge the moral vision of Nevisian girls as chaste and virtuous. This apparent contradiction in terms of what happens in everyday Nevisian life versus the moral ideal is a collective preoccupation among a number of professionals, including the nation's AIDS educators, guidance counselors, and pastors.

Thomas Johnson, a therapist who worked closely with the Department of Education illustrates this concern in his comments about busmen: "They will go and have those girls up and down the roads all day and keeping them from school, some of them. . . . And the real problem is that these adult males will come onto the school grounds and that was one of the concerns I had all the time is how to protect these girls, not only at home but in school in a real way. There should be a wall [around school grounds]".

The coupling of schoolgirls and men, particularly men with social status, was an occupying concern of Francine Baker (who, as I mentioned earlier, is an attorney, the leader of the Girl Brigade, and a returning Nevisian national). Baker implicates not only bus drivers as the moral transgressors but also policemen who, purportedly, at least from her perspective, uphold the law and thus, in some ways might be seen as the moral custodians. According to Baker, bus drivers and policemen are complicit in the decline of Nevisian morality:

BAKER: The bus drivers, they are a big influence on the school kids. But you now see the policemen and the school kids. And I mean if the policemen are chasing the school kids, who else wouldn't?

DEBRA: I was riding with this one woman one day. She's twenty. But she said to me, "See that policeman? He zapped me when I was young." I said, "In your [school] uniform?" And she said, "Yeah, I was sixteen."

BAKER: There was a certain policeman, and he was not thrown out of the police force for this. It was something else. He took pleasure in every year he had a different child pregnant in school uniform under sixteen, and they would come to court for maintenance [child support], and the senior police officers would know. The magistrate would know. All the lawyers would know and he was kept in police uniform.

DEBRA: How many girls did he have? I mean, how many impregnated?

BAKER: Probably about four.

DEBRA: Does he pay child support?

BAKER: There's one girl who actually was a preacher's daughter, and he got her pregnant, and she was fifteen at the time, and her parents put her out. She subsequently had two more kids for him, and he never paid child support. As a matter-of-fact . . . a friend of hers brought her to me, because I do quite a bit of pro bono work for single mothers. And a friend of hers brought her to me to pursue maintenance, which I did, and what she ended up doing was giving him the money to come and pay me; do you understand that? I mean, she would give him the money to come and pay me and make it look like he's paying child support. Eventually, however, after the third or fourth person was pregnant, then she really came in earnest and sued him for all the back child support.

As these interviews suggest, Nevisians such as Johnson and Baker are producers of the dominant Nevisian moral discourse; in other words they are
moral custodians on Nevis. If this is the case, which I believe it is given their
highly visible and influential status, then what kind of norms are they promoting? First, within Nevisian society, they have their own bias and perspectives
as the result of their positions, training, and education. Theirs is a particular
point of view, which arguably is a middle-class sensibility linked to the culture
of respectability that Olwig (1993) maintains Methodist society imposed on
the Afro-Caribbean culture in the ninetieth century. Within this culture of
respectability a certain type of sexuality is promoted while other more permissive forms are disavowed. In this way, Johnson and Baker distance themselves from unfettered adolescent sexuality as well as from intergenerational
sex between men and girls and both sets of comments more than hint at the
exploitative aspects of intergenerational sexual relations. Men who have both
social status and access to goods and resources, namely, policemen and busmen, seek out schoolgirls for sex, taking advantage of the girls' vulnerable
social status and inexperience. Particularly noteworthy is that as intergenerational sexual relations have become normative, girls, too, seek out opportunities to be with older men, as we shall see in subsequent chapters. Baker is
representative of a group of Nevisians that are committed to reforming
Nevisian society and saving it from the social ills produced by the influence of
American consumer culture. The brief narrative that follows highlights a specific focus on moral reform. Cultivating morality and promoting a moral education is the mission of both the Girl Brigade and the Girl Guides program on
Nevis. It should be noted that the forty-year-old Baker, was raised on Saint
Kitts and then moved away to Canada for twenty years where she studied law
and met her Nevisian husband. She returned to Nevis ten years ago.

Girl Brigade: Cultivating Morality

Francine had just come out of the water when it started to rain. The trade
winds had picked up as well. Francine and I, along with a group of girls from
Francine's brigade, were huddled together on the beach under a dilapidated
shelter, a circular structure with an umbrella made from palm branches to provide relief from the sun. Some of the younger girls, including my daughters,
stayed in the water, playing in the light rain. Francine had come to the beach
for an outing with the members of the Methodist Girls' Brigade. As she patted
herself dry with a towel she explained to me how the girls in her group represent the "spectrum": "There are girls on the one end who would walk over
there [gesturing to the group of men gathered around the beach bar] and ask,
'What do you want for a ride in the car?' versus the girls who wouldn't even
turn their heads." We turned our bodies to watch the younger girls play in the
water. Some of the older girls had moved away from the palm shelter back to

their towels on the sand. Pointing to one of the older girls, Ally, a fifteen-year-old who I had just met days before at Charlestown Secondary, Francine said, "She's one of the ones at the end of the spectrum who'd walk over there in a second." As she said this she lifted her chin in the direction of the bar. Francine explained, "Ally takes a lot of risks." Ally was a friend of Jasmine's, and when I met her in the schoolyard a week before, I recalled being impressed by her stature and self-confidence. Ally told me when we first met that she wanted to be a doctor. On the telephone the night before, when I was asking her mother for permission to interview her daughter, Ally's mother told me that Ally barely passes her classes. Francine and I were interrupted by one of the younger girls who couldn't find her towel. Looking over at Ally, I caught her eye and she gestured for me to come over. The local grocery store was sponsoring a Heineken party at another beach and she wanted me to drive her there. She tried to convince me to leave Oualie Beach and drive over to Paradise Beach, explaining, "There's music and dancin'." And then just for extra measure, attempting to appeal to me as an anthropologist, she looked at me and said, "It's a cultural event." Ally explained her plan to me in great detail. She wanted me to call her mother on a cell phone and explain that I was interviewing Ally this afternoon at the beach. Instead of remaining with Francine and the other girls, I was to assure Ally's mother that she would be with me for the afternoon. Ally was hoping that I would agree to this plan so that she could use it as a ruse and have me take her to the Heineken party. When I would not agree to her plan, Ally's disappointment spread across her face; it was followed by a look of disgust.

Months later Francine invited me to her home for a more in-depth discussion about the history of the Girl Brigade on Nevis. She lived with her husband and three children near the fourteenth hole of the Four Season's golf course. There was a massive iron gate at the end of her driveway. I called Francine on my cell phone just outside the property, not quite sure how to pass through the gate. Seconds after my call the electric iron gate began to open slowly. By Nevisian standards, Francine's house appeared massive. The circular driveway abuts a well-manicured green lawn. Francine's SUV was parked in the driveway. It was Friday and she had planned a special night out with her husband; their three boys had taken the ferry to Saint Kitts to be with their grandparents for the weekend. Francine and I had arranged to meet before she joined her husband at one of the elite hotels on the island for dinner. The rooms in her house were spacious and elegantly furnished. The French doors remained open, providing a refreshing breeze so that the tropical evening heat was less oppressive. A security alarm beeped continuously while I was there, triggered possibly by yellow Bananaquits or red-breasted bullfinches fluttering about and through the open doors. Francine talked about her involvement in the Girl Brigade and her concerns about the lack of discipline among youth:

> I am affiliated with the fourth company of the Girl Brigade. It's a group rising out of the Methodist church. We work with girls from the age of three to eighteen. And we do a foursquare program meeting once weekly, which deals with spiritual, physical, educational, and service. . . . [O]ne of the things that it helps to cultivate is discipline and womanhood and all the good stuff, which seems to be nonexistent now. We were very disciplined [when I was growing up]. Now, it's very loose. Discipline was very strong. . . . [Girls] wanted to be a part of it. Now . . . the interest for the girls is . . . not there as it was, I believe, in my time. . . . There are many distractions . . . [and] . . . the community supports are not as strong as they used to be. What I mean by that is, the Girl Brigade was an offshoot of the church. The minister visited [in the past]. He checked to make sure you were there. Your parents sent you along. Now, there are no parents really sending their kids. It's really more of an initiative from the children, more so than the parents. It's very loose as opposed to the way I grew up. . . .

Baker refers to the seventies, when she was coming-of-age, when presumably family and church exerted more control and authority in the lives of girls. She recognizes the current distractions in girls' lives, which I take to mean television and consumer culture, but locates some of the responsibility for the lack of discipline with religious leaders and parents. What she speaks to indirectly is the waning of the traditional forms of authority, particularly the church and the way sexually permissive practices remain in constant competition with notions of sexual propriety.

Indeed, moral discourse rooted in religious doctrine and traditional sexual discourse remain two of the most powerful forces structuring social life on Nevis. The seemingly cultural homogeneity of Nevisian society and its size make the disjuncture between moral and sexual discourses appear huge. In other words, there are no alternative or secular moral discourses on Nevis to compete with the Nevisian religious moral discourse. Because of the sheer smallness of the island society (as opposed to a larger island like Jamaica where there are over 2.4 million people), the contrast between religious morality and traditional sexual customs appears particularly noticeable on Nevis. The absence of anonymity resulting from the size of the population and the island's geography provides Nevisians with fewer opportunities to be discreet when it comes to breaches in moral sexual codes. After all, there are only so many places individuals can meet, and wherever they go, others are likely to recognize them. Consequently, one does not have to look particularly hard to see how the religious moral discourse on Nevis is frequently contradicted by behaviors driven by more potent sexual discourses.

Some locals, particularly community leaders such as ministers and individuals like Baker view the split between the ideal moral discourse on sex and sexuality and traditional sexual discourses on Nevis as wide and increasingly widening. There has been a great deal of emphasis placed on addressing the perceived moral crisis. For instance, UNICEF sponsored a television program focusing on a number of social problems that was broadcast on a local television station. The four-part show, entitled *Pale Horse*, featured a physician who lectured on the social consequences of teen pregnancy, a popular sports commentator who spoke about the global economics of HIV, a teen segment devoted to safe sex, and a prominent minister who spoke about the necessity of moral reform. In this last part, the minister described two major social influences shaping the sexual climate on Saint Kitts and Nevis: television programming and its concomitant "liberal" messages about sex and poor parental modeling. The minister attributes what he sees as the decline in the nation's moral health to the influence of television and the way it promotes sex as "free and all right." In addition, he blames parents for modeling sexual impropriety: "Children see that their father has several girlfriends. They learn early on that's acceptable." To reduce the negative effects of both social influences, the minister recommends establishing a national service program, essentially a two-year training program, designed and implemented by the government to focus on moral development.

By stressing the differences between ideal moral discourse, which focuses on sexual propriety, and traditional sexual discourses, which stresses more permissive sex codes, I do not mean to discount the very real way in which the moral discourse is reproduced and at times inscribed on the bodies of girls in the form of beatings from their parents and teachers. Nor is it meant to dismiss the way the girls themselves reproduce the moral discourse by gossiping and stereotyping girls who are perceived to be too sexually active. There is undoubtedly a public standard of respectability on Nevis with regard to sexuality; however, there is also a very entrenched traditional discourse that influences sexualities on Nevis. Many Nevisian community leaders are attempting to bring about "moral reform" by encouraging after-school programs and by encouraging girls to join church-based associations in an attempt to instill in the girls what older Nevisians consider to be traditional values, such as chastity. This is despite the fact that historically having multiple partners has been commonplace.

In this chapter, we have seen how the simultaneous existence of religious discourse and traditional discourse prescribe competing sexual norms. Sexual actors, like Felicia, consciously or unconsciously navigate the tensions and contradictions between the two. Nevisian girls have the awareness of religious ideals and codes, but they also know what people do—what the women in their village do, what well-respected powerful men do, what schoolteachers do, and what their classmates do. When Nevisians, including the girls themselves, engage in practices that are contrary to religious ideals, which they endorse, they are engaging in transgressive acts in the sense that the acts go against the moral codes, which they have indicated that they accept. My focus, of course, is on how these competing discourses not only inform one another, but also how their competitive engagement affects the ways girls experience their sexual lives.

In addition to the long-standing traditional discourse and religious discourse on sexuality, Nevisian society is also being transformed by an influx of global influences linked to consumer culture that inform the production of girls' subjectivities. It is this increasingly globalized context for the coming-of-age process that provides a point of departure for chapter 4. Chapter 4 allows us to see how traditional sexual patterns, which are highly permissive, are not only accentuated by the affects of consumer culture, but also are made more visible and apparent.

CHAPTER 4

Consuming Global Scripts

MEDIA, SEX, AND DESIRE

THERE WERE some days in the field when events or experiences were presented to me, almost too flawlessly, lining themselves up, one right after the other, in order to tell the perfect story. In the middle of April, I had such a day. I spent a small portion of the morning wrestling a copy of D. H. Lawrence's *Lady Chatterley's Lover* out of the mouth of a mischievous goat. This erotic classic belonged to an expatriate known as the "Goat Lady." I had paid a visit to her home that morning, at her request, as she wanted me to baby sit an orphaned goat later that evening. She had intended to, and subsequently did, drop off the goat, much to my daughters' delight, where it would stay with us, in my living room until later that night. Since the goat was barely a day old, I was instructed to coax it to nurse from a baby bottle. Days later when I shared this story with one of my Nevisian friends, Andrea, she said, quite adamantly, "Debra, this isn't Kansas; we don't keep our livestock in the living room." It was after I had been given instructions from the Goat Lady on how to care for the kid that I had my encounter with the goat and the erotica. I was standing in the Goat Lady's kitchen, making up fresh baby bottles when I turned to find a curious female goat also in the kitchen, sneaking up behind me, or so it appeared. Startled, I let out a yelp, the goat ran through the living room and out the screen door, but not before she grabbed the book from the coffee table.

Visiting the Goat Lady that day was a Nevisian man in his forties, a businessman, who I had come to know. He helped me retrieve the book and upon reading the title he launched into a story about his adolescence. He explained that when he was growing up, he and the other boys his age had little, if any access to pornography or to "anything close to it." Once when he was sixteen, in the early 1970s, a boat captain from the states gave him a copy of *Playboy*, which he circulated among his friends. "Every boy in school had a chance to look at it before I got it back. Believe me, it was well-worn. I could have charged something back then. But it was just naked girls, nothing really, just nakedness." When he lent out the magazine a second time, it was confiscated by a teacher. Later that same day, I was with Tamara, a sixteen-year-old who likes to look at pornography on-line with her girlfriends. "We wait til me mom and sisters go to work and we look up de porn. . . .We started just looking up Victoria's lingerie [Victoria Secret]. She has all the pretty things we want. But den we see de porn. It's all over de place. We see everything. Everything, even de freaky stuff." I learned later that the "freaky" stuff were websites that featured "gang bangs," instances in which one woman is depicted as having sex with several men. A rare and well-worn copy of *Playboy* versus instant access to multiple Internet images depicting a variety of sexual acts, including "gang bangs" suggests that the landscape in which Nevisian sexualities are produced is rapidly changing. As a result of high-speed global linkages—including technologies that exchange bodies and information—new sexual scripts, practices, and repertoires are proliferating on Nevis.[1]

In chapter 3, I examined the long-standing sexual discourse that competes with religious moral discourse. This chapter explores the availability and range of globally mediated sexual scripts. I am specifically interested in exploring the proliferation of network programs, websites, and imported DVDs, including pornography, on Nevis. These media forms, what Reverend Percival of Saint George's Anglican Church referred to as "that which is beaming into the bedrooms and living rooms on Nevis," are part of a global flow of sexual discourse that produce subjectivities that in turn affect and at least partially determine sexual practices and the general concept of the erotic. Before turning my attention back to pornography and its influences on girls' sexualities, I begin by looking at another potentially erotic genre, namely, music videos.

Black Entertainment Television: Consuming Music Videos

Television, particularly Black Entertainment Television (BET), appears to be having a significant effect on how Nevisian girls make sense of the world. As described in chapter 2, over half of the girls I surveyed watch television somewhere between three and five hours a day.[2] Lamenting the impact of cable television on Nevisian youth, a woman in her sixties asserted, "Dey get white culture. Dey get white music. Dey don't sing songs of praise." While the girls may be consuming white culture through soap operas and through other network television programs, the consumption of BET, and specifically, of music videos featuring black hip-hop artists, is by far one of the favorite pastimes among Nevisian girls. I learned firsthand what mattered most to the girls through our discussions in focus groups, during in-depth interviews, and by simply spending time with the girls. During focus group sessions girls of all ages would become giddy with delight describing their favorite musical artists. One question that always prompted enthusiasm was, "If you could watch anything you wanted on television, what program would it be?"

BET, far and away, was the most commonly reported television favorite. Furthermore, once captivated by the music videos, the girls spent even more time listening to music and spending hours writing down the lyrics to their favorite songs or downloading lyrics from the Internet.

Television plays an important role in everyday social life for producing meaning as well as for the way it enables and promotes consumption.[3] I am particularly interested in investigating how Nevisian girls interact with music videos in order to create sexual meanings and to learn about sexual practices. I frame this investigation by assuming that music videos generate an array of identities and roles for Nevisian girls also to perform and provides them with rules for a variety of new sexual acts, desires, and practices.

Much has been written about representations of black female sexuality in hip-hop music videos and the linkages between sexuality and the erotics of materialism, or more specifically, the eroticization of what is known in the hip-hop culture as "bling-bling."[4] In many music videos emerging from hip-hop culture, the eroticization of bling-bling—jewelry, clothing, cars, mansions, and other manifestations of material wealth—is fused with sexuality. Cultural critic Patricia Hill Collins (2004) suggests that the "theme of the materialistic, sexualized black woman has become the icon within hip-hop culture" (126). Representations of black women in many videos featuring male musical artists often depict "oversexed" or "hypersexed" females; women in such videos are scantily clad and their dance movements are dominated by rhythmic gyrations, simulating sex acts like intercourse, masturbation, or oral sex. Black women are represented as having uncontrollable sexual desires which is exactly how they are represented in nineteenth-century colonial discourse. In terms of materialism, it is not uncommon for there to be normative wealth displayed in the form of fancy cars, in-ground swimming pools, and gigantic mansions. Both men and women are adorned with what appears to be jewelry, typically diamond and gold jewelry.

As just noted, hip-hop videos starring male rappers offer a limited range of sexual subjectivities available to black women, all of which link sexuality to materialism. Significantly, these sexual subjectivities also express a particular sexual discourse. Collins (2004) shows us how images of women "who trade sexual favors for jobs, money, drugs, and other material items" dominant hip-hop videos (128). This reinforces the image of the black woman as a gold digger who, as Stephens and Phillips (2003) write: "is a woman who explicitly seeks material and economic rewards above all else, and is willing to trade sex for it. Sex is her commodity because it is the only valuable thing she has in society. Sex may be used to barter for basic needs such as a bag of groceries, getting rent paid, or making sure their lights do not get turned off. However, manicures and pedicures, new clothing, vacations, or having a car paid for are also possible wants that gold diggers may be willing to trade sex to get (17–18)."

A related sexual image depicts women as "skeezers." Unlike gold diggers, "skeezers" trade sex not for material wealth or commodities, but for status (Collins 2004, 128). In contrast to the "gold digger" and "skeezer," women are also depicted in hip-hop music videos as "freaks" who do not inextricably link sexuality with commodity desires, but who will "forego financial gains and [are] satisfied with only sex" (Stephens and Phillips 2003, 20). "Freaks" apparently have no sexual inhibitions or hang-ups. However, the "freak" image is limiting to women in that it re-inscribes the notion of "unnatural" female sexuality. Sex in any position or place, or with any person or number of people, characterizes a "freak" (20). As Collins summarizes, "Freaky sex consists of sex outside the boundaries of normality" (2004, 121).[5]

In addition to the visual images that determine a series of limited and proscribed subjectivities for black women, the lyrics of popular hip-hop songs performed by male artists are filled with new sexual repertories and rules. For instance, in *Mesmerize*, a song popular among Nevisian girls featuring the superstar female artist Ashanti, Ja Rule, a male rapper, offers a new set of sexual rules and expectations about intimate pleasures for the Nevisian girls who consume his music. He establishes guidelines for performing desire and desirability—moan in bed, grab the sheets, and perform fellatio. Ja Rule, like other rappers, attempts to proscribe for women where and how sex can occur. For example, he croons about a particular fetish of having sex in the backseat of his SUV (2003).

While Nevisian girls greedily consume the work of male artists such as Ja Rule, there are also alternative scripts available to them in the work of female rappers. For example, artists such as Lil' Kim offer graphic new ideas about sexual possibilities for Nevisian girls, which very likely serve to sanction new desires. In her song, *How Many Licks* video (2002), Lil' Kim sings: "And Tony he was Italian; he didn't give a fuck. That's what I like about him. He ate my pussy from dark till the morning." Furthermore, toward the end of the song, the following message scrolls across the screen: "She doesn't satisfy you—you satisfy her." Such cultural forms produce new types of sexualities, pleasures, and possibilities for Nevisian girls. These new subjectivities demonstrate the extent to which the sexual landscape on Nevis has changed in recent years. The pleasures imagined by Lil' Kim were unimaginable when my older informants, Eleanor and Ruthie, were growing up. Indeed, Ruthie explained that when she was coming-of-age, oral sex was not at all part of the sexual repertoire; only recently had she come to expect oral sex from her partners.

What is clear from my interviews with Nevisian men and women of all ages is that hip-hop music videos have become the preeminent site for manufacturing desire, that is, for producing the very rules of desire. The videos produce, sanction, and legitimize both new desires and attitudes that are compatible with existing erotic structures and codes on Nevis. The following example illustrates how hip-hop music videos promote a type of masculinity that corresponds to the Nevisian code of masculinity. In *In Da Club*, Rapper 50 Cent (2003) explains how men become more desirable when they have greater access to goods, resources, and wealth. Rapper 50 Cent declares that when he pulls up in front of a nightclub in a Mercedes Benz with unlimited rolls of cash it drives the women to "wanna fuck." That men are more desirable when they appear to possess wealth is a dominant theme in hip-hop that is tied to the eroticization of "bling-bling." Similarly, references to trading sexual encounters for goods and cash, which is implicit in *In Da Club*, are abundant in hip-hop videos. One of the best examples of this is the music video *P-Poppin*, by Ludacris (2003). The scene is a dance contest where female contestants are required to perform cartwheels and splits for the male spectators. Toward the end of the video, a female dancer lies on the floor, wearing a thong, with her legs spread wide as the male spectators throw money at her. As the bills land between her legs and come to rest near her crotch, a look of ecstasy spreads across her face. I surmise that the rapture the dancer displays is generated less from the potential excitement she experienced during her dance and more from the erotics of the cash.

What, then, can be said about "the relation between representations of sexualities and their lived forms" to borrow a phrase from Purnima Mankekar and Louisa Schein (2004, 4)? How do new sexual rules and expectations about intimate pleasures affect a girl's subjectivity? Sixteen-year-old Felicia offers this explanation:

> I think that when Nevisian girls, like myself, watch videos on BET, we admire and aspire to look like the girls in the videos, and most of us want to get that same attention from men. I know that I get ideas about clothing and fashion from videos on BET, and my friends do too. I think that we are influenced to a limit, though, because of our society. In Nevis, certain types of clothing for young girls are not acceptable, but because of what we learn from the videos we know how to get away with other things, things like sneaking around behind our mothers' backs and having more than one boyfriend. There's a lot of songs that talk about having a boyfriend, but being "in love" with someone else. I had a friend who could relate to that, and I could also relate. I was actually caught between two [boy] friends and that went on for a while, until I realized that it was a bad situation when they [the boys] started fighting. I also think since we don't have any other ways to learn about sex and stuff we go to TV. When I was younger, I really wanted to be like the girls in the videos; I really wanted to be sexy and have guys trying to get my attention and all that stuff. As I got older and all that stuff was actually happening I didn't really like having all of the attention all of the time, mostly because some guys were just awful. The guys even get a lot of their lines from the videos, like some guys

use this really cheesy line, "I wish you were my kid, so I could spoil you rotten." I don't even know where that came from, but definitely the TV.

Felicia's comments illustrate an important point about media and the production of subjectivity. When Nevisian girls, like Felicia, interact with and consume music videos, they attempt to locate themselves in the stories. In other words, through the process of identification, some girls recognize themselves in the narratives and images produced through the music videos, to the extent that they "aspire to look like the girls in the video." Consuming music videos is part of the ongoing process of constituting subjectivity, and as a result of that process the sexual images and scripts consumed though music videos have the potential to arouse and incite new sexual desires and practices. In Felicia's case, she wanted to be "sexy" to gain boys' attention, so much so that she had two boyfriends at once. Felicia's experience suggests the very practical ways in which media participates in the construction of subjectivity.

In order to fully understand the manner in which media create subjectivities, we must first recognize the degree to which imitation is a powerful aspect of the observational learning that is involved when Nevisian girls cultivate their sexualities.[6] Media sites, such as BET videos, offer adolescent girls exemplars to follow; girls are exposed to and observe sexual mannerisms and styles—how to move, how to dress to get boys' attention, how to caress, and how to kiss—and these are all important aspects of girls' sexual subjectivities. However, when girls enact the verbal and visual messages they consume on BET, existing cultural norms constrain their behavior.[7] This means that the practices, postures, and mannerisms that constitute a girl's subjectivity are formed by the normative sexual order, even as the girls themselves rework that order. Felicia, for instance, emulated the girls in the videos. She learned from the videos what it meant for a girl to act "sexy." Felicia's enactment of the observed music video performance naturalizes the new normative sexual order. In essence, social learning is constrained by existing rules and standards but is also introduces new ideas (e.g., oral sex). The standards and rules gradually change as more people adopt new practices.

On Nevis we see competing sexual normativities as prescribed by the ideal religious morality and traditional sexual discourses. However, with the influences of global mediated scripts, like those on BET videos, Nevisian sexual norms are also increasingly reworked. The fact that there are competing sexual normativities on Nevis suggests that sexual orders become destabilized and can radically change.

IMPORTED DESIRES: WATCHING PORN

Not only is BET a resource for self-production, but so are imported adult X-rated videos. After learning from several girls that adult videos were not only accessible on the island, but also that they themselves had viewed them with men from their villages, I decided to assess the available collection at various rental stores. Most of all, I was curious about how these imported commodities might be affecting the changing sexual culture on Nevis and competing with or complementing more long-standing sexual discourses and patterns. In 2003 two shops opened that rented DVDs and videos. The first store I visited was also the newest. Available for rent were the latest Hollywood blockbusters. I asked a well-dressed store clerk if she had any X-rated films available. Excusing herself, she went into a back room to call the manager. After they were both assured that I was not a customs agent, the clerk showed me five X-rated DVDs that she stored in a desk drawer. In this particular store, four of the five were in a series entitled, *Quickies: My 19th Birthday Party Vols. 1–4*. There was an additional caption that read: "Beautiful Black Babes in the Hottest Sex Scenes." The fifth DVD featured a gangster theme.

Later that week, while shopping alone in Soloman Square, I came across a shop that rented videos, and after perusing the small collection, I noticed two films (out of a collection of twelve X-rated videos) exclusively about gay sex, entitled, *Bi-ology Homosexuals* and *Hombres: Gay Sex Scenes*. The clerk working in this particular video store explained that there was a small market for such films on Nevis. For various reasons, not the least of which was her apparent discomfort in talking with a stranger, she was not willing to offer further details on the subject except to say that the owner tries to "stay on top of his customers' requests." As noted previously, Nevis, like many West Indian societies, is marked by a high degree of homophobia. For example, health workers and teachers told me repeatedly that if a male student was perceived to be the least bit "feminine," his peers referred him to as an "anti-man." Anti-gay sentiment is expressed in popular discourse and especially in the lyrics of dancehall music, which is largely imported from Jamaica. Thus, what is surprising about finding this collection of gay pornography in this shop is not that there are individuals on Nevis who take pleasure in watching men have sex with other men, but rather that a small business owner would seek to capitalize on a sexual practice that is highly stigmatized and risk offending potential customers. This suggests to me that there is a demand for this type of genre on the island and that there are shifts taking place within the dominant sexual order.

The availability of video pornography has been significantly impacted by the increased availability of television itself on Nevis. As just noted, it is only in the last ten years or so that television has come to Nevisian households. DVDs and video players are relatively new commodities that only recently have become affordable goods. This means that the availability of images to which the average Nevisian is exposed has exploded in a relatively short period of time.

My informant Ruthie's story illustrates this shift in the type of media and technology to which a Nevisian might have access. When Ruthie was growing up, girls were supervised closely; they were permitted to leave the yard alone only to collect water at the village pipe or to walk to and from school. The opportunity to view TV with neighbors was considered a luxurious novelty. Ruthie recalls how in the 1980s, after the evening meals and chores were completed, multiple families from her village might gather around a second-hand black-and-white TV, the only set in the village, to watch programming from St. Thomas or St. Martin. Here is Ruthie's recollection of her early exposure to television: "Once in awhile I go to de neighbors to watch *Another World*. You have to make sure you bathe, because de neighbors don't want to be smellin' dirty children. I take me bath and I always have good manners so dat dey would let me stay and watch *Another World*. De TV was on de porch and ten people from de village would reach dere [arrive there] before me and I done stand dere. I would say, Good evening. I be so happy to watch Stacy on de TV. She was quiet wit de glasses. Lance scared me."

Ruthie, often the youngest in the crowd, was asked to hold the antennae, which she said she did willingly if it meant that she had a chance to "see TV." By contrast to Ruthie's experience, many of the Nevisian girls I interviewed reported watching imported adult videos and DVDs, unsupervised, with men in their villages.

Without rehashing the U.S. feminist debate on pornography, I would assert that adult videos affect Nevisian girls; they provide a graphic demonstration of sexual variety and as I already mentioned, provide a resource for self-production. For example, consider how pornography features mostly nude people, and incorporates close-up images of penises, vaginas, breasts, and anuses. One of the goals in producing pornographic images is to maximize the visibility of, and exposure to, bodies. Unlike the music videos girls consume, the content of pornography portrays people engaging in a variety of explicit sexual acts, such as oral sex, anal sex, intercourse, masturbation, and group sex.

A segment of an interview conducted with one of my informants, Varshnie, draws attention to the influence of imported adult films on Nevisian sexualities. Varshnie was a sixteen-year-old whose parents immigrated to Nevis six years ago from Guyana. It should be noted that Varshnie was also newly married, which as pointed out earlier, was not a common occurrence among Nevisian girls or women.

DEBRA: Has he ever wanted you to watch "dirty" movies?
VARSHNIE: He bring a porn home one day and said to me, "Let's watch it." And he was watchin' it, and then I am not watchin', he goin' to put my face in it [in front of the TV set] and I'm goin' to close my eyes, and then I open

my eyes, and I'm goin' to watch a little of the picture, and then I'm goin'
to close my eyes.

Debra: So did he watch it at the house?

Varshnie: Yeah.

Debra: Where did he get it?

Varshnie: He said he bought it from one of his friends.

Debra: Where was your mama when you watched it? [The young bride and
her new husband live with her parents in a two-bedroom house.]

Varshnie: She was not home.

Debra: Did he watch the whole thing or just a little of it?

Varshnie: The whole thing.

Debra: And what were you doing?

Varshnie: I was hidin' my head. I was closin' my eyes. (laughs)

Debra: Where were you sitting?

Varshnie: Right beside him.

Debra: Did he get . . . um, excited?

Varshnie: No. (shaking her head from side to side)

Debra: He didn't?

Varshnie: No. He said movies like that don't turn him on.

Debra: Did he want to have sex after?

Varshnie: Yeah.

Debra: And did you?

Varshnie: No.

Debra: Why?

Varshnie: I said I had work to do. [She cooks and cleans for her parents and
husband.] I didn't allow him.

Debra: When was this?

Varshnie: I think it was Wednesday afternoon. Yeah.

Debra: Oh, your parents weren't home.

Varshnie: No, my parents workin' the same shift.

Debra: Were the people in the movie light skinned or dark skinned?

Varshnie: Both.

Debra: Did you see anything that surprised you?

Varshnie: Yeah.

Debra: Like what?

Varshnie: When the girl sucked the guy's penis.

Debra: What were you thinking?

Varshnie: I was like thinkin' "That is so nasty." And then the guy cum in the
girl's mouth, and I thought, "That is so nasty."

Debra: And did you see anything else that surprised you, that you thought
was different?

Varshnie: No.

DEBRA: Did he see anything on the video that he said he wants to try with you?

VARSHNIE: There was almost everythin' he tried.

DEBRA: Was there ever a scene where there were more than two people?

VARSHNIE: Yeah.

DEBRA: What did you think?

VARSHNIE: I say I can't believe it, somebody havin' sex with the people next to them and then with them.

DEBRA: So you watched a little.

VARSHNIE: Yeah.

DEBRA: Was there a scene with two women?

VARSHNIE: No.

DEBRA: Because they have movies like that. Has anyone ever talked to you about that?

VARSHNIE: No.

DEBRA: No one's ever said that, um, have you ever heard the word "lesbian"?

VARSHNIE: Yeah, I heard lesbian, and bonk, gay, and. . . .

DEBRA: Bonk?

VARSHNIE: Bonk. Yeah, like a guy, he's a bonk.

DEBRA: When was the first time you heard those words?

VARSHNIE: I was fourteen.

Varshnie's comments are interesting for many reasons. They hint at the complex process of subjective mediation. Understanding subjective mediation brings to light how external social forms, such as imported pornography, shape subjective interiorities, which articulate with sexual practices. Importantly, this three-way interaction among external social forms, subjective interiorities, and sexual practices is missing from theory, generated from globalization studies on sexualities (Povinelli and Chauncey 1999, 445). Consequently, it is important not only to track the flow of global commodities, like pornography, but also to understand how external forms are reshaping intimate spaces and affecting subjectivities.

In Varshnie's case, the effect of pornography on her subjectivity is complex. Her new husband introduced her to pornography that he procured from a friend, and as she states, "He going to put my face in it." It is unclear from her comment if she feels obligated to watch. For example, Varshnie's husband may have cajoled her or even possibly threatened her verbally or physically. However, if she felt that what she was doing was transgressive, she might have felt required to deny her interest in pornography. Nevertheless, Varshnie's interaction with, and consumption of pornography, is mediated by her husband's desire to consume porn. He, as well as the graphic images, are likely to shape Varshnie's notions of, and experiences of, pleasure. What's more, the conflict embedded in her remarks may be suggestive of competing Nevisian sexual normativities. For example, on the one hand, Varshnie is curious and wants to watch, but on the other hand, she looks away, possibly out of shame and embarrassment, or possibly because she was aroused, or repulsed, or both. After the movie, when Varshnie's husband initiated sex, she told him, "I have to work" which meant that she had to complete her chores. She was surprised by a scene involving fellatio and what appeared to be group sex, but was familiar with some same-sex practices. These varieties of responses to pornography all suggest that as a recent emigrant to Nevis, Varshnie is coming-of-age in a climate that is marked by changing sexual codes and expectations.

Another one of my informants, Tamara, also suggests that girls on Nevis have a dynamic and interactive relationship with pornography. Tamara's comments, which follow, are also suggestive of the difficulties in understanding the domain of erotics; it is not always accessible through interpretations of discourse and language (Mankekar 2004, 404). Tamara is sixteen and has watched pornography on a number of occasions with her thirty-something boyfriend. As Tamara relates: "I see porn all de time at my boyfriend's brother's house. We watchin' it and den when everybody gone, he all sexed up and ready. At first me nervous; now me watch to see what de girl goin' do."

Both Tamara's and Varshnie's comments point to the girls' curiosity about pornography, and indeed, suggest the way such interest might incite new desires. Tamara admits in so many words that she wants to see what the girl is going to do next while Varshnie moves back and forth between repulsion and the desire to see more. An interesting aspect of sexuality is that so much of one's sexual desires is constituted in relation to others. So that, in this case, for instance, it might prove difficult to try to distinguish between Tamara's new pornography-inspired desires and her desire to please her boyfriend.

With the consumption of pornography, erogenous zones are remapped in ways that affect how the girls experience their sexualities. Pornography, in this context, has the effect of promoting a Western sexual discourse among Nevisians. Foucault (1978) would suggest that pornography has normalizing effects on sexuality.[8] The importation of a Western sexual discourse simultaneously exists with, and competes against, older more established sexual normativities. The comments that follow illustrate these competing sexual normativities as well as how they affect the eroticization of new bodily zones and reshape sexual subjectivity. Here are Ruthie and Eleanor commenting on new sexual trends:

RUTHIE: Years back my grandmother knew nothin' of tongue kissin'. All dat dey know was smack, smack, smack [pushing her lips together tightly]. Honestly. And all dat "booty lickin'" . . . if dey heard about dat, dey go crazy and tell de police to lock us up in de prison.

ELEANOR: I had a Trinidadian boyfriend. De first time he do dat to me ["booty lickin' "], I shocked. Ohhh, but me love gettin' dat now.

Both Ruthie's and Eleanor's comments are suggestive of how Nevisian sexual norms have changed. "Booty lickin'," a practice Ruthie described as "lickin' somebody's asshole," would be considered deviant by Nevisian standards twenty years ago, in Ruthie's estimation. Ruthie asserts as well that "tongue kissin' " was not part of the sexual repertoire of her grandmother's generation. The key here is Eleanor's enactment of a new sexual practice, in this instance, "booty lickin'," produces not only her changing sexual subjectivity but a new normative sexual order as well. This is similar to the way Felicia's imitation of the postures and mannerisms of the girls on the BET videos reworks the sexual order.

NEW CODES AND REGULATIONS: FEMALE PLEASURES

As these newer sexual normativities emerge as the result of global influences from media, migration, and tourism, I wondered what the impact would be on female sexual pleasure, given that within Nevisian society there did not, at least historically, appear to be any coded discourses of female desire or pleasure.[9] This issue occurred to me one night after I had spent the early part of the evening reading by the light of a flashlight. Our village lost electricity, as did most villages, at least once a week. Sometimes we lost power three or four times a week, and these outages could last anywhere from one to ten hours. On this particular night, as I peered out the window, the entire village was dark. I could hear voices singing in the not so distant Pentecostal church up the hill. In the distance, where the Four Seasons Hotel was located on the beach, a string of lights that received power by a generator could be seen. That evening I happened to be reading a book by James W. Sutton (1987), a Nevisian who vividly describes Nevis in the 1920s. Here is Sutton's description of Nevis: "shrub-lined footpaths wound their way to a few peasant houses that nestled here and there. . . . With no electricity in the houses and no public lighting on the village paths, the place was pitch-dark at night and we traveled more by memory and by feel than by sight, on nights when there was no moon (18)."

Sutton's account of the night captured the stillness and darkness of the nights when our village lost electricity. On the nights when this occurred, I often reflected upon Ruthie's stories of what it was like coming-of-age in the early 1980s when most homes had no electricity; there was little in the way of public lights in the countryside, telephones were a rare commodity, and TVs even rarer. Battery-operated radios played calypso music and featured the music from local and regional string bands. Many locals described Nevis

during this time as "very, very sleepy." When the electricity was restored a little past eight o'clock as I ruminated about the Nevis of twenty years ago, I was
taken aback by the images that quickly reappeared on my television, which
appeared so out of place on the Nevis I had been envisioning. I now imagined
Nevisian girls, unsupervised, in various villages throughout the island, sitting
in front of their TVs and watching these images while their mothers and
grandmothers worked late shifts at the hotels.

On this particular night, the American Movie Channel (AMC) was show-
ing a film in which a teenage girl was lying on the floor holding a large white
vibrator. The camera stayed on her face while her hands moved the vibrator
presumably between her legs. There was a shot of the ceiling fan, and then the
camera moved back to the teen's face as her eyes rolled back and a slow smile
appeared across her face. The next shot featured her flowered cotton panties
around her ankles as her toes curled. This scene was from a popular American
movie, *Slums of Beverly Hills*. It aired several nights during the month of
March. The image of the young girl masturbating fascinated me because of the
way it drew attention to female pleasure in the absence of men and because
not that long ago, these images were not available to the majority of Nevisians.

Another movie, which captured my imagination for the same reasons,
focused on female same-sex desires and pleasures. It was aired at seven o'clock
on another movie channel. In this movie, a couple experimented with a
ménage à trois, although most of the show focused on the wife's affairs with
other women. In one particularly graphic scene, the husband, who appeared
tired of sexual activity, got out of bed, leaving the two women to continue
without him. While he was in the kitchen preparing a snack he listened to the
sounds coming from the second floor—women moaning and the sound of
headboard thumps. The husband finished making a sandwich, climbed the
stairs, and entered the bedroom—the camera shot was of a headboard banging
against the wall. The wife and her partner sat up and he asked them if they
needed any refreshments. The scene was repeated a number of times, with a
number of different female participants over many nights and lengthy sexual
encounters. Sometimes it was the wife and other times it was the guest who
sat up in response to the husband's inquiry, but in either case the women
always said, "No, thank you." This was immediately followed by one woman's
hands pushing on the shoulders of the other woman who had appeared
upright when the husband interrupted them. The woman leaning up against
the headboard pushed her partner back down, seemingly between her legs.
Given the visual cues, the viewer is left to surmise that one female partner was
performing cunnilingus on the other. Both of these scenes—the masturbating
teen and the female couple in bed—are marked by the absence of men;
importantly, both scenes focus on female pleasure. In a similar vein, Lil' Kim's
music video, *How Many Licks* focuses on female gratification. If we assume that

media becomes a "site for the production of erotic subjectivities" (Mankekar and Schein 2004, 359), then what is the relationship between images depicting sex and the Nevisian girls' desires, practices, and pleasures? I would argue that BET images, pornography, and American films serve a similar function; (1) they offer girls new sexual repertoires and rules; (2) they offer girls visual and verbal guidelines on what is desired and how to be desirable; and (3) they offer new sexual scripts that spotlight female pleasure. Fictional sexual narratives, such as Lil' Kim's video, which spotlight female desires, offer new ideas about the significance and possibilities of pleasure for Nevisian girls, sanctioning the girls' desires or creating new ones. What else can be said about the codification of female pleasure and Nevisians girls' sexualities? The codification of pleasure encourages girls to pay attention to their bodily sensations. Once they do this, they become attuned to the differences across internal states. The girls begin to become more discerning—more able to recognize which states or sensations are more pleasurable. To the extent that pleasure is codified, we have to assume that there will always remain ambiguity as to whether or not girls have the same experiences. My point, however, is that now Nevisian girls are increasingly exposed to coded discourses on female pleasure that are affecting how they experience sexual encounters. Like music videos, pornography, and film images, women's fashion magazines and romance novels offer yet another possible venue for changing sexual scripts.

PRINT CULTURE: FASHION MAGAZINES AND ROMANCE NOVELS

Between 2000 and 2003, with the opening of Rams Supermarket, Sherry's Beauty Salon, and Chapter One Bookstore, there has been an increase in the availability of women's magazines on Nevis. While the Four Seasons' gift shop and other hotels might have stocked fashion magazines, they did not become widely available to Nevisians until recently. Most of the girls on Nevis cannot afford EC $20 (US $7) for a copy of *Glamour* or *Ebony*. They have the opportunity, however, to peruse them at Rams, Chapter One, and the beauty salons, which they visit during their lunch break and after school. It is not uncommon to see groups of girls on their lunch breaks from school standing around the magazine racks at Rams at 11:45 a.m. Or, if they can afford to pay EC $25 for a haircut, they can look at recent copies of a wide selection of women's magazines imported from the United States. I found articles covering a range of topics related to sex that were typically heralded with sensational headlines such as "25 Ways to Have Your Best Orgasm Ever." This particular article included this tip, "Bring yourself to the brink with your fingers, then insert a dildo before your finale" (*Marie Claire* 2003, 235). In one well-read issue of *Cosmopolitan* (2003, 176–179), there were explicit instructions on how to improve upon the quality and character of your male partner's orgasm in an article entitled, "Seven Ways to Please a Man." In this instance guidelines were offered for promoting sexual pleasure in a male partner. The reader was instructed to, for example, "sit backward" or "use more tongue" on their male partners. The article also suggested: "As he's climaxing, gently pump a finger or two into his perineum, the smooth skin that separates his balls from his butt. It will make his orgasms go on and on" (178). What is the significance of this type of sexual tutoring for Nevisian girls?

Writing on the relationship between sexual pleasure and fictional sexual narratives, Edward-Laumann and John Gagnon (1995) describe the nature of the sexual tutoring in women's magazines in two ways. First, such texts implicitly and not so implicitly suggest that women are entitled to sexual pleasure and gratification. Second, women's magazine articles suggest that if readers follow through and exercise their newly acquired sexual skills, then they have a better chance at "getting and keeping men" (203). Might the sexual tutoring offered in women's magazines reorganize Nevisian girls' sexualities in other ways?

Here, I am suggesting that women's fashion magazines are sites where female sexual pleasure is codified. Over the past twenty years, there has been a proliferation of articles in women's magazines that have to do with female pleasure, specifically female orgasms (Laumann and Gagnon 1995). As Carol Vance (1984) suggests, this might be interpreted in many ways and not necessarily in a positive light. Concerning clitoral orgasms and cunnilingus, two areas of female sexuality that have been covered extensively in women's fashion magazines over the past two decades, Vance argues: "It can be seen as a liberating expansion beyond the bounds of procreative heterosexuality, enabling women to learn about and experience a type of pleasure not connected to reproduction or even to the penis. . . . On the other hand, the anxious question, 'Did you come?' may demarcate a new area of women's behavior men are expected to master and control—female orgasm (12)."

Like other forms of mass media, women's magazines might have the effect of codifying bodily sensations so that girls come to recognize their pleasure in different ways. The best example of this is the way girls talked about "orgasms." Tamara, a sixteen-year-old, was able to assure me with great confidence that she was having orgasms with her older boyfriend, having "read these things" in women's magazines. What's interesting here is that she had come to recognize a specific sequence of bodily sensations while reading women's fashion magazines. In declaring "I read these things," Tamara receives a form of textual legitimation (Gagnon and Simon 1973) that helps make sense of her bodily pleasures. Similarly, along the lines of what Vance is pointing to, Varshnie mentioned how her husband asked her repeatedly about her orgasms. Varshnie explains: "He say, 'A woman cum too, sometimes.' So he asks me, 'How many times did you cum?' and I say to him, 'One,' because I don't know when the hell I cum." The flood of sexual tutoring that appears to be changing the sexual landscape on Nevis stands in sharp contrast to the 1970s, when according to one forty-five-year-old Nevisian man, foreplay was nonexistent. "Looking back," he says, "being with a girl was more like a simulated rape scene." He continued by explaining that there was no mention of foreplay and discussions of female pleasure; references to female orgasms were nonexistent.

In addition to the proliferation of sexual tutoring in women's magazines, romance novels sold at Rams and at Chapter One offer Nevisian girls new ways to organize their sexual subjectivity. What girls learn from romance novels is a specific language about relationships—the language of "romantic love stories." Girls use romance novels as guides to romance as well as sources of fantasy. When Sula Mae, a twenty-one-year-old self-described connoisseur of Harlequin romance novels, recounted her first sexual experience, she explained, "I wanted to see what it was like. . . . It was horrible. . . . It wasn't what they picture on TV. . . . it definitely wasn't what the romance novels say. It was painful. Yeah, I could remember it all right now." Sula Mae, like several other Nevisian girls, explained that her initial experience with sex was motivated, in part, by her desire to "see what it was like." She had imagined that her first sexual experience would be similar to what is described in many romance novels. There was an obvious disjuncture between what Sula Mae imagined sex to be like based on her consumption of romance novels and her first sexual encounter. Her experience prompts the question: How has the consumption of romance novels and other mediated scripts that promote romantic love shaped the girls' understanding of their sexual relationships or their desire for relationships?

Girls who admitted to being sexually active framed their first sexual experiences around "love," much as social psychologist Deborah Tolman (2002) suggests American girls do (179). Ironically, in Nevisian society where men openly and somewhat brazenly have multiple partners, love and commitment were popular themes in the girls' sexual narratives. When girls talked about relationships and boys, they framed their discussions around a specific set of experiences, especially their first kisses or their first loves. Repeatedly, I heard stories about how "He kissed me outside of church," or "He was my girlfriend's older brother and we kissed sometime during Culturama for the first time." All of this makes me wonder if romance had become the lens through which Nevisian girls organized their sexual relationships. Is romance a "code word" for sex, as Tolman suggests? Is it an "amalgam of relationship, passion, sex, and desire" (355)?

The topic of romance was noticeably easier and more pleasurable to talk about for the girls than their sexual practices. When they talked about their hopes and aspirations, most girls, with few exceptions, described living in a two-story house with a washer and dryer and with the father of their children. While the girls rarely mentioned marriage, they repeatedly articulated the desire to live in the same house as the father of their future children. Girls who did not focus on a house and children crafted alternative scenarios revolving around moving "off-island" and going to Canada or to the United States to further their education. Nonetheless, both sets of girls—those who dream of living in a two-story house and those who want to move off-island—appear to be taken with, and consumed by, the anticipation and possibility of romantic involvement and attention.

Most of the feminist literature on romance and adolescence focuses on the negativity of heteronormative scripts (cf. Fine 1988; Tolman 2002). These scholars argue that sex cannot be separated from gender structures and that most romance narratives derive from and reinforce gender inequalities and heterosexuality.[10] If I were to stress the negative aspects of romantic scripts in romance novels, fashion magazines, and music videos by focusing exclusively on how gender inequalities are reinforced, then I would fail to account for the moments when Nevisian girls craft new sexual subjectivities as well as experience pleasure and gratification, however long-lasting or short-lived. For instance, Sula Mae's reading habits are particularly illustrative of the effects of consuming romance novels. Raised by strict Baptist parents who prohibited her from watching television or playing with other girls in the village, Sula Mae devoured romance novels, which she hid from her mother and father in her school bag. Ironically, her father's sister supplied her with the Harlequins. At night, while her parents looked after the family-owned store, Sula Mae took pleasure in her clandestine reading habits. When she was thirteen, inspired by Harlequin novelists and authors like Danielle Steele, Sula Mae wrote her own romance novel, entitled, *She Cries at Dawn*. Her dream was to "become a millionare." Throughout her adolescence, Sula Mae kept journals and composed lyrics to several songs. She explained that her personal favorite, one that she wrote in church, was entitled, *Eleven O'Clock*. Here is what it meant to her: "I matured very quickly. I had the boob thing going on while my classmates were like sticks. I was the fat kid. I write things like, 'Back in school you used to say this about me . . . that I was a figure 8. You stopped and watched me.' It [the song] speaks about me. In the song I'm trying to say, my parents had me so protected but now I have so much talent . . . so just look out . . . something big is coming. I'm mature now. It's like a climax . . . so I'm going into my climax until I burst kind of thing."

Reading romances proved to be an integral aspect of Sula Mae's coming-of-age experience. It shaped her understanding of herself as a young woman. In many ways her experiences as an early and avid reader incited her passion for writing, an expressive tool that helped her make sense of her body image, her relationships with boys, and her future aspirations as a writer.

IMPORTED SEXUALITIES: RE-CATALOGING SEXUAL PRACTICES AND DESIRES

Not only does the proliferation of images and scripts, such as the ones described promote new sexual forms and desires, but it also increases the cultural references to same-sex relations circulating on Nevis. Cultural references to Western categories of sexual behavior appear to be affecting the way youth catalog sexual practices by linking them to sexual identities. The National AIDS Coordinator Andrea Nisbett explains: "I hear them [young people] say from time to time, 'This person's a lesbian.' So there is a culture, but I think it's more like a fashion thing. I think . . . for young people it has to come from television. I know it's a medium that their parents don't know much about. And I'm sure if there is a show that's coming on, a lot of them won't be sitting around there watching it together. Or the Internet or watching porn and getting into those sites and stuff like that—Parents don't know how to use a computer. . . . They're not hip to all of that."

When Nisbett states "there is a culture," she is referring to the importation of cultural references to lesbians, gays, and bisexuals that circulate in a globally produced popular culture. As suggested previously, one effect of this enhanced global flow is that it suggests to girls that specific pleasures and bodily encounters can be organized or indexed. However, this way of cataloging sexual practices does not necessarily translate into widespread tolerance and can even be viewed as promoting intolerance, as evidenced in a conversation with sixteen-year-old Felicia.

DEBRA: Let's change the subject a little bit. Let's talk about television. There are American shows that are now depicting gay relationships. Take for instance, "Will and Grace." [Will and Grace is a sitcom on NBC set in New York which focuses on the relationships of four adults, two of whom are gay men.]

FELICIA: Yeah, I love that show.

DEBRA: Do your friends watch *Will and Grace?*

FELICIA: Yeah, we love that show.

DEBRA: Do you think it's influencing the way in which people on Nevis see homosexuality?

FELICICA: No. People on Nevis just are close-minded to homosexuality. I think it's because we're still predominantly religious. Everybody's thinking about religion. Everybody goes to church and if you go against what is in the Bible, then that's it. They don't want you and you are cast out.

DEBRA: So you don't think that it's making same-sex relationships more acceptable by making gays more visible?

FELICIA: No, one of my social studies teachers told me never to watch that show, and if she should hear that I'm watching that show, she would minus five marks from my mark sheet.

DEBRA: What does that mean, minus five?

FELICIA: Marks. We get a percentage at the end of each, like, in a couple of weeks. If she should hear I'm watching *Will and Grace*—she's going to take off from my mark.

DEBRA: Did she tell you that or everybody in the class?

FELCIA: Everybody in the class.

No doubt there is an acquired cosmopolitan sensibility projected on the sit-com *Will and Grace* that has its roots in urban American pop culture. The show may be seen as spotlighting gay lifestyles, as well as affecting viewers' notions and perceptions of gay culture. For some Nevisians, like Felicia's teacher, the program represents a threat and an unwanted cosmopolitanism. Agnes, a white expatriate who has lived on Nevis since the 1980s, once remarked, "Nevis has become very worldly, partly as the result of American TV." The nature of this "worldliness," which is characterized in part by an influx of sexual discourses, is the cause of intense debate on Nevis and generates conflict between Nevisian youth and older Nevisians. Agnes tells a poignant story about how, when a group of businessmen and government leaders got together in 1988 to discuss the introduction of cable television to Nevis, a fistfight broke out among the opposing sides.

Older Nevisians readily denigrate what they perceive to be the negative influence of TV, particularly BET. They blame recent social changes on television and on other global influences, including the tourist industry and information technology—all of which are contributing to what they perceive as an increase in sexual promiscuity and unruly youth. Jefferson Wallace, however, a community worker and state employee who has worked with youth on Nevis for over twenty years maintains that the markers used to examine sexual activity remain relatively stable. For example, from 1965 to 1985 the teen pregnancy rate remained steady (20 percent); in that same period the incidence of STDs with the exception of chlamydia and HIV also remained stable.[11] Wallace asserts that some Nevisians use American television as a scapegoat for what they see as the demise of Nevisian morality. In addition to, and perhaps in response to, the influx of American TV shows, Nevisian state-sponsored programs, focusing on teen sexuality, have also developed over the past ten years. The most prominent are public health programs that focus on teenage pregnancy and HIV prevention. The development of these programs, as well as the affect they are having on girls' sexualities, are the topic of chapter 5.

CHAPTER 5

The State and Sexualities

IT WAS a hot day in June around the time the flamboyant trees bloom and show their bright red flowers. Natie and I had moved our metal folding chairs under the tree for shade. Before we began our interview, I fiddled with the tape recorder, checked the batteries, and tested the sound quality. When I looked up at Natie she was sucking her thumb and tugging on her short denim miniskirt that I assumed was riding up the back of her thighs, causing her to stick uncomfortably to the seat of the metal chair. Natie was a thirteen-year-old girl whom I had met in one of the focus groups. She wore her hair pulled back in pigtails, with pretty pink bows covering the elastics. She told me she took time to pick out just the right outfit for our outing. With her denim skirt she wore a white cotton blouse with capped sleeves, embroidered with pink and blue flowers at the neckline. As our interview progressed, she described her first consensual sexual experience while intermittently sucking her thumb.

Two days before Christmas, Natie had left her schoolmates in Charlestown, where they were participating in the holiday festivities, to go for a ride with Dylan, an eighteen-year-old boy she knew from her parish. They went to Pinney's Beach, and there, in the backseat of his Nissan, she had sexual intercourse for the first time. She described it as painful and quick; she reported that they had used a condom. Dylan had at least one other girlfriend of whom Natie was aware; since having sex, she had seen him, but they had not had sex again, nor had he displayed much affection toward her. Her sexual encounter had been six months ago.

As Natie explained, fear is an integral part of her understanding of sexuality: "AIDS scares me more than pregnancy. You get pregnant, you get a child, and you live and de child live. You get AIDS and you die." While Natie measured her fear of AIDS against her fear of becoming pregnant, both fears seem to play an essential part in shaping her sexuality: "De fact dat me mother got me when she thirteen young [thirteen years old], she couldn't go out. She didn't have much privilege. I want privilege. I want to see me sixteen party and all dat. Everybody thinkin' dat I was goin' to get pregnant at thirteen and I went to thirteen and didn't get pregnant."

Natie's desire to enjoy her adolescence, to celebrate her sixteenth birth-day, to take pleasure in her favorite pastimes, which include going to the horse races with her girlfriends as well as playing netball, appear to be strong deter-minants in shaping her sexual practices. Like Natie, many girls discussed the threat of an unwanted pregnancy and its consequences, a threat that appeared to be a deterrent to engaging in sex. Also like Natie, the girls talked about their fear of contracting HIV. Given these girls' fears, it seems critical to examine public health programs among the disparate but overlapping discourses affect-ing the production of girls' sexualities. It is remarkable that a thirteen-year-old Nevisian girl has come to narrate her sexual subjectivity in light of her con-cern over an unwanted pregnancy and HIV. This brief vignette about Natie reveals the complexity of the linkages between public health programs, including those aimed at reducing the rate of teen pregnancy and HIV prevention on the one hand, and the production of sexuality on the other hand. In this chapter, public health programs that focus on teen pregnancy, HIV prevention, and sexual violence will be examined to suggest that public health is not only a site for the struggle to construct a particular type of sexuality, but that it is also a site of social ambivalence and discomfort around sexuality.

As a result of globalization, the social regulation of sexuality on Nevis has become more diffused. Weeks (1986), writing about modernity and sexuality in general, argues that there has been a "move away from moral regulation by churches to a more secular mode of organization through medicine, educa-tion, psychology, social work, and welfare practices" (29). Nevis, over the past ten years, has followed a similar trajectory in terms of the social regulation of sexuality. Nevisian sexualities no longer fall exclusively under the domain of the church. Public health programs have become increasingly more organized and well-established within Nevisian society. While public health does indeed represent a new mode of organizing sex, it is far from secular on Nevis. Thus, this chapter also will examine how public health discourse on Nevis is not completely free from religious and moral underpinnings and influences. In other words, public health education on Nevis is really a form of moral edu-cation. Given the history of Nevis, specifically the influence of the Methodist society and the significance of religion in everyday life, the connection between public health and religion is not unexpected. Public health ideology appears driven by the desire not only to improve the overall health and wel-fare of the country's populace, but also to create a type of Nevisian who will be morally upstanding as well as economically productive. Public health dis-course on Nevis is notably framed by the tenets of biomedicine, but also by Christian morality and development ideology, a confluence of discourses that is most apparent in the health and education programs that focus on teen pregnancy and HIV and their subsequent implementation.

My focus on public health and sexuality deviates a bit from a new trend in anthropology. Let me explain. In their new book *Sex and Development* (2005), coeditors Vicanne Adams and Stacy Lergh Pigg, both of whom are anthropologists, examine the way the globalization of development-orientated health programs, such as HIV prevention and family life programs have become powerful means for remaking sexuality. They raise important questions about the medicalization of sex and the way in which "(f)actual claims about sexuality, reproduction, and health" (27) masquerade as morally neutral and objective. By asking provocative questions such as: "What is at stake for various actors when, in the name of health, equality, and improved life, sexuality is foregrounded as a target for intervention" (17) they caution us to be concerned when "hopes and visions" are invested in sex education programs that after all may not represent the "tools for empowerment" (21). This is a classic Foucaldian formulation. Foucault warned his readers to be suspicious when sexual openness is conflated with liberation (1978). The disparate queries in *Sex and Development* critique, in one way or another, how the conjoining of science and sexuality is deployed to advance various political agendas in modernity projects in different places around world. I, however, want to ask a different question, namely, what is at stake when the state fails in its effort to modernize through public health interventions? What are the implications of this for Nevisian girls' sexualities?[1]

TEENAGE PREGNANCY: A NATIONAL OBSESSION

Over the past ten years, the Nevisian Ministry of Health has attempted to develop a system for tracking and measuring sexual practices and behaviors. The number of births to teenage mothers is 19 percent of the total births each year, or one in every five births annually (Martin 2001). A mini-cottage industry is emerging that looks at whether teens are using condoms, the age at which they first have sex, their knowledge of HIV prevention, frequency of sexual partners, travel history, and sexual experiences while traveling. The subject of teenage pregnancy was regularly discussed in television broadcasts, newspapers, government meetings, and in other civic forums. However, despite the attempt at the surveillance of teen sexuality, particularly girls' sexualities, which the Ministry of Health hoped would aid in their efforts to alter the dominant sexual patterns, public health programs, while affecting some change, cannot compete with both the traditional sexual norms and the influences of consumer culture. What follows is a discussion of a particular civic forum that spotlights how teen sexuality is viewed among Nevisian leaders and how it is discussed in public venues. Examining this forum in detail is important because it highlights the seemingly minute moments of discursive formation that are easily overlooked, in this case, in the domain of public health discourse.[2]

"LET'S TALK:" DEFINING THE PROBLEM

Let's Talk is a weekly radio program in which a well-known radio personality, Everett "Webbo" Herbert, interviews guests from the community to discuss public policy, as well as current social and political issues. The motto of the weekly program was: "This is your voice in the community. Talk that gets results." On March 25, 2003 Von Radio televised a radio program whose subject was the "nonacademic side of education." The guests for this particular program were Vance Amory, premier of Nevis; Mrs. Hodge, headmistress of Charlestown Secondary School (CSS); Mrs. Jones, a guidance counselor at CSS, Mr. Brantley, a local attorney and social activist; and Pastor Maynard, a church leader. Each guest was given a few minutes to comment on the significance of what the host referred to as the "nonacademic subject of education," a subject not clearly defined at the onset of the program. Mr. Amory noted that the nonacademic side of education was important to the development of Nevis, describing it as the process of "inculcating certain values" such as self-control, self-discipline, good manners, and neatness of dress into students in order to "create well-rounded persons who can be useful citizens to help with the further development of our country." Following the premier, others talked about the conspicuous lack of civility as a sign of the moral decline of the nation. Mrs. Jones implied that poor manners indicated a permissive sense of morality. Mrs. Hodge described the number of extracurricular activities that the school offered to enhance nonacademic skills, including sports, drama, Christian fellowship, and vocational training. In her estimation, however, "students run from these opportunities." Mr. Brantley called upon parents to support the teachers' efforts in instilling the "essential skills," which he had defined similarly as self-discipline and common courtesy. Additionally, Mr. Brantley added one other value that he thought deserved serious consideration, which was patriotism or a "love for one's country." According to Mr. Brantley, Nevis has "suffered a breakdown" as a society. He reminded the audience that "In the not so distant past, we saw it was a community effort, the essentials were taught in school and enforced at home and *that* is the Nevis we ought to be looking to, the country we are seeking to develop where children know that there is a standard of behavior required of them . . ." (NTV [Nevis Television], March 25, 2003). Pastor Maynard agreed with the sentiment, asserting that there were "serious problems" in Nevisian society; however, he maintained that the school could not be counted upon to rectify the problems since "most of the teachers were bad examples." He was just as pessimistic in describing the church's inability to cultivate morality among Nevisians, including youth. "The churches are now like hotels. People check out of one and into another; if you do not get good service in one you check into another." He referred to this as "church sampling."

The assembled guests suggested that parents' unwillingness and inability to foster self-discipline and good manners in their children were the primary causes of the recent decline in civility and weakening of the moral constitution of Nevisian society. What's more, this state of affairs could be attributed to the fact that, according to one outspoken panelist, "children were having children." Mrs. Jones described this by saying that today's "grandmothers are thirty years old, wearing hot pants and short skirts. Grandparents, parents, and children [all] end up at Sanddollars [a popular dance club]." Packed into Mrs. Jones's comment is the idea that today's grandparents are not equipped to perform their duties as moral custodians, a role that they apparently performed in the past. By claiming that multiple generations are gathering at Sanddollars, an establishment associated with unruly sexualities, permissive dance forms, alcohol, and violence, Mrs. Jones is painting a picture of the epitome of moral indecency. Other panelists agreed. Mr. Brantley explained that teenage pregnancy is a very serious problem that plagues both the schools and society at large. Within a very short period of time, the discussion on *Let's Talk* had moved from a general discussion of the lack of civility among teens to their unruly sexualities. Soon after the panelists debated the issue, the radio station was inundated with callers. Many callers suggested that an alliance be formed between parents and schools in order to repair the moral health of the nation. One caller warned that teaching moral values and principles required a valiant effort in order to "fight the evil forces" of television that promote lewd behaviors among the youth. Before the show was over, a caller spoke passionately about social change, invoking Christian allegory. "Our community continues to reap what it sows and I am wondering when we will change the seed so that we could reap the right harvest. Those of us who grew up in the church . . . we produce; we work; we have that right discipline. Do we have the will to change the seeds, to reap the kind of harvest we need in the next ten years?"

How does a seemingly mundane or ordinary event, like a televised radio talk show become a vehicle for the state in its effort to advance social reform? It provided a public forum to debate the issue of who is responsible for the nation's health, morality, and future. Its participants and the majority of those who called to comment, indicated that parents should be held at least partially responsible for their children's uncontrollable behavior and lack of self-discipline, particularly when it manifests itself in teen pregnancy. In many ways, this particular program represents a critical struggle to construct sexuality; it also reveals the power dynamic embedded in the production of sexuality. Taken together, these statements, produced by a government official, school personnel, and community leaders are reflective of a discursive formation specific to public health and teenage pregnancy. In other words, the guests' statements can be viewed as a collection of authoritative statements about teen sex and its consequences. According to the experts, teenage mothers signal unruly sexuality, and thus a decline in the nation's morality that will impede the course of its development. Moreover, community leaders, such as those featured on *Let's Talk*, determine not only the terms of the debate regarding teen sex, but more significantly, they also organize the moral issues, thus shaping the range of possible social reactions and solutions. Given that discourse produces meaning and assigns value, it is critical to ask what it means that sexually active girls are viewed as agents of moral decline and impediments to economic and social development. How does this figure into the way in which girls produce their sexualities? Before addressing these issues I will lay the groundwork for answering this question by looking more closely at the character and influence of public health programs.

The issue of teenage pregnancy has been an increasing source of concern for the Ministry of Health on Nevis. In 1983, the topic of "human sexuality" was included in the school curriculum as part of the health program. Prior to that, aspects of sexuality were supposedly taught during hygiene class. Over the past decade there has been a concerted effort by the Ministry of Health, particularly by the Department of Gender and Social Affairs, to conduct seminars for teachers, parents, youth groups, and school counselors on the subject of teen sex. However, the long-term policy goals for health promotion do not always reflect what is taking place on the ground, so to speak. The story and interview segments that follow highlight the disjuncture between the policy goals and their implementation.

HEALTH AND FAMILY LIFE EDUCATION: TEACHING SEX

On January 16, 2003 I attended a curriculum guide review meeting on the family and life syllabus. This meeting was sponsored by the Ministry of Health and the Department of Education. In attendance was Shirley Wilkes, the nation's health educator, Mrs. Liddy, a representative from UNICEF who had been working on St. Kitts to evaluate the family life curriculum, and eight guidance counselors from the secondary and primary schools. The UNICEF representative spoke at length about a one-week training workshop on family life that had been conducted in March 2002 with guidance counselors on St. Kitts. During her introductory comments, she held up a 200-page curriculum on family life education produced in 1990 by Nevisian health care workers, including Wilkes, who was at this meeting, and a number of local doctors and nurses. The impressive thirteen-year-old guidebook was passed around the room for closer inspection. Its topics ranged from sexual wellness, to anatomy and physiology, STDs, and sexual violence. None of the guidance counselors had ever seen the document or been made aware of its existence. This surprised the counselors since it was part of their responsibility to teach family life, a responsibility that many said they could not fulfill adequately. The counselors took turns conveying their strong reservations about teaching a topic that they felt ill-prepared to teach. A few expressed openly that not only were they not prepared to teach sex education, but also that they felt uncomfortable with the topic in general. It is important to point out that on an island as small as Nevis, these eight counselors are representative of the state in its effort to implement policies.

This disjuncture between the Ministry of Health's long-term goals for family planning and the implementation of these goals is a sign of Nevisian society's general ambivalence about sexual matters. On the one hand, Nevisians talked openly and joked freely about sex; on the other hand, there was reluctance for cross-generational talk, the kind that would characterize a classroom environment, between a teacher and her students. This reluctance and discomfort was made clear in an interview I conducted with the minister of health, Jean Harris. In trying to pin down some of the cultural barriers to family planning, Mrs. Harris noted what she saw as the ineffectiveness of the teachers. Mrs. Harris told me that "Years ago we started to teach reproductive health in the schools and I always thought the teachers were not comfortable with their own sexuality. That's where the problem is. I kept saying, You don't send somebody there to teach something that they themselves have a conflict with. They have a conflict with their own sexuality. A lot of people come in to teach health, but [they] are not competent with the children . . . and they don't even call things by their proper name because they're not confident talking about it."

Rather than focus on what may appear to be some individuals' conflicts with sexuality, I chose to interpret Mrs. Harris's observations as an indication of how public health is a site of much social ambivalence toward sexuality. More importantly, the state's reluctance to implement a health and family life education program that would educate the girls makes it more likely that they will become susceptible to the demands of consumerism and give men with access to cash and goods, the upper hand. Consequently, the girls become the state's foil for its own inability to manage sexuality. Community leaders, including some of the schoolteachers tend to hold the girls responsible for aspects of their lives rather than point to the social and economic circumstances that produce certain effects, in this case, teen pregnancies. Perhaps the ultimate way this manifests itself is in the school policy in which girls who become pregnant are expelled from school and are not allowed to finish their education. Such tension and ambivalence around sexuality is quite evident in some of the public health programs geared toward HIV prevention and condoms as well.

2. Charlestown Secondary School, a view from the schoolyard.

HIV PREVENTION: CONTESTING SEXUALITIES

Between 1987 and 2003, the Ministry of Health documented fifty cases of
HIV on Nevis (Statistical Report, Health Information Unit, 2003). Health
officials suspect that this figure does not reflect the actual number of people
with HIV living on the island, since many Nevisians are very likely to be
tested elsewhere in the Caribbean or in the United States. In response to the
potentially disruptive effects of HIV on both individuals and society, the government of Nevis has initiated a national strategic response. This response has
involved a tremendous intensification of internationally generated and state-
sponsored public health programming devoted exclusively to HIV/AIDS.
Currently, the government is working to establish a volunteer testing and
counseling program. At the maternal health clinics, testing pregnant women is
not mandatory, but doctors strongly encourage pregnant women to be tested.
HIV testing, which is voluntary, is free at government laboratories for all
nationals. In 2000, the Ministry of Health, in collaboration with church
groups and representatives from the private sector, including the hotel industry and chamber of commerce, proposed a number of programmatic initia-
tives, including a recommendation to develop programs for youth which
would incorporate teen perspectives on various health and social issues.

In 2001, based on these recommendations, Andrea Nisbett, the nation's
AIDS coordinator, received a grant from UNICEF to develop and produce

Get Real, a television program that is best characterized as a reality/talk show. One hundred teens were interviewed from varying backgrounds, and twenty were cast to appear on twelve episodes. The topics were fashion, teen pregnancy, HIV/AIDS, peer pressure, music, juvenile delinquency, education, relationships, religion, health and beauty, communicating with parents, and discrimination. The thirty-minute show aired every Tuesday night and garnered great attention. Charmaine Howell, who helped to develop the program and served as its moderator, addressed the objectives of the program as a well as a few production issues:

> This show actually was Andrea Nisbett's idea. . . . She had done some seminars and workshops with young people, and from those sessions, she thought that a talk show would have been a very good way to get their views out to the public. . . . What we really wanted to do was to get people to understand how young people think; and use it as a base from which to develop programs and understand how to deal with young people and the challenges that they're going through. . . . [The] average age was about fifteen . . . that to me was a little bit disappointing, because I would have preferred to get a wider age range. . . . We wanted people who were articulate, people who were logical, people who had a certain look and presented themselves well—you know, who weren't slouching and shy looking, and people who seemed to be upfront and positive, if you will. I was hoping to get . . . like I said, a cross section of people, so I didn't want just the smart kids. I wanted people who have boyfriends, who don't have boyfriends, who live with their parents, who don't live with their parents, a lot of different scenarios and situations that young people find themselves in. I was hoping to get a good mix of that. I don't think we achieved that. I think the majority of people were from what we call the brighter classes, and you know, everyone was more from stable family homes. No troubled youth really ended up on the panel. And to me, I think the show might have had a little bit more substance if we had a good mix of people.

Get Real was an innovative program by Nevisian standards. In the past there had been a number of health education seminars geared toward youth, but this was the first time a public forum was created so that teens could discuss and debate important social issues. The emphasis was on "getting people to understand how young people think." At its inception, the show was described by its producers as a "medium through which young people can exchange information about education, careers, finance, lifestyles, sex, sexuality, HIV/AIDS and related issues. This is their voice, their chance to be open and expressive and represents the first step toward opening the communication lines with parents and guardians" (*Get Real*, proposal).

Get Real was met with resistance and ambivalence throughout the community. In part, the negative community reaction was due to the fact that teens themselves were setting the terms for the social debate around teen sexuality and HIV. Rather than being perceived as "opening lines of communication," the program instead posed a threat to the community. The fact that teens spoke openly and publicly about private matters, such as the practice of men having multiple partners and condom use, was highly controversial. A high school guidance counselor told me that the show should be censored. Howell was repeatedly told that she had recruited the "wrong kind of girls." A passerby on the street explained to her that "You need better people, more exemplary people." This kind of public feedback is interesting given the fact that Howell herself had thought that the show actually lacked a "good mix," and that in her estimation, they wound up with girls who were from the "brighter classes" and more "stable homes." A participant on the show described the show's reception this way: "*Get Real* was a unique show for Nevis and we did give a lot of good information to the public, because we were actually getting real, but as usual in Nevis, they always look for a negative and oddly enough, the Nevisian public felt that the cast wore too much makeup. But the public both in St. Kitts and Nevis tuned in to see it with their families and it did spark conversations."

On the show teens were accused of talking too openly about sex and the girls were accused of wearing too much makeup that must have signaled a type of excessive sexuality. Some teens even were ridiculed in their villages. In the episode on teen relationships, for example, a girl described how common it was for girls to exchange sex for money and clothes. After the show was aired, people interpreted her comments to mean that she was taking money in exchange for sex. People harassed the girl on the streets, hurled insults at her, and called her a whore on several occasions. For days, the girl was afraid to be seen in public. The girl's mother and pastor called Howell demanding that she intervene "to clear the air and to tell the people what's going on." According to Howell, the girl's comments had been misunderstood. During the show the teen explained, "Young people want money. That's what they mainly want. That's why they go with older guys. And if I can get clothes, if I can get shoes, I will take it." What was misunderstood was that the girl was representing not her personal experience, but her impression of how popular this sentiment was among girls her age.

By talking about sexuality and issues related to health, teens were challenging Nevisian norms and notions of what is considered socially acceptable. The teens' involvement in the program itself represented social change. This is revealed by the comments of another female participant on the show:

> The sex show was very big, because the consensus on the show was that we thought that people should have sex when they are emotionally ready

and shouldn't be forced to abstain; rather they should be taught about safe sex. The public felt that we were telling all the young girls to go out and have sex. The public missed the whole point of the show, but a lot of the teens at school absolutely loved the show. I guess it was kind of a sense of relief to hear someone else say exactly what they were thinking. The parents for the most part were quite upset, and I had actually heard a mother say that the show needed to be pulled off the air. It was really crazy that week when that show aired, because the cast was getting a lot of backlash as well as our parents; they were being blasted. The older folks were saying that we should have been talking about waiting until marriage for sex, but that's just not the way we feel about the whole issue of sex. That way of thinking is quite simply extinct.

For this girl, the positive reception by other teens is a signal that the episode's discussions legitimated their desires, including their desire for more sex education. The negative reaction expressed by older Nevisians is attributed to the apparent disregard that the youth have for the value of "waiting until marriage for sex." However, contrary to the participant's interpretation, marriage, historically, has never been normative within Nevisian society (Olwig 1993). It is not difficult to imagine, however, that older Nevisians would want younger Nevisians to postpone sexual activity. Perhaps what *Get Real* represents is a public display of the tensions between the ideal religious discourse and the traditional discourse described in chapter 3. In addition, the fact that the teens themselves were exposing the contradictions more than likely fueled the controversy. For instance, Ruthie, who I regarded as somewhat of a broad-minded Nevisian, once told me that *Get Real* scared her. She was concerned that her nine-year-old daughter would soon be an adolescent facing similar issues and she was troubled with how rapidly social change had occurred in her lifetime. For Ruthie, social change was marked by how openly and candidly girls spoke about matters related to sexuality and by how much information girls seemed to possess about sex: "When me was fifteen, I didn't know all dat teen pregnancy stuff. Me get on with some of de girls in *Get Real* and me ask dem, 'You so smart on de TV, but when it come time, are you goin' know what to do?' "

Ruthie's poignant query calls attention to an important issue, namely, that awareness about safe sex practices does not always translate into actual safe sex practices. In Ruthie's estimation, just because the girls know how to prevent pregnancy (e.g., using condoms) does not mean that the girls will act accordingly during sex. The disjuncture between the girls' "knowledge" of sex safe and their practices needs to be viewed in light of the larger Nevisian attitudes about condoms. In other words, one way to illustrate the conflict between safe sex discourse and the girls' practices is by looking at how condom use and the promotion of condoms has been received on Nevis.

CONDOMS: COMPETING RULES
AND EXPECTATIONS

Like other public health issues, the subject of condoms was a contentious issue on Nevis. Public health recommendations to use condoms compete with and challenge local sexual rules and expectations. First, while advocating the use of condoms was a major component of HIV prevention efforts on Nevis, the accessibility and distribution of condoms were a major source of contention. Health workers were frustrated by the fact that while condoms were sold at local pharmacies and distributed at health clinics, it was illegal to distribute condoms to teens under the age of sixteen. As a result, condoms could not be distributed at schools or at clinics to this age group. There was also a gender-based stigma associated with procuring condoms, as noted by the minister of health:

> If a girl shows up at a pharmacy (we do have . . . cellular phones here on Nevis) and someone calls her mother and says, "Do you know who I saw in the pharmacy today? Your daughter." They [parents and the community members] don't see that the girl is trying to be responsible, that she is trying to protect herself. They look at it like she is too hot. If a man picks up a condom in the drugstore, then he is a smart man. But on the other hand, if a lady picks up a condom, she is a whore. They think that a woman is being promiscuous, even if you have a boyfriend and want to have sex. But nobody seems to mind if the boyfriend has six girlfriends. If they see a woman picking up a condom, they think, "Oh, she probably wants to go with somebody else." It would be so much better to have the attitude that you could buy all the condoms you want because you are smart and you want to protect yourself and your future. But if a woman has a steady boyfriend, she's not supposed to want to have a condom.

As Harris explains, girls and women on Nevis buying condoms appear to display a type of aggressive and promiscuous sexuality, whereas men buying condoms represent a responsible and mature type of sexuality.

The fact that Nevis is a small island society turned out to be a recurring theme in discussions that I had with Nevisians about sexuality. Residents linked the surveillance of sexual practices to the island's small size. On the subject of buying condoms at a local store, a fifteen-year-old in one of the focus groups explained: "You gotta understand, it's tough, everybody sees, and everybody knows; you gotta be careful of what you do and who sees you doin' it." Many of the girls voiced similar concerns about the accessibility of condoms. However, according to community youth workers such as Howell, accessibility was just one of the deterrents that kept girls from using condoms. Howell maintains that many girls view condoms as the man's responsibility.

What's more, she maintains that the girls' resistance to condom use was linked to their ideas about sex and, in some cases, to romance. In the following she shares her understanding of how girls view condoms:

> A girl turns sixteen, she grows breasts, and all of a sudden somebody's paying her a lot of attention. And I think that kind of goes to her head. And they [the girls] get clogged up with these notions of love, such as "I'm a teenager and I'm supposed to fall in love." And they get confused with the puppy love thing. They're stuck in that stage of thinking, because they don't have anyone else to help them through that stage and tell them, "Yes, you have a crush. But it doesn't have to be the end-all thing. I think a lot of them feel that "I've found my forever love." And they get stuck there. And this man, the kind that's just a predator, he's not going to use a condom. He's the man. And he tells her don't worry; he doesn't have AIDS, and they trust each other, and it's this whole brainwashing. And the girls get sucked into that, because they don't have the education they need. I remember a young girl saying, when I asked; "Would you buy a condom? She said "No. that's the man's job." And that's how they think." It's the man's responsibility to buy the condoms. If he doesn't buy condoms, I'm not going to buy condoms." And that's the end of that. And that's a serious thing. I think a lot of girls this age would be a lot more forceful in protecting themselves if they weren't embarrassed to go into the store and buy the condoms. Because it's such a small society, they think, "Oh, so-and-so will see me, and she will tell her mom, so I don't want her to see me. I don't want to be seen doing this."

Howell's comments reflect how attitudes about condoms are constrained by traditional gender roles. Furthermore, her comments hint at the nature of the coming-of-age process on Nevis by telling us that the girls do not have adequate support from older Nevisians, such as parents and teachers. The absence of cross-generational talk, specific to sexual matters or romance appeared to be characteristic of Nevisian society. Not only are most guidance counselors reluctant to talk about health and teen relationship issues with teens, but the majority of Nevisian girls with whom I met did not discuss sexual matters with their parents. For example, the majority of girls whom I interviewed rarely had detailed discussions about reproduction, pregnancy, or menstruation with adults, including grandparents, mothers, and fathers. As one sixteen-year-old said, "we talk about sex with our friends but never our parents or anyone older in society." A fifteen-year-old girl explained to me that when she "saw" her period, her mother simply warned her to stay away from boys. "Dey just want one ding, me mother tell me. She say, 'Keep you legs crossed and you skirt down.'" As discussed earlier, the absence of cross-generational talk about sex was one of the motivating factors in the development of *Get Real*. And this was one of the reasons why *Get Real* was so radical in its approach to sexuality; it incited public debate about sexuality that cut across generations.

Howell's comments are also suggestive of the cultural expectation that women and girls should be sexually available to men and that Nevisian men are in control of sexual activity. Such expectations are also illustrated in a story that Nisbett tells about men's resistance to using condoms:

> Out of the blue, I have people call me on the phone and abuse my ear. One day a taxi man came up to me and said, "Why do you insist on telling people that they're not to supposed to have sex?" I say, "Well, I'm not telling them that they're not supposed to have sex." His response was something to the effect that using a condom and having sex is just the same as not having sex. He said, "You're going around telling women to hold out from their man if they don't want to use a condom." [This guy was] close to fifty . . . he went on and on about what is sex and what is not sex. And the option that I'm giving [the women] is not sex in his mind, you know. [People are mad] that I am telling married woman to use condoms with their husbands. [They tell me] I don't have any right to be telling married woman to have sex with their husband using condoms.

Nisbett in her role as an AIDS educator was seen as intruding upon the private domain of "domestic" sexual relations. Her story raises interesting questions about how Nevisians set the boundaries between public and private health and how public health discourse competes with traditional scripts. Apparently, when girls or women request or demand that their partners use condoms, it disrupts the cultural expectations that girls and women should be sexually available to men. Nisbett's narrative also reflects Nevisian men's unwillingness to give up control of sexual activity. I believe that not only does resistance to using condoms reflect men's reluctance to jeopardize their opportunities for physical pleasure, but wearing a condom also suggests that a man is being considerate of a woman. With that consideration may come other obligations, including the obligation to attend to a woman's sexual satisfaction. Such an obligation is likely to diminish the dominance that men want to feel about who's in control.

Nisbett's story also hints at another issue regarding how internationally generated public health HIV programs overlay on Nevisian sexual norms. It is clear that the Nevisian health promotion model borrows from U.S. models. Most U.S. public health programs that focus on safe sex are based on the assumption that partners talk about sex. But recall that Vanessa, an informant mentioned in chapter 3, never knew, although she may have suspected, that her boyfriend was married. Another girl explained to me that she never talked about "intimate matters" with her new boyfriend. Thus, while U.S.-generated HIV health promotion programs on Nevis promote the idea of negotiation and dialogue, encouraging frank discussions about sex and sexual health is a relatively new practice on Nevis. Bear in mind that I am not assuming that frank discussions about sex are liberating; instead what I am interested in is how new public health programs that are aimed at altering the dominant sexual ideology compete with older more established ways of conducting sexual relations.

The stigma associated with the purchase of condoms, the consequences produced by this stigmatization, and the disarray of public sex education all shapes the girls' sexualities. Felicia's comments are suggestive of how these cultural factors get played out in a girl's life:

> I got my first health course in First Form [seventh grade]. It wasn't very in-depth. The teacher pretty much just taught the parts of the body and how to keep them clean and healthy, stuff like that I guess. I didn't have a health course on birth control and reproduction. I learned about reproduction in my biology class in Third Form [tenth grade] and everything that I know about birth control is from *Get Real*, books, magazines, and what I've read on the Internet. . . . Contraception was never discussed by the teachers in high school, but every so often when my class got to Fifth Form we would talk about that sort of stuff, but mostly I talked about that stuff with my friends. . . . Most of the Nevisian men that I talk to say that they hate condoms; they claim that it doesn't feel the same. . . . Girls in Nevis don't buy condoms. It is pretty safe to say that not even women in Nevis buy condoms. There is just too much of a stigma on sex in Nevis. People talk about everything because there is nothing to do in Nevis. So even if a woman went to the drugstore and bought something as common as a condom it would be the talk of the town. . . . I don't think that girls are willing to get the necessary alternative types of protection because they still have to hide the fact they are having sex. In Nevis there is no such thing as doctor patient confidentiality; even if the girl decided to get contraception in St. Kitts, she would still have to worry about the Nevisians living or visiting in St. Kitts that may say something. The only possible way I think that a girl can get contraception is by having her boyfriend get it for her. People expect the guy to be buying those kinds of things but not the girl.

Felicia's comments illustrate the overlapping cultural constraints that impact how girls learn about issues related to sexuality and birth control. I learned that despite the fact that sex education was not taught in the schools; the girls still possessed an awareness of contraception. For example, 126 out of 153 girls surveyed were able to list an example of a form of birth control. All of the girls over 14 provided at least one example. The girls surveyed at Lynn Jeffers, the private secondary school, were more likely to list a wider range of birth control methods. With the exception of 27 girls who indicated "don't know," most of the other girls listed condoms and 40 of the girls were able to list condoms and one other method, such as "the pill" and "the patch." In every focus group, at least two or three girls explained how girls on Nevis, if they were seeking an abortion, could take a ferry to St. Kitts and have the procedure performed by a local physician. It became clear within the focus groups and within in-depth interviews that the girls' awareness of contraception came from sources outside of school and rarely, if ever, from their parents. These sources include men, magazines, the Internet, and older siblings. Furthermore, it is still illegal on Nevis to dispense contraceptives to girls under 16 years old. The legality of contraceptives needs to be viewed as another cultural factor shaping girls' sexual practices, in the sense that it has the potential to constrain behavior. With limited options for contraception and under intense surveillance, girls who opt to engage in sex are forced to rely on their partners to procure and use condoms. Some girls limited their sexual activities, as I found the younger ones often did.

In general, public health discourse on Nevis, which circulated, however unevenly and inconsistently, on local television programs, in pamphlets, on billboards, and on the radio, competing with older more established sexual codes, partially determined new social/sexual practices for girls. The girls talked about monogamy as well as not "making a habit of sex" for fear of getting pregnant or contracting STDs. On one survey, a 14-year-old, when asked how old she wanted to be when she had her first child, wrote: "It depends when I meet the man that is loyal to me and after I get married I'll have a child." I point to this particular example because while monogamy was a strong theme among the girls, marriage was not. It was also interesting that this particular 14-year-old framed her desire for children around her future partner's loyalty.

The influence of public health discourse could be seen in other ways as well. Out of the 12 girls I interviewed between the ages of 12 and 17, 11 girls engaged in sexual activities, including sexual intercourse. Six of the sexually active girls reported using condoms, although not every time they had sexual intercourse. Two girls over 16 described having used condoms when they first started having sexual intercourse with their boyfriends, but said they stopped after the first few months, having established what they considered to be an intimate long-term relationship. (One of the girls had been with her boyfriend for three months and the other six months.) One of the girls had been tested for HIV. At least 3 of the girls I interviewed reported that their boyfriends were allergic to condoms and as a result did not use them.[3]

The younger girls, those under 14, reported that they did not want to "make a habit of sex." For instance, 13-year-old Kayla asserted that she "tried it" but that she did not want to "get used to having it." She was afraid of being "careless." One 15-year-old girl described being in the backseat of a car with a boy who was "just a friend" and letting him "do other things," but because he did not have a condom, they did not have sexual intercourse. She was proud of herself in this instance because they had been drinking alcohol, so she was very vulnerable. To avoid getting pregnant, some girls deliberately resist sexual intercourse as indicated by one 13-year-old girl: "I let him touch me in me privates and all dat but we not going to have sex all de time. Even when he tells me dat he get sick if he don't get it. Doctor tells he dat he got to have de sex or he get sick."

The idea that men or boys become ill from a lack of sex is a popular belief I had encountered repeatedly. It suggests the Nevisian belief that not only is it natural for men to have strong sexual desires but it is a requirement for masculinity.

In the opening segment of this chapter, I described Natie, a 13-year-old who used a condom, when she had sex for the first time with a boy she knew from church. Recall that Natie had had sexual intercourse one time with an 18-year-old boy. As described previously, Natie's life aspirations were structured around her desire not to become pregnant. In the following section Natie summarizes her interactions with men/boys: "When I was in de sixth grade I was fat. I got slim because I didn't want to have a heart attack. I get slim and de boys start askin' me to go wit dem. Nevis men, dey no good. All dey want to do is to have sex wit you. Most of dem, if you get pregnant, dey scorn you. I want my first child when I am twenty, and if de man I wit don't use a condom, I won't have sex wit him."

I asked Natie to tell me her impressions of why other girls her age were sexually active. In response, she declared, "Dem girls, dey nasty. Dey don't go to church to listen. Dey go to church to meet wit de boys." Caught somewhere between religious discourse, public health discourse, and a local culture in which girls engage in sexual activities at a young age, Natie manages to constitute her sexuality. Still very much tied to the conditions that structure her sexual practices and acts, her sexuality emerges as both an effect of competing discourses and her own agency.

In the experience of this 13-year-old, it also becomes evident that she sees Nevisian men as potentially dangerous and as posing threats to her sexuality, a threat that is not overestimated. That sex is a possible site of danger for Nevisian girls is a theme that I encountered throughout my fieldwork. The threat of sexual violence or the possibility of being coerced into having sex was a powerful force in Nevisian girls' lives. One of the most complicated aspects of understanding Nevisian girls' sexuality is the way in which sexual coercion and violence created a culture in which it becomes difficult to disentangle consent from the girls' inability to refuse sex.[4]

BODILY VIOLATIONS: SHAPING
PUBLIC HEALTH DISCOURSE

In 2003, the prime minister of St. Kitts and Nevis, Dr. Denzil Douglas, addressed the UN Special Session on Children, during which he spoke about prioritizing the well-being of children within the twin island federation. Dr. Douglas pointed to "traditional structures" that require attention and reform, specifically structures that impede the overall health and welfare of Nevis' children. He cited new legislation, the Domestic Violence Act, passed in 2002, and described the concerted effort to train police officers, guidance counselors, and child-care workers in matters related to sexual and physical abuse.

While it has been difficult to enforce the Domestic Violence Act on Nevis, a handful of community activists continue to make matters such as physical and sexual abuse matters of public health. Their aim is to change the "traditional structures" that Dr. Douglas invokes, such as the community's permissive attitudes toward sexual relations between close relatives, forms of sexual exploitation, such as encouraging girls to exchange sex to help offset the cost of household bills, and rape, all of which have historically been underreported. In the past and continuing today to a large degree, these aspects of Nevisian culture have been regarded as private matters. This section will examine local attitudes regarding sexual violence and exploitation, and how these attitudes might shape the climate in which girls come-of-age.

According to the majority of Nevisians with whom I spoke, children's bodies on Nevis are exposed to a range of acceptable and not-so-acceptable practices. Without a doubt, beating children falls within the range of acceptable practices. Indeed, most Nevisians viewed the practice as tolerable and reasonable. In fact many Nevisian adults, both parents and schoolteachers alike, fiercely defended their rights to physically discipline children. Beatings were inflicted on children using a hand, fist, or an object. I listened to numerous stories from my adult informants who beat their children, as well as stories about and by children who had been beaten. In some instances, when my informants were describing how they used beatings to discipline their children, I asked them if there might be a difference between using a beating as a form of rational discipline versus using it to vent frustration. I discovered that physical punishment was *such* an acceptable means of discipline among Nevisians that even beatings conducted as the result of an angry outburst were often described in rational terms and justified.

The nature and extent of the violence became most apparent to me from listening to stories from my informants about beatings in their homes and at school. Two of my closest informants who had children of their own told me on numerous occasions that they beat their children, sometimes with their hands, and other times with objects like brushes or straps. My informants also recalled incidents from their own childhood when their mothers or other adults had beaten them. Anna, a twenty-three-year-old woman with two children, who worked as a sex worker provided the most detailed account:

> I used to get some serious whoopin's from me mother, real serious . . . she hit me anywhere on my body. . . . I remember one time, she pressin' me down on de bed with her feet in me chest and she give me a couple lashes. . . . I been hit with hoes, de back of a machete, de wooden clog shoes. I was fourteen goin' on fifteen . . . [the day I ran away]. . . . Dere was dis Rasta guy I was very much in love but he always respected me. De Nevisian people, we have dis slang, "Family, how you doin'?" Everybody's family. Dat's how he would address my mom. When she hit me we was up by de court house and [after] she went to Daniel's Deck to buy some salt fish; she left me and me brother in de car sittin' dere. It was a sports day and dere be people sayin', "Oh God don't hit her in town." I knew if she goin' beat me dis bad in town when we get home in Barnes Ghaut I gonna really get it worse. . . . I ran away. I came down to a place at dat time called Nok's Bar and he was dere [the Rastafarian] and he say, "Anna, oh God what happened to your eye?" . . . I say, 'Me go home with you please.' . . . I saw her comin' down the road and I sneak inside . . . while standin' behind dere, dere was dis white lady dat owned de Nok, she says "Let's go to de police." I say, "No, she goin' to kill me."

Anna explained to me that she sought refuge at the Rastafarian's house that night, but that someone from the village had informed the police. The man was taken in for questioning the next morning while Anna was examined at the hospital. Apparently, her mother accused the 27-year-old Rastafarian of raping Anna, which Anna denied. Anna returned to her mother's house and lived there until she was pregnant with her first child, which occurred three years later when Anna was 17. She moved in with the baby's father, an older man from her village, who beat her as well until she left him for another man with whom she had her second child. Anna's oldest, who is now 6 years old lives with her mother and Anna's daughter, who is 2 years old, lives with a neighbor. Despite Anna's desire not to treat her children the way she was treated by her mother, Anna told me that once, she purposely put her son's hand on a hot stovetop and burned it, leaving scars. While this appears as an extreme situation, I would argue that this type of multigenerational abuse is not uncommon within Nevisian society.

It was also commonplace to learn from girls that their schoolteachers or principals had hit them on their hands and bottoms using wooden sticks.[5] Kayla, for example, told me that she and her friends were caught drinking rum during sports week. As she relates, the school principal deployed a customary disciplinary technique: "He called a group of us and had us sittin' down. Most of dem were girls. But we not tell him about dem others. And den he talked

to all of us by ourselves. He write down our names . . . and told us he goin'
beat us and give us two licks each . . . but I didn't get any . . . because we had
to go run and me had on jean pants . . . so he didn't beat us because we not
feel it. . . . He say on Monday when we come back to school he beat us but
he forget . . . me not tell him. . . . So everyday me come home from school
and me mother say, "He beat you yet?" Me say "he forget." She laugh.

At this point, I asked, "Why didn't you get beat while you were wearing
your jean pants?" Kayla explained, "Cuz me no feel it . . . we get it on de bum.
Everybody bend over and put she hands on the chair." As she said this, Kayla
stood up and demonstrated what she meant by, "we get it on de bum." Kayla
bent over and rested her hands on the seat of the chair and spreads her legs
apart a bit. In order to ensure that I understood the situation correctly, I asked,
"You have to bend over and lift up your skirt?" Kayla replied, "Oh yeah, and
de last time he beat me, he beat me slow. Five times."

The ordinariness with which forms of aggression are regarded on Nevis is
unmistakably revealed in the quality and character of Kayla's tone, and in her
mother's laughter after she asks her daughter, "He beat you yet?" Moreover,
that Kayla was instructed to return for her beatings when she was wearing her
uniform so that her skirt could be raised, which would allow direct contact
with the upper thighs, recalls the West Indian tradition of beating children
when they were naked. This custom may in fact be a legacy of the way over-
seers and slave owners beat slaves, particularly female slaves (Clarke 1998).
Furthermore, the linkage between violence and sexualized Nevisian girls with
raised skirts also requires us to consider how social violence and aggression,
which permeates daily life on Nevis, extends to, and affects sexualities. Such a
view prompts the question: Can contemporary patterns of sexual violence be
viewed as the legacy of slavery, particularly if, as Diana Fuss (1994) asserts, sexual violence was "imbricated in an entire economic and political system" (31)
of the slave economy?

"UNTOLD STORIES ARE UNTOLD STORIES FOR A REASON": NEVISIAN GIRLS AND NONCONSENSUAL SEX

Anthropologists have noted that it is not uncommon in the West Indies
for a girl's first sexual experience to be traumatic and non-consensual (Smith
1988, 137; Sobo 1993, 167). What is missing from my research are quantitative
data on sexual violence: the actual percentage of girls whose first sexual experiences were nonconsensual, the number of girls who have been physically
forced or coerced into having sex, and/or the number of girls who live with
the threat of sexual violence. Unfortunately, incomplete data on the nature
and extent of sexual violence in many West Indian societies limits our ability
to understand the subject matter. However, by completely ignoring the extent

to which many girls confront sexual violence growing up on Nevis, this project would fail in its understanding of the range of conditions that produce girls' sexualities. Elsewhere in the Caribbean literature, Jacqui Alexander (1996) has observed that the "normalization of violent sex inside and outside the family [has] produced a real existential dilemma" (71). The subject of how sexual violence, subjugated to greater political and economic needs of the postcolonial state, is the focus of Edwidge Danticat's fictional narrative *Breath, Eyes, and Memory*. Danticat's primary goal is to retell the social history of Haiti by focusing on the erasure of sexual violence committed against women and girls (Francis 2004).

What follows may not represent Nevisian prescriptive ideals but reflects the actual patterns of many girls' sexual experiences. The stories of sexual violence on Nevis that I use to understand girls' sexualities represent more than just the mythologies of growing up in the West Indies; they represent untold cultural stories that affect girls' lives in general and their sexualities in particular. Given how widespread sexual aggression is on Nevis, I am willing to maintain that girls growing up on Nevis fall into two groups—those who have experienced sex forcibly and those who know the threat of sexual violence. Writing about rape and Jamaican girls, Sobo (1993) maintains,

> Girls are warned from early on that men and boys must be avoided because they want nothing but sex. They learn that men seek young, tight "needle-eye pum-pum" and that rape is frequent. . . . Girls know rape may happen, and like those who care about them, fear encountering "man gangs" on the road. They wear clothing to bed partly so that night prowlers cannot trouble them and do not find them "easy fe rape." Some even wear shorts under the slips or nightdresses they sleep in. Two sisters, forced to seek refuge in a neighbor's house during a hurricane, fear that, even in a room with twenty-five others, the boys and men there might "fingle" or "interfere" with them if they tried to sleep (166–168).

The stories I collected are similar to the ones Sobo tells. The girls' stories were filled with tales of men hiding behind trees or in *ghauts* (a local term for a valley or a ravine located near a mountain). One thirty-year old woman recalled having to collect water from a public standpipe in the village when she was a child. One day, a man whom she knew from her village, hid in a ghaut, took her by surprise, and handled her roughly by pressing himself against her. Another woman, who was regarded as a "village prostitute" by many, told me that she was brutally raped when she was thirteen years old. Early one morning, dressed in her school uniform, while walking through a pasture, she was beaten and raped by a man who had been hiding in some shrubs. Soon after the attack, her brother attacked the man with a machete. The brother, subsequently spent thirty days in jail and the woman's attacker was set free. Another woman I knew from a nearby village who left her daughter in the care of neighbors discovered that the man of the house had raped her daughter. Right after I returned from the field, a schoolgirl who had been the baby-sitter of a friend of mine was reportedly raped by a family friend. Stories told by my male informants also indicate the extent to which Nevisian girls were subjected to the threat of sexual violence. Nari, a busman, was convinced that "dem schoolgirls like to be had by lots of men at once." In the past, he explained that he "lined" up his friends on the beach to "take on" a schoolgirl. He stressed the point that the older girls "grow out of the phase" and don't take more than one man at once. It was difficult to discern the extent to which Nari might have been describing "gang rapes," which were not uncommon on Nevis, versus consensual sexual activities, although even consensual sexual activity in this context needs to be examined more fully. Under what circumstances can a fifteen-year-old Nevisian girl truly consent to having sex with multiple men in one night, particularly, if as Nari explains, they are lined up and taking turns? Not surprisingly, given the normalization of sexual violence within Nevisian society, Nari, was neither ashamed nor embarrassed by this admission, nor did I sense that he was boasting. It was simply, according to Nari, a matter-of-fact. The tenor of his story reminded me of another story I had heard from Sally, an expatriate and longtime resident on Nevis. Sally explained:

> I know this guy, this affable guy. He is a poor guy. He drives a beat-up truck and picks up garbage. One day he is at my house and a little girl walks past and he says in a nice way, "That's me daughter." I said to him, "I didn't know you had a daughter." He says, "Yeah her mother lives in the village. She a young girl." He tells me that the mother of his daughter is very young and that he used to lie in the ghaut and "steal the sex" from her while she was walking back from school. I said to him, "You mean you raped her?" To which he replied, "Yeah, I guess I did." And he was not ashamed of this at all. They did take him to court but in the end he paid a little money.

How does sexual violence shape a Nevisian girl's subjectivity, if subjectivity is formulated as one's desires, one's practices—essentially one's lived experiences? First, the patterns of sexual violence that impact Nevisian girls needs to be seen as a form of social suffering. Arthur Kleinman and Joan Kleinman (1997) maintain that social suffering is a part of what it means to be human: that "suffering is one of the existential grounds of human experience" (1). However, they remind us that "there is no single way to suffer" (2). If Nevisian girls experience the trauma and pain associated with sexual violence differently and as individuals, then what does it mean to talk about sexual violence as a form of social suffering on Nevis? Together in a study of violence and subjectivity, Veena Das and Arthur Kleinman (2000) write, "One cannot draw a sharp line between collective and individual experiences of social violence" (5). Thus, we cannot separate the girls' individual stories from the larger cultural truths, namely, the way the state (e.g., police, judges, state-employed physicians, and schoolteachers) has historically neglected or ignored incidences of rape, incest, and sexual coercion. Similar to what happens in many places around the world, social suffering on Nevis results from "the devastating injuries that social force inflicts on human experience" (Kleiman, Das, and Lock 1997, ix).

In the girls' short narratives that describe their lived experiences, I looked for traces of how the threat of violence and/or the experience of violence press itself into their everyday lives. The threat of violence, as well as its naturalization, is a consistent thread running throughout their stories. Natie explained it this way: "Me personally, I flex like a boy. Sometimes I girly like dis [gestures to her short skirt and to her pigtails], but me I flex like a boy. Most people know dis, but you got to walk wit a weapon. If I goin' up de road I got a knife in me pocket and I normally carry a stick. Me mom don't have to worry about me dat much. Some boys bang up de girls. Once dis boy he be bangin' up me classmate and I hit him good."

What experiences has this girl had that she has learned to carry a knife or a stick? From a young age, Natie explained that she watched as men took "advantage" of the women in her life, namely, her grandmother, her mother, and aunt. Growing up, Natie overheard and witnessed violent fights between her mother who, as you recall, was thirteen when Natie was born and her mother's boyfriends (none of whom were Natie's father). Natie recounted an incident that occurred when she was around nine years old when one of her mother's boyfriends beat her mother to the point that she was sent to the hospital. Natie is convinced that she overheard this man raping her mother as she stood in the yard. This terrified Natie and had a lasting impact on how she viewed boys and men. Somehow Natie used her fear to fuel her courage. She was unusual in the sense that she took pride in being strong and capable of defending herself. As she explained, she "flex like a boy." Natie raised her arm and proudly displayed her bicep. On several occasions, she was disciplined in school for getting into fights, all of which, in her estimation, were justified because she was protecting a classmate from a boy's aggressive behavior.

Given Natie's story and others like it, I was also interested in understanding how knowing about others' sexual traumas insinuates into the lives of young girls. For instance, I am convinced that when some Nevisian mothers admonish their daughters, particularly once they learn that their daughters have begun to menstruate, to keep their skirts down and their legs closed, that these warnings reflect the mothers' own harsh realities and past experiences of sexual violence. On Nevis, like many places around the world, sexual violence becomes a collective experience shared by mothers and daughters: a mother's memory becomes her daughter's fears.[6]

Quite honestly, and in retrospect I must admit shamefully, the pervasiveness of the sexual violence got to me to the extent that I began to refuse to accept the legitimacy of the people's stories. I began to wonder whether I could take my informants seriously. As I sat across from a woman who told me her memories of being raped on the way to school, I wondered if she were lying to me. On a different occasion, while sitting with a fourteen-year-old girl, who was talking about being raped by a neighbor, I questioned (in my mind) if she really were raped. She appeared untraumatized and unaffected. As she was telling me this story, she continued eating her French fries. In these moments of doubt, knowing full well the spectrum of emotions and disassociation that are linked to sexual traumas, I, too, became complicit in the violence: By rendering the sexual violence as unbelievable, by quietly discrediting the girls' stories of abuse, I committed a form of violence, and that is why as incomplete as this ethnographic account is, I chose to retell fragments of the girls stories—to bear witness to the girl whose mother's drunken boyfriend stood outside her bedroom, mumbling the girl's name, over and over, long after everyone else has gone to sleep; to the thirteen-year-old girl who scribbled on her survey, "Yes, my brother" in response to the question: "Do you know the person who forced you to have sex?" and to Natie who listened, too often, to her mother's cries as the mother's boyfriends beat her.

Not only do many of the girls have a difficult time telling pieces of their stories, but once they do, they run the risk of being blamed for whatever might have happened, for instance, when I explained to a Nevisian friend how I learned that a thirty-six-year-old man refused to let a schoolgirl out of his car and then threatened to beat her if she told anyone, my friend responded, "Why she accept a ride wit him in de first place, dumb girl." In part, when girls are held responsible for the sexual traumas that men inflict, it serves to downplay the trauma, to make it less significant than what it might have been, particularly in the eyes of others. I would argue that trivializing sexual violence or the threat of sexual violence creates social conditions in which the girls themselves are unable to recognize the extent of their social suffering. This certainly was not the case with Natie, but we cannot rule this possibility out for other girls. This becomes clear in a story Grace told about her best friend.

Grace, who is fifteen years old, described how she and her twenty-one-year-old boyfriend were particularly concerned about Sharmera, a girl I knew well and had talked with extensively, and who, according to Grace, was being "troubled" (a local expression that connotes unwanted sexual advances and sexual conduct) by her mother's boyfriend. After the mother left for work, the mother's boyfriend would go into Sharmera's bedroom while she was sleeping and start kissing and fondling her. According to Grace, the mother's boyfriend stayed, off and on, in Sharmera's house and provided financial support to the family. Grace described the situation in detail to me:

> She finally told me and I told my friends. Well, a friend who I trusted, the same twenty-one-year-old guy I told you about, because I figured he's an adult. He can do something about it. So we went and we told her mom, but the thing is he [the mother's boyfriend] was providing money and support for the family, and her mom—her mom was kind of softhearted, I guess you could say. The guy promised he'd never do it again, but then he did it again. Sharmera's mom didn't believe her at first when Sharmera told her and then we called her. There was one night when he and she were alone, and we were afraid he would rape her or something. Sharmera and her mom don't get along well, because she's [Sharmera] been boy crazy, I guess you could say. She's kind of looking for attention, kind of looking for love and stuff from other people, guys and things, so she will go out and she'll talk to men and her mom gets upset and then she will get upset with her mom. They don't really have a relationship. . . . So her mom at first didn't believe her, thought she was just doing it to get attention; then we told the mom and she finally believed it. What happened was that one night we tried to get a cell phone to Sharmera, so she could call out if anything ever happened, [but] because the guy put a bar on the phone, . . . she couldn't call anybody. She and him were alone in the house. So we gave her a cell phone, but the guy found out and he got really upset and he told her he was going to come back, and he's going to do all these things to Sharmera and so all of us went up to the house and took her out of the house, down to a friend's house and then we called her mom who was in St. Kitts and told her everything and she came, but she didn't kick the guy out of the house and then the second time he beat up Sharmera and she got bruised all over and then we had to call the police and get the guy out of the house. The mom actually called the police. I mean, it happens a lot, and even when we went down to the police station, they were saying, "Well, there's nothing much, not much we can do unless there's real evidence." The guy still goes up to Sharmera's house and spends time there. But Sharmera tries to get out of house and all of us really hate him, you know, but there is nothing much we can do about it.

Grace's story indicates the extent to which both Sharmera's family and the state denied Sharmera's abuse. Such disavowal speaks to a cultural reluctance to make sexual violence a part of the public health discourse. Importantly, the marginalization or disavowal of sexual abuse affects girls' sexualities and prompts the question: Is the effect of violence on individual girls mitigated? For example, if incidents such as the one involving Sharmera get reported, and then go unacknowledged by the police or by the state, it appears that the cultural expectation that violence is unavoidable, regardless of what the girls do, is strengthened. Indeed, due to the cultural reluctance to view certain forms of sexuality as exploitive, sexual coercion and violence remain, if not socially acceptable, than at the very least, accepted as inevitable by a society that tolerates it. In this instance, girls like Sharmera and Grace appear resilient, yet they have learned that there is little girls can do about sexual violence on Nevis and this is a pattern that is continually reproduced in the lives of other girls.

In a place as small as Nevis, it is difficult to draw a clean line between the state, as an institutional power that is complicit in the social suffering of the girls and Nevisian society at large. It was clear that many people knew about the pervasiveness of sexual violence but despite the prime minister's public admission of the problem, the majority of Nevisians continue to avert their gaze. The extent of sexual violence has been described on Nevis as an "open secret," something that is widely known by members of the community, including its leaders, but something that is not talked about publicly or addressed officially, with of course the exception of the prime minister's comments in his address at the UN. In certain instances, like the state, the family or more precisely, mothers, play an integral role in the perpetuation and normalization of sexual violence. Francine Baker, who you recall, is a prominent lawyer, maintains that many mothers do not pursue legal action against men who force their daughters to have sex for a number of reasons that are primarily economic. In situations where a girl becomes pregnant, the girl's mother's priority is to secure financial support from the baby's father. If the mother proceeds with legal action and the man ends up in jail, then he cannot support the child; if the perpetrator is also the mother's boyfriend and father of one or more of her children, then she runs the risk of disrupting the family's financial support. There have been some mothers who have pressed charges on behalf of their daughters. However in the majority of these cases the male perpetrators are found not guilty; in the few cases where they are found guilty, they typically receive light sentences.[7] Baker maintains that this is due to the general attitude of Nevisians toward such violence. She reports that in her experience, judges and jury members do not view incidents when girls are forced or coerced to have sex, as serious.

Incestuous relationships between girls and family members also involve coercion and must be considered in understanding the context for the production of Nevisian girls' sexual subjectivities. When I first learned of this from a white American expatriate female who had lived on Nevis for over ten years, I dismissed it as racism. Then I began to hear more and more from health educators, doctors, teachers, guidance counselors, and from the girls themselves that some fathers have the idea that they are "entitled" to their daughters. Locals described such practices as "breaking the girls in" or "training girls."[8] Over time, I found it difficult to dismiss the phenomenon as a form of racist stereotyping. I also found it difficult to dismiss this accusation as a class-specific stereotype because the Nevisians who described it as a problem maintained that men from "all walks of life" engaged in the practice. Girls also told me stories of how their friends from various socioeconomic backgrounds were sexually abused by fathers. While incest is not the norm, it is believed to be widespread.

Hilary Beckles (1996) argues that understanding the multiple forms of male violence against women in the Caribbean requires a historical perspective that seeks to locate enduring social and ideological structures in the slave system. Recognizing the similarities across the region and trying to make sense of the legacy of the New World Caribbean slave system as it relates to contemporary sexual violence, Aldrie Henry-Lee (2000) reminds us that

> the principal concern of the slave system was with maternity, fertility, and the management of the slave household. Slaveholders had no interest in black fatherhood. Moreover slave masters had the right of sexual access to all their black slave women, and black men could not confront or question this right. Relations with a slave man and a slave woman could only be maintained within the context of force, power, and opposition. It is in the context of the culture of violence that colonial masculinities took form and this violence . . . maintains an essential feature of an insecure and subordinate black masculinity. (3–4)

Melba Wilson (1994) takes this historical context a step further, linking the legacy of slavery to contemporary incestuous practices: "Black fathers historically performed an 'opening up' of their daughters. As the words imply, the fathers literally sexually open them up, in preference to allowing an overseer or slave master to do it" (12). Furthermore, Wilson writes, "historically, since slavery and other forms of colonization, black men have felt a need to exhibit the male strength and power which is denied them in the wider community, and to compensate by demanding it within their own communities, by whatever avenues seem appropriate to them. . . . (Moreover), some black men consider their children to be their possessions, and consequently have no remorse about their actions" (22–23).

According to such scholars of history, contemporary black Caribbean masculinity is produced by a number of social factors, thus further complicating sexual violence in West Indian societies. In other words, sexual violence in the homes, to paraphrase Jacqui Alexander (1996), draws its strength from a number of larger cultural attitudes (72). Alexander identifies three predominant cultural attitudes in her analysis of sexual violence: first, the subordinate form of masculinity is not only based on sexual prowess and virility but also rooted in ownership. Second, there is the cultural notion that children are the property of men and therefore are sexually available, even in light of the fact that the men do not live in the same house as their children. Third, there is a common belief that schoolgirls entice or tempt men, even their relatives. Girls are discouraged from appearing "too womanish" in front of their fathers, brothers, or uncles. West Indian mothers may see their daughters as "too womanly for her good" and therefore one "can't have two women in one house" as it breeds competition (99). Expanding Alexander's insights, I would also argue that there is also a common Nevisian perception that even when girls are not "seductive," they require forcible sex as a way to initiate sexual relations. Finally, and I already hinted at this, there is an impression held by some Nevisians (including members of the public sectors, including lawyers, judges, and health care workers) that the U.S. idea that trauma is inevitably associated with sexual relations between fathers or mothers' boyfriends and daughters or girls living in the home is overestimated.

There is nothing simple about the production of sexualities. With that said, there is one further aspect of incestuous familial relations that requires closer examination, and that is what Wilson (1994) calls the "fine line between the giving and the receiving of love and comfort, and the perpetration of abuse" (94). My invocation of Wilson's formulation here is not meant to reproduce the Nevisian attitude that people in the United States overestimate trauma associated with abuse. Rather, Wilson's insight serves to inform the analysis of the production of sexualities that characterizes Nevisian girls' lives, which incorporate the conflicting emotional states that might be produced from incestuous familial relations. These feelings can include a sense of pleasure in being desired, and pleasure that comes from sexual attention from a father, caregiver or any older man, particularly if material rewards are exchanged. Such an interpretation of incest points to the complexity of sexual subjectivities and to the way in which sexuality can be a site of multiple tensions and contradictions. As described here, Nevisian girls' sexualities are conditioned by coercion and violence that are likely to render them powerless or at least, create the impression that they have few if any options available.

Before closing, what should be clear at this point is the uneasy and competitive dynamic between multiple discourses and how this affects the production of girls' sexual subjectivities. For instance, experts and community leaders have organized and deployed a particular type of public health discourse embedded in religious teachings that attempts to compete with consumer culture. The effects of established traditional practices of men having multiple partners, women having children with more than one man, and youth initiating sex at a young age is not considered by Nevisian elites in their discussions of how to remedy the effects of consumer culture and the girls' unruly sexualities. Not surprisingly, the dominant culture views sexually active girls as agents of a declining morality and as impediments to Nevis' development efforts while men who physically force girls or coerce them to have sex remain unstigmatized.

Girls coming-of-age are caught in a web of cultural contradictions and competing discourses. This is most evident in the girls' stories; for instance, we see this in thirteen-year-old Natie's desire to maintain control over her sexuality. Despite the fact that Natie knows that men force women to have sex, she insisted that her partner wear a condom, in a society where the use of condoms is met with ambivalence and resistance. In addition, Grace refused to give up on her friend Sharmera and persisted in getting Sharmera's mother to believe that her daughter was being sexually molested by the mother's boyfriend. In doing so, Grace and Sharmera both rejected Nevis' marginalization of sexual violence. These stories serve as compelling evidence of the tension between subjective ideas and practices versus larger cultural discourses.

Girls on Nevis have a range of sexual encounters and interactions that offer the possibility to resist traditional structures and discourses. One of the most significant factors in considering such a resistance involves the impact of Nevisian economic development on girls' sexual subjectivities. Viewing the girls' resistance through the lens of a changing sexual-economic system provides the subject matter for chapter 6.

CHAPTER 6

Rethinking Sexual-Economic Exchange

LAWRENCE, A PLUMBER, was someone I'd come to see every-day walking through Charlestown. Rumor had it that Lawrence was once the best plumber on the island but that years of drinking and smoking crack had slowed things down for him. One morning, as he climbed the back steps to the laundromat, Eleanor jumped off the counter where she was sitting reading her romance novel and greeted Lawrence at the screen door. With her head tilted up a bit Eleanor sniffed Lawrence's neck. "You took a bath, Lawrence!" Eleanor declared. Soon both Ruthie and Eleanor were at Lawrence's side, sniffing him. I was sipping coffee and sitting on the steps inside the laundromat that led up to the washers and dryers. To me, Lawrence looked like he did every day. He was wearing faded jeans and a ripped t-shirt; his long dreadlocks were pulled back in a rubber band. Eleanor insisted that she had to remind Lawrence to bathe. They playfully teased Lawrence about how good he looked and how nice he smelled. Out of the blue, Ruthie threw in a comment about a broken shower pipe in her house that required repair. Cleverly, she shifted back and forth, one minute telling Lawrence how good he looked and how sweet he smelled, and the next interjecting comments about her plumbing needs. Still sitting on the steps, Lawrence gazed over at me and smiled, revealing his blackened teeth. Noticing this, Eleanor scowled at Lawrence, admonishing him for looking at my breasts, a gaze Eleanor apparently witnessed. Lawrence made a face of disgust, as if to deny he was looking at me. Ruthie shouted out, "Oh come Lawrence, me know you like white women. At Sunshine's [a popular beach bar] you tell me dat de most beautiful ding in de world is white pussy. Right? Right!" Then Ruthie switched gears. Touching his shoulder, she lowered her voice and said, "Come fix me pipe. Come on mon, fix it." At this, Lawrence became visibly upset: "Quit troubling me woman about de dam pipe." Ruthie remained cool, knowing that it would come to no good if she upset Lawrence. In a last-ditch effort she smiled sweetly at him, pushed out her lips, lowered her eyelids, looked him over seductively, and said, "Please fix me pipe, mon."

The brief exchange between Ruthie and Lawrence falls within the range of what is considered socially acceptable on Nevis; it is an interaction predicated on a complex and elaborate sexual-economic system that is built upon reciprocity. Ruthie's gestures and comments, particularly her flattery and comments about "white pussy," are more than just congenial comments: they are enticing and pleasurable to both Ruthie and Lawrence. More significantly, the interaction is symbolic of a larger network of sexual/social meanings. In all probability, Ruthie will not have sex with Lawrence, nor will she overtly offer Lawrence sexual favors in return for his plumbing services and expertise. Still, the interaction plays on the idea that a sexual liaison between them is not completely implausible. This type of symbolic play, which is embedded in gender expectations is structured by a sexual-economic system. It is the very nature of this system that forms the central point of departure for this chapter.

In this chapter, I document the manner in which girls aggressively initiate relationships with men who have access to goods and resources. Many of these men are gainfully employed as police officers, teachers, and politicians. Their positions of power in the community matter to the girls, who by and large are both powerless and impoverished. Yet, they have agency and experience pleasure, and neither should be denied in an analysis of their coming-of-age. Yet, it is also the case that prevailing attitudes, which promote girls as highly desirable, combined with the immense gender disparities, give rise to exploitative conditions that affect girls' sexualities. How then, are we to understand the interplay between dominant and dominating structures and personal agency in contemporary Nevis? To explore this complex issue, this chapter discusses various forms of sexual-economic exchange, the concept of "commodity erotics," and instances of sexual exploitation that result from trading sex for goods and services in a society that is marked by poverty and gender inequality.[1]

The current pattern of sexual-economic exchange on Nevis is derivative of an older more established pattern typical of normative gender/sexual relations in the West Indies. This is best understood by examining West Indian family forms.[2] In the West Indies, legal and non-legal unions, in all variations, whether they are referred to as marriage, common-law marriage, visiting unions, or conjugal unions, involve some form of sexual and economic exchange between partners. The fact that West Indian women have historically lacked the same economic opportunities as men has put them at a disadvantage in terms of securing a means of subsistence, thus encouraging a system of exchange based on a sexual division of labor that involves women exchanging sex and domestic services, such as washing laundry and cooking meals, for access to money, goods, and other resources linked to subsistence. Up until the tourist industry expanded on Nevis in the 1990s, women had very little access to economic resources and relied on men and extended family for the basic subsistence needs for their own survival and for their children's survival. In this context, sexual-economic exchange, as Barbara de Zalduondo and Jean Bernard (1995) argue, becomes normative. I am reminded of an informant's poignant remarks about the father of her children. She explained to me that she did not have time to "figure out if he was a good man or not" before they became sexually involved, as he gave her goods she needed, goods she could never have afforded on her own. My informant's comment more than hints at the impoverished conditions to which most Nevisians, especially women, are exposed.

It is important to keep in mind that up until the 1990s, prior to the increase in revenue and employment opportunities generated by the tourist and offshore finance industries, the standard of living on Nevis was different than what it is now. With unemployment at 64 percent for women and 25 percent for men, daily subsistence needs were difficult to secure.[3] Claudia Weisburd (1984) notes that women generally raised children alone with some financial assistance from the father and that very rarely did a mother and father live together with their children (62).

Now with the expansion of the tourist and offshore financial service sectors, the unemployment rate has been reduced to 4.9 percent making it the lowest in the Caribbean, thus ameliorating some of the effects of poverty. This shift from a relatively impoverished and economically unstable agrarian society to a rapidly growing consumer society—as discussed in chapter 2—has affected the character and dynamic of the sexual-economic exchange system on Nevis. While the current pattern of schoolgirls exchanging sex for access to goods, services, and cash is reminiscent of the older, more established pattern, there are key differences. Within the anthropological literature on Caribbean family forms, Elisa Sobo (1993) offers a clear description of how sexual-economic exchange underpins West Indian *traditional* conjugal unions:

> The traditional model [is one] in which sexual relations are initiated by men, [they are] ongoing, and only indirectly paid for. Money is properly and respectably exchanged, with a time lag. It serves not to compensate but to attract—"to keep the women . . . coming back." It becomes part of the expression of kinshiplike altruism that traditionally overlays sexual relations. . . . Ideally, each woman has her own man, and each man supports [all of] his women. . . . Mystifying the instrumental aspects of sex by adding expressive dimensions to sexual relations (on top of indicating that they were initiated by men and involve long-term commitments) protects women from being considered prostitutes. Women should be monogamous. . . . Since women supposedly do not need as much sex as men, only the base need for money could spur them to casual copulation. . . . Non-monogamous women all too overtly expose the tension between the cultural ideal of moral relationships and the instrumental side of sexual liaisons (185–186).

In the traditional model that characterizes conjugal unions and sexual liaisons, the emphasis is on long-term reciprocity, a sense of obligation between the partners, rather than on a tit-for-tat reciprocity where "accounts" are settled quickly. When reciprocity is invoked, it is done with an appropriate time lag and the goods and services involved are seen as necessities, or at the very least, related to the domestic sphere. For instance, in exchange for preparing meals, doing laundry, and engaging in sexual relations, women expect their partners to contribute income to buy food and household goods, such as clothes and school supplies, and to provide money for both necessities as well as items that might be considered luxuries.

Although exchanging sex for money or goods has long been a part of the social life on Nevis, commercial sex, where women might live together in one house with their sole means of supporting themselves being sexual solicitation ("houses of prostitution") is relatively new on Nevis. Contrasting the traditional model of conjugal unions to prostitution, Sobo (1993) writes:

> Only prostitutes accept money when sexual services are given and only they have no debt to their partners, who are truly their customers. . . . Men hire prostitutes for sex and sex only, relieving themselves of responsibility of any progeny. . . . Prostitutes refuse to mystify the instrumental dimension of sex. They do not develop expressive, intrinsically fulfilling, kin-like relations with customers and do not limit themselves to one man's money. They invert or overturn cultural tradition and are held in disdain as antisocial. . . . Because they do not seek to infuse their heterosexual liaisons with kinship qualities, prostitutes do not create bonds of obligation with men. While their sisters establish a moral dimension in their unions, women in "that harlot business" have no "claims" on any man's money in late life, having "tied" no one to them with kinship altruistic bonds. (182–184)

The women who refuse to mystify the instrumental dimension of sex were well-known on Nevis. My friends and informants readily pointed out "whorehouses" and sex workers to me. For instance, "dat's de Spanish whore house," Eleanor would say, referring to the small, brightly colored, pink house with the black iron gates off the main road in Charlestown. On another occasion, I was reproached for spending too much time with the "Spanish prostitute" on Caddrock Road. The woman who reproached me had two children with two different men, entertaining one on the weekends who came to visit her from another island bringing goods and cash, and seeing the other man during the week. It was clear from our conversations that in exchange for sex this woman expected money from both men. But because of the kinship-like bonds between them, namely, their children, she differentiated herself from the "Spanish prostitute." Moreover, Nevisians blame "Spanish women" for bringing

HIV/AIDS to the island. More so than any other cultural group, people from the Dominican Republic are viewed as promiscuous and immoral. When some Nevisians stigmatize women from the Dominican Republic as immoral and dangerous, it serves to reinforce Nevisians' own sense of morality. For many Nevisians, the system of sexual reciprocity, which is so much a part of the fabric of the society, shaping family systems and gender norms, is viewed as very different than "foreigners" trading sex for money.[4] So how does the pattern of sexual-economic exchange that was occurring among schoolgirls differ from the variations just presented?

Similar to what is happening throughout the Caribbean and the larger world, Third World girls and women are just as caught up in the effects of consumerism as are their First World counterparts.[5] However, Nevisian schoolgirls, unlike their mothers and grandmothers who are benefiting from the economic changes through employment opportunities in the growing tourist and professional sectors, have few ways to earn the income required to satisfy their consumer desires. There is a great disparity between the goods that are desired and the resources needed to purchase them. This appears to be the determining factor in shaping new sexual trends among girls on Nevis. This, along with the fact that sexual coercion is normative needs to frame the analysis of sexual-economic exchange if we are to understand the complex relationship between sexual agency and the dominating discourses that constitute the girls' lives.

The system of sexual-economic exchange on Nevis can be viewed along a continuum, with the exchanges taking many forms. For some girls, their sexual relationships are grounded in romance and love. For instance, they describe the men with whom they have sexual relations as their "knights in shining armor." I also met girls for whom love is secondary to more economical, short-term interests. Many girls told me that in order to initiate these brief liaisons, schoolboys, presumably modeling the behavior of men, will often say to the girls, "I give you dollar, if you give me wifey." The expression "wifey" is common slang used to imply sex. In a society where legal marriage is not the norm, the term *wifey*, and the role associated with it, has come to represent various sex acts.

Viewing the sexual-economic system along a continuum, it is clear that there are multiple manifestations. In other words, the practice of girls letting men fondle them in exchange for a cold drink or bus fare can be viewed alongside the practice and dynamics of the more traditional conjugal union where sex is exchanged for subsistence needs. Admittedly, the quality and the character of the relationships differ, but, nevertheless, they represent the range of practices within the larger cultural system where the organizing principle is sex in exchange for goods and services. No doubt, many Nevisians would disagree with this interpretation. The moral critique of schoolgirls, sexuality, and consumer culture reveals that many in the older generation do not view the two types of exchanges as anywhere near equivalent. To a causal observer it may appear that the older generation is being hypocritical, but it is not viewed as such by the older Nevisians since they do not see the types of exchanges as the same.

When considering the current sexual-economic exchange patterns among girls, it is important to pay attention to where Nevisians draw the line between certain forms of sexual solicitation, as this reveals much about the links between sexuality and morality. When, for instance, sexual liaisons are not long-term, when children are not involved in establishing kin-like relations, and when money and goods are exchanged too close in time, the instrumentality of sex is exposed and people see moral collapse. This, I think, is the best way to describe how some Nevisians are responding to the current situation.[6]

CONSUMPTION, DESIRES, AND SEXUALITIES

Initially, fifteen year-old Sharmera appeared distracted when I began to interview her. I asked her several times if she wanted to meet at another time, but she always declined the offer. But something happened when I asked her about Leon, her new boyfriend. A smile appeared on her face, she giggled, she seemed to finally relax, and became a lot more animated. She told me that finding a place to have sex was tricky, particularly when she was supposed to be in school. Sometimes three or four of her girlfriends would leave the schoolyard together walking up toward Nell's Bar. That way, once they reached the end of Park Road, she could slip into the backseat of Leon's Toyota Rav4. As her friends made their way back to school, the few teachers standing in the schoolyard inside the fence would fail to notice that Sharmera had not returned. Lying in the backseat of Leon's car was a strategy that Sharmera resorted to several times. That way, while her mother was at work in Charlestown, she could ride, without being noticed by other family members or other women from her village, to a remote beach on the other side of the island to have sex with her twenty-nine-year-old boyfriend. Some days, Sharmera returned to school. Other days she was dropped off on the road to wait for a bus to catch a ride back to Bath Village, where she lived. Leon, according to Sharmera, was generous. In the past he had given her a cell phone, CDs of her favorite artists, and new shoes from Simon's Contemp, new shoes her mother could not afford. "Someday" Sharmera told me, "Leon will take me to St. Martin for some real shopping—name brands and everything."

In what follows, I explore the linkages between consumption, desires, and sexualities by looking at the distinguishing features of the more current pattern of sexual-economic exchange in which Nevisian girls participate. For a number of women who are raising children alone, sexual-economic exchange is still a means of subsistence. Many schoolgirls on Nevis, however, who exchange sex for goods and cash, do so to have access to what may be considered "non-essential" goods and services, such as cell phones and rides in cars. The focus seems to be less on subsistence goods and services and more on consumer goods and luxury items. A service, such as transportation, is highly regarded by the girls. The local expression "ride for a ride" connotes a sexual favor in exchange for a ride in a car. Charmaine Howell, a community youth worker employed by the state, repeatedly offered unsolicited advice to the girls, warning them not to accept rides in cars driven by men, even if it's "terribly hot and one is wearing high heels." Charmaine explained, "I tell them, 'You don't want to owe anyone anything, you don't want to be indebted.'" Such straightforward advice speaks volumes about an unspoken rule: that often when men offer goods and services to girls and women, the females incur sexual debts that obligate them to the men. As just stated, a system of reciprocity is the basis of gender relations in the West Indies, and girls at a very young age learn the rules of reciprocation. The assumption embedded in Charmaine's advice is that the men are the sole solicitors. However, based on what I was told and what I observed firsthand, this is not always the case.

One of the most distinguishing features of the more current pattern of sexual-economic exchange is that the girls, at times, initiate the interactions. Many locals criticized girls and what they saw as the girls' increasingly aggressive sexuality and impropriety. On numerous occasions I watched girls approach men and initiate interactions, and while I was never privy to the intimate negotiations and dialogue, what was clear was that girls could be very persistent. For instance, while driving through town with Jasmine and her cousin, Jasmine, on numerous occasions, would direct me to stop the car so that she could talk to various men, men who in my estimation were either in their twenties or thirties. One afternoon in particular Jasmine jumped out of the car I was driving to pursue a man who she wanted to see, leaving her little sister for whom she was responsible, in the car.

When talking about how common it is for girls to solicit liaisons with men, Thomas, a returning national with a steady income and British citizenship, said, "It's like the old children's game called 'Chinese whispers.'" In the United States this children's game is called "telephone." The implication of Thomas's comments is that some girls initiate liaisons in exchange for resources and that everyone is talking about it. Thomas insists that girls and women will often say to him, "I want to have your baby so that I can go to England." For Thomas, this solicitation has contradictory effects. "On the one hand," he says, "if I was willing to dish it out, I could have sex for life." Later he lamented, "It's hard to find out what women genuinely want because they are just after material things. . . . They want material things that they've never had before and sometimes it's for themselves and sometimes it's for their families." Here "dishing it out" refers to cash or goods. Similarly, Tobaa, who, as you recall, lived in the same village as I did, told me how girls often approached him in town asking him for EC$50; promising him "a bit of something in return." Jean Harris, minister of health, described girls' desires for material goods this way: "I discovered that the girls are so strange in their way of thinking and their behavior. They are also unpredictable. You have some who say, 'Mom and Dad are not able to buy me what I would like to have.' So if a girl sees a skirt that she likes or earrings or if she needs to get food, she wanders off. And then the girl says to herself, 'What else do I need?'"

"Wandering off" can be understood as drifting away from a moral path and engaging in practices that violate Nevisian notions of a virtuous Christian girl. Many Nevisians, particularly shopkeepers, observed that girls have become consumers on this small island, and often speculate as to where the girls get access to cash. Simon, the owner of Simon's Contemp, once remarked to me about the buying power of girls: "Some girls get money from their parents, others save the money they earn from odd jobs, and still others, well God only knows where they get it from." Simon receives regular telephone calls from angry and concerned mothers who wonder where their daughters got the money to purchase new clothes. Simon explained, "I have to be diplomatic. I have a policy not to give refunds, but in these cases I have to show consideration." Other shopkeepers who maintained that they "had a business to run" did not always share Simon's attitude. When I shared this perspective with Eleanor, she reflected on the 1980s when she was a schoolgirl: "If you went into a store with money, de shopkeeper would ask, 'Where you get dat money?' Den dey would tell your momma. Now it doesn't matter where de money comes from. Plus, if I not home by four o'clock I get a beating. . . . we couldn't be out on de street [shopping or meeting men] . . . my time growing up we went home for lunch because we had no money to buy lunch or visit stores."

One local businesswoman, the owner of the first beauty salon on Nevis, described it this way:

From what I've seen and from what I've heard others say [in my shop] a lot of them girls, [are not] virgins. . . . The way they walk and the way they talk, they think that they are desirable to big men, because I've heard big men talk about them. They will give them a ride . . . because the young girls like cars. . . . They like to know they're talking to somebody that has a car. . . . They [were] not like that when I was growing up. If my dad passed me in a man's car and I went home, there's big trouble. [When I was growing up] you were not supposed to be in a grown-up's car, but now, it's no problem. It's okay for them to flag down a car and go and when they do that, that's when they get themselves in trouble. . . . I've heard men talk, and they say [the girls] offer themselves . . . a lot of my friends will tell me that they give them rides and the girls say, "You taking me home? You don't want to go someplace?" [My friends] are giving them an innocent ride home and [the girls] are not ready to go to home . . . I've even heard of married men giving kids a ride home, and the girls [say] "Let's go someplace else or whatever." . . . It's up to that person to say, "No." . . . I guess some men [won't say, 'No'] and don't want to be called an anti-man [homosexual]. . . . The girls are more aggressive. . . . Back then [when I was growing up] it was the guy who was the aggressor. But now the girls are aggressive. . . . I guess a lot of them are doing it for money because they keep begging—a lot of young girls are into this begging thing. . . . It's not a shy thing anymore. It's real.

SEXUAL SOLICITATION: "GIRLS GO BEGGING"

What begins to emerge from these stories is that the girls embody a type of aggressive sexuality and that they have a strong sense of entitlement to, and desire for, consumer goods. Younger girls will "beg" for rides, soft drinks, pencils, or lunch money, in other words, "small ticket" items that if added up might incur a debt and obligate them to men. As girls become older, there seems to be a range of goods and services that are exchanged and that determine the nature of the reciprocal relationships, which clearly are not all the

3. A view of Pinney's Beach, a popular site for sexual encounters.

same. Some girls, like Sharmera, may be involved in a romantic relationship with an older man and as part of the dynamic of the relationship, gifts and cash are offered. Likewise, Vanessa had a boyfriend who was married who often gave her cash to buy new clothes. In other situations, girls might get cash and gifts, such as cell phones and jewelry, from multiple men in their villages for whom they have no great affection, but to whom they might be obligated to offer sexual favors. One of my fourteen-year-old informants, who had just recently received a cell phone (that she hid from her father) from a man in her village, told me quite directly, "If you work, you should get paid." She explained unequivocally that if a girl has sex with a man she should get "something in return." During the focus groups girls listed "ride for a ride," "whoring," and "sex for money" as sexual practices they imagined other girls engage in.

Several girls told me stories about schoolmates who would "beg" for free chips and soda from the men who ran various snackette shops, and in exchange, they would let the men have sex with them. These liaisons might be fleeting or might occur with regularity. Whether it is the girls or the men who initiate these relationships is not always clear. The following story illustrates how complicated these situations can be. Francine Baker worked on a legal case that involved a schoolgirl, the girl's mother, and a proprietor of a snackette. She explained:

> There is one case with the child, but you see a lot of these incidents happen. The mother was not providing the child with lunch. She [the child] was going to a bar shop . . . [and] . . . the proprietor there was giving her a lunch and a drink every day and for the lunch and the drink, she paid him in kind. . . . Then, of course, she ends up pregnant. She's, of course, as well fourteen, and what I gathered, looking at the letters and stuff that he wrote to her, he was insisting that she have sex with him, and if she doesn't come, he's not going to give anymore free lunch, and eventually, she gave in and then she got pregnant. Now, the mother was at the time trying to pursue action against him. The child refuses [to provide testimony]. She [the child] insists that he did not force her, but then there is correspondence or letters that he wrote to her which, you know, can be taken as "force" . . . [or] . . . coercion, you know . . . not fully voluntary, but—and that goes down the drain, because you can't get the child to give evidence.

Is Baker's story about a hungry fourteen-year-old girl who is coerced into having sex with a sexual predator or is it a story about a precocious schoolgirl who exchanges sex for food and attention from a local businessman and winds up pregnant? Or is it both? Given the economic conditions of poverty combined with the cultural expectations surrounding sexuality, how are we to understand the line between consent and coercion? If we overstate the girls' willingness to take part in the exchange of sex for a snack are we underestimating the social determinants of her behavior? Paul Farmer (1996) demands that we consider the way in which "people's life choices" are limited by poverty (33), and thus, we should not overestimate her personal choice in this matter; on the other hand, we cannot discount her agency altogether. This complex dynamic between structural effects and agency will be taken up later in this chapter and in chapter 7.

DESIRING MEN AND COMMODITIES

According to many sources, including guidance counselors, community health workers, pastors, and the girls themselves, there are two groups of men that seem to especially appeal to schoolgirls—busmen and policemen. Apparently, policemen are desirable because of their steady income and their positions of authority. Ally, a fifteen-year-old girl from Charlestown explains why girls are attracted to busmen: "De girls go for dem. De busmen dey look nice. Most of dem dress in real modern stuff, nice pants, big shirts, and dey drive de bus. Most of dem, dey attractive. We have some old ones with gray hair, but most of dem dey nice. Dey drive de bus with music and all dat. Dey [play] BET [Black Entertainment Television] songs dat de girls want to hear. A lot of girls like de busmen, Gingerland girls, Charlestown girls." Ally's assertion that girls are attracted to busmen because of their sense of style implies an erotic dimension to the girls' sexualities. Their desire for men who look nice and wear "modern stuff" indicates that girls find pleasure in, and might get excited by, the busmen's presence. Given that many girls rely on local vans for transportation and given that it is in the nature of their work for busmen to have a constant supply of cash, it is no surprise that they attract a lot of girls. The complexity of the production of sexuality makes it almost impossible, however, to disentangle what might compel the erotic in these instances. Is it the busman's attractive clothing, his access to cash, the rides in his bus, or the promise of the goods that might be acquired as the result of a liaison with a busman? Before attempting to address this issue I want to look closely at an excerpt from an interview with Nari, a thirty-three-year-old man who drove a bus for a living. His comments capture the complexity of interacting sexual scripts:

DEBRA: What do the girls want?

NARI: Sex.

DEBRA: Do you think they REALLY want sex or do you think they want the clothes and cash?

NARI: Dey might need a bit clothes, but down to de bottom line, dey want sex because dat's de discussion in de end.

DEBRA: When I talk to people, they say the people who get the most sex [with schoolgirls] are the policemen and the busmen.

NARI [laughs loudly]: Dat could be true. Dere's a lot of girls since I get de bus, dat I could make love to but. . . .

DEBRA: What do the girls say to you?

NARI: Some will be brave and say it straight up, "I want to make love to you." . . . I see dis girl on de street, back and forth. . . . I been watchin' she on de street. . . . One day she come in my bus and sit behind me and say, "Rasta man you [dread] locks look good; I love to see you." And ever since dat day we be real close.

DEBRA: Are the younger girls that bold?

NARI: Oh yeah, mon, even bolder sometimes. About two months ago, de Seventh Day Adventist had de tent up in Gingerland; you remember dat? And dey doin' baptism on de beach. A young girl, she not more den fifteen or sixteen. She get baptized on de beach and on de way back to de tent, dere she go tellin' de busman who's my friend, dat she want to give him a blow job and she just got baptized. . . . Dey would like to put us in jail for sexin' de underage girls in de states but down here it different . . . if you see a girl with big breasts and a good body and she come over to you, you won't resist, if you a man, believe me, you might say, "leave the schoolchildren be." As a man who really sexually active and thinkin' de same thing de lady thinkin'. . . . It's just want happens. I just pray to God dat the police don't find out. Some of de girls are brave enough to ask for somethin'. If dey see me wearin' one or two gold chains, dey say, "Lend me one." I mean as a man, if you sexin' dem and de chain worth nothin', you give it to dem and dey glad for dat. Right away you have an opportunity for sexin' she, when you want sex because gave she a chain. To she, she get somethin', and den she think, "Oh maybe I ask for somethin' again." . . . If you sexin' a schoolgirl you always have to be ready. Because she go and tell her friend dat he penis is soft and he penis short. He can't do nothin'. So you always have to be ready for de schoolgirl.

Despite what Nari asserts, I would argue that the girls want *both* sex and the goods, and most importantly, that they sometimes conflate the two. Embedded in Nari's comments is the principle of reciprocity that structures sexual-economic exchange. Nari maintains that if he gives a girl something, like a gold chain, then "right away you have an opportunity for sexin' she." He is expressing aspects of reciprocity, namely, the obligation to give, but also the sense of entitlement that is accrued.

In order to understand the way sexuality shapes and is shaped by commodity desire and consumption, two questions still need to be fully addressed: What influences commodity desire among Nevisian girls and what do commodities signify among Nevisian girls? What the growing consumer culture and its concomitant consumer desires mean to girls on Nevis is potential access to a wider variety of goods and services. The most desirable goods and services—designer sneakers; the latest fashions such as sports jerseys, platform shoes, jeans, and peasant blouses; beauty supplies; cell phones; computers; televisions; imported foods and rides in cars signify status to the girls who consume them. Embedded in this understanding of the significance of consumption is the understanding that goods convey social meanings (Appadurai 1986) and that consumption is linked to identity production.

Writing on Thai women in Bangkok, Mary Beth Mills (1999) asserts that commodity consumption is about how young women wish to acquire status—a type of status that is linked to an urban sense of modernity (12). Nevisian girls also want to acquire status, and they do this by conveying a particular sensibility—one that is reflected in the American urban hip-hop culture. This particular form of style, urban hip-hop, has been referred to as aspirational dressing. It involves dressing "for the position in society you aspire to be in."[7] Commodity desires and consumption in the context of Nevisian girls can be viewed as this type of aspirational dressing. In other words, among many Nevisian girls, consumer desire is an expression of what some scholars view as consumption fantasies (Belk, Güliz, and Askegaard 2003, 327).

For instance, many girls on Nevis want to be the girls they see in the hip-hop music videos. They want to be one of the girls Sean Paul, a famous hip-hop artist, surrounds himself with; for example, when talking about their favorite male artist, a common expression heard among the girls was, "I wanna have so-and-so's baby." Sometimes it was Sean Paul, and at other times it might have been Nelly or Mario, two other well-known hip-hop celebrities. I interpret this to mean that the girls not only wish to have sexual relations with these men, but that they also fantasize about the lifestyle associated with wealthy hip-hop stars. Not only is the statement, "I wanna have Sean Paul's baby," about a girl's infatuation with the male artist, but it also reflects a girl's desires to be connected socially and to be taken care of financially. Even among the more socially reticent Nevisian girls for whom the desire to have a baby with a popular figure like Sean Paul is not a strong or preoccupying sentiment, being connected, belonging, or looking like they could fit in on the streets of Miami or New York was a driving factor in shaping commodity desire and consumption practices.

What evidence do we have that consumption practices, or more specifically, the girls' obsession with fashion, is an expression of a desire to fit in not just among other Nevisians but to fit in within urban centers in the United States as well? Girls repeatedly remarked that they acquire their sense of fashion from television. As one fifteen-year-old explained: "My ideas about fashion come from TV. I watch soaps not just for the story but to get ideas about what to wear and how to wear my hair." Similarly, a sixteen-year-old reflecting on the popularity of BET music videos among Nevisian girls explains: "We admire and aspire to look like the females in the videos." Among Nevisian girls, there is not only a desire to conform to new fashion conventions but there is also a desire to express a personalized sense of style that others might admire. For example, girls noticed and recognized trendsetters among their fellow Nevisians. Two sisters who owned a store in town were referred to time again as women who could be counted on to set the fashion standards on Nevis and "to be up on all the latest styles."

Fashion is about cultivating a sense of distinction and sense of identity; however, it is also about fitting into a larger cultural group. The girls want to emulate the girls they see on BET and on other networks, signifying a desire to be identified with the girls on television. The following statement illustrates this sentiment perfectly: "If I dress up in me best dress and go to Charlestown, nobody knows I from de country." Similarly, commenting on her peers, a fifteen-year-old asserted, "Girls dress to be noticed by men and dey dress to fit in; nobody wants to look like dey from de country." Among Nevisian girls, in general, commodity desire signifies both a desire to be a part of a group of stylish women but also a desire for alterity. These Third World girls desire to be different, not necessarily non-Nevisian, but a different kind of Nevisian, a connected, wealthy, and well-respected Nevisian. For Nevisian girls, commodities promise transformation. Framed in this light, commodity desire is about the desire to be transformed into a prestigious, respectable woman with all the appropriate cultural markers for prestige.

LINGERIE AND THE EROTIC

Unlike the range and quantities of commodities and goods to which their mothers and grandmothers had access, the girls with whom I engaged, had access to, and experienced, an influx of commodities and goods. Consumption practices have become a means by which Nevisians construct their lives and produce subjectivities—who they are, how they want to be seen, and the range of social practices they consider performing.[8] By consuming a newly available array of goods such as lingerie or other desirable clothing items, girls and women create new scripts for themselves. In other words, they consume goods that may not only alter the way they think about themselves, but also change their sexual practices. This became very clear to me through my interactions with Ruthie and Eleanor.

By the time she was sixteen, Ruthie had dropped out of school. Her great-grandmother, with whom she lived, had died and she was taken in by family friends. Ruthie's mother died when she was a child. When Ruthie was eighteen, with money earned from working at a shop downtown, she was able to buy herself a pair of high heels and what she called, "sexy panties." Growing up, Ruthie owned one pair of panties, which she washed nightly. She had church shoes, but no school shoes. Buying high heels and panties had a huge impact on Ruthie. She told me on several occasions that she felt different from the other children because she was "so poor" and that this was the reason why she dropped out of school. By the time she was able to buy lingerie and high heels she felt transformed. She described herself as a "lady." The following stories reveal how significantly the influx of imported goods and consumption practices are affecting the production of Nevisian sexual subjectivities.

The laundromat was quiet and even the mango tree's shade offered little relief from the midday sun, so Ruthie, Eleanor and I once again sat inside in the laundromat on top of the counters. On this particular morning, Von Radio was playing *When I Fall in Love* sung by Nat King Cole. Ruthie and Eleanor talked over each other as usual. The tape recorder rested on my lap. My friends had grown accustomed to its presence and they were well aware that I taped our conversations about men, sex, diets, and fashion. I told them that the schoolgirls were searching the Web on their home computers at nights for sexy lingerie and coveting the expensive items they see on the Victoria's Secret site. Unlike the days when Eleanor needed undergarments and she had no choice but to buy bulky products from vendors peddling imported goods at the open market, the teenage girls I interviewed have a number of small shops to patronize where shopkeepers do their best at stocking Victoria's Secret knockoffs. Without a bit of hesitation or embarrassment, Ruthie unbuttoned her blouse revealing her red sateen bra. I considered that it would be impolite not to look. Eleanor was critical of the way the bra shaped Ruthie's breasts, "Ruthie, they're like cones—too pointy." Absentmindedly, Ruthie reached into her bra and pulled out a small piece of paper that she unfolded, read and then stuffed back into her bra, nodding to herself in a gesture that told me she'd remembered its contents, probably something she needed from the market later in that day. Her blouse was still unbuttoned, so Eleanor, who was never one to be upstaged, lifted her loose blouse, exposing a lacy black bra designed for her large breasts. They laughed as I lifted my blouse to display my sturdy beige bra, but their comments revealed how impressed they were with the support it apparently provided. Eleanor bragged that she paid as little as EC$30 (U.S.$10) and that in her estimation her bra compared favorably to mine; she noted that Ruthie's was by far the sexiest of the three. She reminded us how when she was a girl there was no selection of "sexy panties and bras" on the island. Eleanor explained: "My time growin' up we had no black or red bras dat was all soft and silky. Dos bras was made from some white cloth dat was rough." While buttoning her blouse, Ruthie told us that she wears lingerie everyday and that it makes her feel "sexy." She explained that wearing lingerie "puts her in the mood." Later that afternoon and on several other occasions, she and Eleanor admonished me for wearing what they considered to be "ugly bras." These admonishments usually coincided with my husband's impending arrival. The assumption was that when my husband visited me after a long separation that I should make myself more desirable for him by wearing lingerie. But that was just part of what they were hinting at. Wearing lingerie, at least according to Ruthie, not only makes one more desirable, but also makes one more desirous. This conflation of sexual desire and commodities is evident in another story, which features Ruthie.

In the middle of March, Ruthie and I stood in the yard together looking at an Oprah magazine I had purchased at the new bookstore. Holding the magazine in front of us, I pointed to an ad for Jenny Craig's weight loss program. In the ad there are two types of women's white underpants. On the left was a pair of what Ruthie called "big lady underpants" and on the right there was a pair of lacy, skimpy panties. The ad read, "Do you want to change your underwear this year?" I laughed aloud and repeated, "Ruthie do you get it, do you get it?" She kept pointing to the lacy panties and almost pleading, "I want dose; I want dose." Another piece to this story is that, later that day, Ruthie told me that she had been having what she considered to be "phone sex" with a man in her village, someone she knew from grade school. Ruthie described that in the late afternoons when her two older children were visiting friends and her baby was sleeping, she called this man and they talked "sexy" to one another. Ruthie told me that initially she never anticipated that she would ever "do anything with dis guy." They carried on with their phone calls for a week. Ruthie explained: "For five days we did dis and me was so horny I couldn't take it anymore. He ask me, 'Are you kids around?' I tell him to come up and we fucked all afternoon. Me be wearin' my prettiest panties when he walk in the door."

Ruthie's stories along with the ongoing admonishments that I endured from both Ruthie and Eleanor about my undergarments hint at the effects of commodity erotics. Ruthie's sexual subjectivity cannot be separated from the erotic significance that she attaches to her red sateen bra or to her "prettiest panties." Nor can Ruthie's sexual desires be separated from commodity desire. Ruthie's stories and my interactions with her represent intimate moments in daily life when commodities seduce individuals, thus inciting both consumer desires and sexual desires. While this was clear in my interaction with Ruthie, I was also curious to learn more about how these imported commodities affected the formation of girls' sexual subjectivity, coming-of-age as they were in an increasingly consumer-oriented society. Naaz, who is a sixteen-year-old, told this story:

"When I was little, maybe eleven, maybe twelve, me aunti come from de Bronx wit suitcases filled with pretty clothes. We share a room, me and me aunti and de little ones. De suitcases dey filled wit new clothes wit de tags still on. Pretty things, like new Sunday dresses, shoes, ponytail things, and underclothes [bras, underpants, and lingerie] all wit de tag still on. When me aunti went out, I go in de suitcases, lookin' and touchin' de underthings.

She bring matchin' sets of de bras and panties. Before dat I see only white panties. Me auntie bring wit her red, pink, black, all different colors."

When me mother say to me aunti, "Are you still with Martin from work?" I know auntie is lyin' when she say "No" because why else she be wearin' de matchin' sets. Me aunti works in a office buildin' and has de money to be in the latest fashions. After primary school I go to Charlestown and me friends, we look at de *Cosmo* magazine. I tear out perfume pages and de pictures of de girls in de matchin' sets. On Nevis dere is some stores sellin' panties and bras like dose my aunti has and dose in de *Cosmo*. Someday I get some too when I have me own money but if I do and me mother finds out she might think me messin' with a boy.

Lingerie or matching sets, as Naaz calls them, have multiple connotations ranging from romance and sex to economic freedom. It is by way of the lingerie that Naaz imagines her aunt's sexuality. The associations between lingerie and sex that Naaz makes as a child were reinforced in women's fashion magazines that she consumed as an adolescent, complete with enticing scents and images of scantily dressed women. In many ways, the objects of desire, namely, the matching sets, which stir Naaz's curiosity, promise pleasure as well. There is one more story worth telling about the social significance of lingerie in the imaginations of Nevisian teenagers, boys and girls alike.

Wearing tight-fitted low-riding jeans and a fashionable peasant blouse, Loida, a fourteen-year-old from Brown Hill village, had caught my attention one afternoon in Charlestown. I was driving in my car with Ally, one of Loida's classmates. Ally, an outspoken fifteen-year-old, pointed to Loida saying, "That's who you should interview. That one over there. We call her the Spanish whore." Ally proceeded to tell me a story that I heard again practically word-for-word from a mild-mannered and trustworthy Guyanese classmate who happened to be the daughter of a friend. The story, apparently fresh on the minds of both girls, was told to me spontaneously by the girls. In other words, I have no reason to doubt its validity in that both girls had apparently witnessed the same unfortunate event and on separate occasions decided to share the story with me. One day a boy in the girls' class rummaged through Loida's book bag looking for Loida's cell phone. Before Loida could stop him, he took out a black thong panty and tossed it around the room, announcing to those present that the item was stained with "cum." According to Ally, Loida wore the thong under her school uniform for a rendezvous with a busman the day before. Apparently, before Loida returned home, she removed her thong and put it in her book bag and had forgotten to take it out of her bag.

The gossip circulating about Loida and how she allegedly wore black thong panties for a bus driver interests me for two reasons. First, Ally, more so than the Guyanese girl, wanted to demonstrate to me that she understood what was expected of Nevisian girls and that she recognized sexual impropriety. It was her way of telling me, "See I know a 'bad' girl when I see one." It was also a sensational story with incriminating evidence, namely, the "stained" black thong panties, which suggest a particular kind of unruly and aggressive sexuality, but clearly a type of sexuality that is promoted in popular culture.

While highly controversial and the source of intense debate on Nevis, girls enjoy the opportunity to self-fashion. Despite the fact that we do not know if the story is completely accurate, what is interesting is that Loida and other girls her age have more of an opportunity to craft their sexualities around commodities like thong panties. Such choices in dress represent an augmentation and expressive aspect of girls' sexualities, particularly in light of the fact that dressing provocatively may increase a Nevisian girl's chance of gaining attention and increase the possibility for sexual experiences. More importantly, focusing on self-fashioning and the desire for goods allows us to see how the erotic significance of commodities incites new sexual subjectivities.

COMMODITY EROTICS: UNDERSTANDING DESIRE

The relationship between commodities, sexuality, and the erotic crystallizes around one particular cultural pastime. Girls and young women alike enjoyed having their pictures taken while dressed in an array of fashions and then assembled into photo albums. This was more popular around festivals like Culturama. In preparation for the weeklong event, Nevisians might travel to St. Martin for an all-day shopping trip where clothes are cheaper. Thomas, a photographer, explained to me that picture taking is a favorite form of entertainment in which the girls get to show off their new clothes while getting their photographs taken; they then have pictures to give to their boyfriends. Thomas, speaking more specifically about girls, described it this way: "It's self-gratifying. . . . They [the girls] like people to see them. It's their way of saying, 'Don't I look good?' . . . They want to say, 'I look sexy'. . . . It's all about looking sexy to attract the boys. . . . Because if you attract the boys, the boys will buy you stuff or the boys will give you money to buy more stuff." Linking the girls' procurement of consumer goods to sexuality, Thomas's straightforward interpretation of the girls' behaviors follows a common trope, one in which sex is viewed as instrumental: sex yields access to goods and services.

If sex is viewed purely as instrumental, the way Thomas views it, then the connections between the production of girls' sexual subjectivities and commodity desire become obvious. When girls trade sex for access to goods and services, their sexualities are influenced in a variety of ways. Their desire to consume commodities brings them into situations where they have sexual encounters more often, with multiple partners or with the same partner. They are more likely to adopt new sexual practices to maintain their partners' interests. Perhaps they are more open to performing and engaging in sexual repertoires that include oral sex, anal sex, or sex with more than one partner at a time—common themes suggested in hip-hop music videos or in imported pornography. For instance, Ally explained that it was only after she received a new cell phone and calling card from her boyfriend that she had sexual intercourse with him. She insisted that the new phone demonstrated her boyfriend's commitment to her and insisted that she was not "trading favors," but that she did feel obligated to have sexual intercourse after she received the cell phone.

There also are the less obvious effects that commodity desire might have on the production of girls' sexual subjectivities. In the case of Loida, a fourteen-year-old who received a cell phone from an older man in her village, the instrumental view would focus on her willingness to exchange sex for goods. However, is it possible that the sexual pleasure that Loida experiences with her partner might be enhanced by the promise of goods, like the cell phone? Is it also possible that the pleasures associated with a caress or kiss increases vis-à-vis the caresser's or kisser's relation to the desirable goods? Such a perspective allows for a more diffused notion of the erotic, as discussed earlier in the introduction. It also allows for the possibility to imagine that specific goods become infused with erotic significance, that desire for commodities can be erotic, and finally, that the erotic association between commodities and those who provide them affects sexual practices and desires.[9]

Some readers may question the focus on eroticism. Such a focus is required however, if it is assumed that sexual-economic exchange is the organizing principle of gender relations on Nevis. If this is the case, then the production of sexualities cannot be separated from the materialism in which it is embedded. Some commodities and goods are endowed with eroticized significance because of the rewards and pleasures the commodities and goods secure—rewards and pleasures that matter most to the girls, such as social status, a sense of belonging and, for some, an increased notion of sexual self-confidence. Take, for example, the cell phones, a popular commodity among Nevisian teenagers. To the extent that the girls' self-fashioning or self-presentation is tied to creating public impressions, or, as Erving Goffman (1959) suggests, that the presentation of self is a type of performance for others, then it is not difficult to understand how Nevisian girls rely on commodities like cell phones to convey social messages. The focus then becomes not so much on the cell phones but rather on the imaginary and real associations linked to the phones. Certainly, there are some real-life advantages to using these phones. Girls can receive calls from their boyfriends without their parents' knowledge or consent. Girls often described how they stayed up late in their bedrooms secretly talking to boyfriends and that cell phones provided them with the means to communicate privately with their partners to arrange rendezvous.

It appears, then, that certain commodities also have instrumental value. But cell phones are significant in that they serve not only this practical or instrumental purpose but also serve a symbolic function. They convey social prestige and garner admiration; they are also associated with "players" who can provide the girls with more goods. Girls using cell phones convey the message, "I am connected." Other commodities, such as "bling-bling" or hip-hop jewelry, convey other types of messages. The most popular type of bling-bling on Nevis includes watches, name pendants (e.g. "2 Pac Don't Judge Me"), dog tags, bracelets, earrings, and crosses. If the jewelry the girls wear is perceived to be valuable, it enhances their self-image. A piece of jewelry that costs U.S.$100 conveys a greater sense of wealth than a piece of jewelry costing U.S.$25. Such distinctions even possess an ability to make ontological statements: "I am valuable enough to wear this jewelry." This social and individual investment in objects or, more precisely, luxury commodities, is strongly emphasized in the media texts that the girls consume, particularly hip-hop music videos. It is worth reiterating that the sexual forms portrayed in hip-hop music videos rely on an excessive display of accoutrements, like jewelry, beautiful clothing, and expensive cars. In a prototypical video, *Tip Drill*, starring Nelly, one of the scantily clad female dancers passionately licks a large gold diamond pendant as if the object of her desire is no longer Nelly, the mega-hip-hop celebrity, but the diamond pendant. This scene epitomizes what is meant by the eroticization of commodities.

Nelly's video centers around a party scene in what appears to be a mansion. The rooms are filled with dancing bodies; there are scenes of naked women bathing and rubbing against each other and repeated images of women simulating sex on other women. The final scene involves a woman bending over so that her bare buttocks fill the screen and a man kneels down and slides a credit card between her buttocks. Taken together, these multiple images exemplify what is meant by commodity erotics; namely, the eroticization of goods. Furthermore, and more interestingly, Nelly's video suggests that not only is there a strong attraction to material goods, but that the goods have erotic affects.

Given the compatibility between the existing sexual-economic exchange system on Nevis and the sort of commodity erotics displayed in music videos like Nelly's, it is not difficult to imagine how an ideology of the eroticization of bling-bling circulates on the island. Recall, for instance, Vanessa, whose married boyfriend picked her up in his car, took her out to dinner and dancing and showered her with cash on the average of EC$250 (U.S.$100) once a week. Vanessa enjoyed the cash lavished upon her as well as the forms of entertainment her lover afforded her. What I want to assert is that we cannot disassociate the goods, forms of entertainment, cash, dinners, and the rides in the car from the sexual pleasure or excitement that Vanessa might experience in her lover's presence.

Considering that the production of sexuality on Nevis is intricately tied to material goods and services, then we can assume that the goods and services have more than a mediating effect on sexualities—that sexual, excitement, arousal, and pleasure, if they are experienced within the sexual encounter, are not limited to the encounter and may, in certain instances, become associated with the goods themselves. Earlier, I had positioned commodity erotics as a way of considering how certain pleasures that are associated with goods like jewelry, clothing, and rides in cars, fall within the scope of the erotic (Schein 2003, 21). Here I am taking the argument one step further to suggest that sexual interactions with a man become more rewarding, desirable, and/or erotic as a consequence of the man himself being associated with certain goods. If the man acquires the cachet of the goods and services, it is therefore conceivable that his ability to produce positive affective value is enhanced, whatever its duration.

The significance of this is that there is potential for the girls to conflate sexual pleasure with the pleasure associated with the goods. This situation is analyzed usefully by a well-established framework within psychology, specifically, associationism, which is based on the single notion that one entity can acquire the same affective value of another object through association. Social psychologists explain it in these terms: "Two experiences that occur closely together in time are likely to be associated" (Schwartz, Wasserman, and Robbins 2002, 12). This principle pertains to making connections between two or more sensations, ideas, or images. For instance, the pleasure the girl associates with money affects the pleasure of the sexual interaction. Fifteen-year-old Sharmera likes the way she feels when she is with Leon, her new boyfriend, because consciously or unconsciously, she associates her interactions with him, including sexual interactions, with the rewards he gives her.

This dynamic relationship between material goods, sexualities, and individuals is what makes up commodity erotics, thus providing a framework for understanding the impact of consumer culture on sexuality—a dominating structure affecting the personal agency of girls. Commodity erotics allows us to analyze how consumerism shaped the interior spaces of Nevisian girls' consciousness, and specifically, it allows us to see how commodities shape sexual subjectivity. Furthermore, and just as significant, it allows us to understand how sexuality propels the market. Commodity erotics demonstrates that the eroticization of commodities exposes the mutually constitutive relationship between sexuality and economics.

Thus far, I have suggested that commodity erotics increases pleasure and intensifies the erotic domain. What about the downside of sexual-economic exchange and the exploitative conditions that influence the girls' lives? This brings me to what the local intelligentsia considers to be the negative social consequences of the current sexual-economic pattern.

"Nobody Knows This,
But This Ain't Paradise"

As mentioned previously, most of the community workers I interviewed and with whom I spent time did not ignore what they saw as the "moral decline" of their society. They believed it was essential to be actively working against the social elements—both traditional influences and global influences—that they view as contributing to the growing "social ills" of Nevisian society. Most of these community workers view global influences, such as cable television, which promotes foreign goods as desirable, as contributing to, and accentuating, the pattern of sexual-economic exchange that I have described.

In the spring of 2002, an American journalist, Kevan Goff-Parker, employed as a features editor for the *Observer*, published a three-part series that focused on the "Girl-Child." The series highlights many of the social conditions that girls face while coming-of-age on St. Kitts and Nevis, including what many Nevisian community and government workers consider to be the widespread and socially sanctioned practice of sexual exploitation. Taken together, the three installments outline a number of unintended consequences produced by the sexual-economic exchange system. The topics in the series range widely in subject matter from teenage pregnancy and HIV to the practice of mothers accepting bribes from "sexual predators" for access to their daughters. In essence, the series looks at how the "cycle of poverty" is perpetuated when some girls, after becoming sexually active at a young age with older men, become pregnant and then abandon their education to raise children with very limited means of subsistence.

The first installment looks at the rise of consumerism throughout the Federation and what local experts see as an increase in materialism among girls, which sets the stage for men to "take advantage of the poverty and innocence." The second installment features an interview with a twenty-year-old man who recounts his sexual relationship with a fifteen-year-old. He describes how he ended the relationship after the girl's mother repeatedly asked for money and expected the young man to pay a household bill before she allowed him to see her daughter. The last installment focused on the "sexual abuse within the family unit," drawing on the insights and experiences of Michele de la Coudray-Blake, a mental health care worker employed by the Ministry of Social Development, Community and Gender Affairs. La Coudray-Blake suggests that the enduring sexual-economic exchange system may give rise to another set of social circumstances that seems to be prevalent on Nevis, one that was previously discussed in chapter 5. This involves cases in which girls are "troubled" (a local expression that connotes unwanted sexual advances and sexual contact) by their mothers' boyfriends. Similar to Francine Baker's interpretation, la Coudray-Blake views mothers as reluctant to intervene in the situation because it might disrupt the flow of income into the household provided by the men. La Coudray-Blake explains it this way, "I've heard of situations where girl children have been harmed and sexually molested by their stepfather or someone else and the mother may respond, 'Well, he's taking care of the family, so maybe we could find a way to deal with it without it getting out of hand.'"

Then there are other cases in which mothers and other caregivers have been known to play a different role in the production of girls' sexualities. The "Girl-Child" series published in the *Observer* touched upon an issue that one local described as "volcanic": the practice of women soliciting men to have sex with their daughters in exchange for money or the practice of overtly encouraging their daughters to have sex in exchange for resources that will benefit the household.[10] Baker described a situation that she was involved with as an attorney:

DEBRA: There was a series of articles published in the *Observer* right before I came, about mothers profiting from their daughters.

BAKER: I'm well aware of that, and that happens quite often. There is one lady I know who would religiously take her daughter for service. That's what she called it. It's a service. And she would be paid.

DEBRA: How old was the daughter?

BAKER: The daughter was probably fourteen at the time. She was at Charlestown Secondary.

DEBRA: And how did it come to your attention?

BAKER: How did it come to my attention? Oh, the child found a boyfriend, [and] ran off to live with the boyfriend and then [the mother went] to court to get the daughter back, because she was underage, but then in the course of taking statements, it was discovered that it's not that she loved the daughter and wanted her away from this man, it's that she was profiting herself having the daughter serviced by different men. . . . There are several instances as well where the wife has a husband, who's not the daughter's father, and she gladly gives the daughter up for use by the husband or boyfriend or whoever [in exchange for resources].

I heard other stories of mothers soliciting men to have sex with daughters who usually lived at home with their mothers and/or grandmothers. Like other children in the village, these girls went to school. Typically, however, at a young age, at around twelve or thirteen, their mothers would encourage or force them to have sex with older men in exchange for money. One such instance gained the attention of the police and courts and it was brought to my attention by an expatriate social worker who had retired on Nevis. Apparently her counseling skills and expertise were sought by child advocates when it became officially known to the police that a twelve-year-old girl was being forced by her mother to have sex with neighbors and strangers, alike.

According to the social worker, there were days and evenings when men would line up to take turns with the girl. Having lived on Nevis for over twenty years and having had a number of other encounters with school age girls, the social worker was adamant in her assessment of the situation of Nevisian girls and sexuality. "Here on Nevis," she explained, "sexuality does not start because girls get breasts or when they get their first period. It starts because girls are pursued and these same girls are ambivalent because they are frightened but they want the good stuff in life that comes with sex. Oftentimes the girls tell me, 'Momma ask me to do it for de fish. Papa ask me to do it for de fish.' These girls want the good stuff in life, like the fish."

The practice of mothers encouraging or coercing their daughters to exchange sex for money is not unique to Nevis. In fact, this form of sexual solicitation has been increasingly well-documented in several Caribbean societies and around the world.[11] The topic of child prostitution has gained a great deal of visibility over the last two decades. Many argue that its prevalence can be attributed to the impact of globalization and its destructive effects on local economies around the world.[12]

Several scholars have tried to capture the perspective and experiences of the children who trade sex for access to goods and resources. Researchers have gone to great lengths to understand the various levels of coercion, exploitation, and willingness on the part of children engaged in commercial sex.

Kevin Bales's (2003) provocative essay, entitled, "Because She Looks Like a Child," opens with a description of a fifteen-year-old Thai girl who was sold into prostitution by her parents. With time, Bale notes, the girl's resistance weakens and her desire to escape grows less intense. Gradually she begins to accept her fate. The girl lives in fear of getting AIDS and becoming pregnant. After severe beatings and repeated rapes she convinces herself that "she is a very bad person to have deserved what has happened to her" (209). Faced with extreme conditions of sexual violence, other girls in similar circumstances, according to Bales, display a wide range of reactions, from suicide attempts to full-blown psychoses and aggression.

Also writing about child prostitution in Thailand, but within a very different set of circumstances, Heather Montgomery's (1998) research focuses on Thai children who live with their parents in a small tourist resort. These children have sex with foreigners in order to gain access to goods and money. Montgomery explains, "These children worked because they felt a strong obligation towards their families and believed that it was their duty to support their parents" (143). According to Montgomery, the children, boys and girls alike, develop an alternative set of ethics to account for their situation in which trading sex for money is not as immoral as betraying one's family. The largely foreign clients offer what the children refer to as "gifts" and in some instances paid in kind by fixing up the child's family house. Montgomery argues that while it is undeniably a form of exploitation and that conditions of poverty constrain their choices, we need a better understanding of the children's agency, however diminished.

How does the current research on child prostitution shape our understanding of what might be going on among Nevisian girls who are coerced into having sex by their mothers? Again, how do we tease out agency for some Nevisian girls when sexual coercion appears normative? What is the potential for Nevisian girls coerced into sex to constitute sexual subjectivities? Before we can begin to address these questions, there are a range of possible experiences that require consideration.

Understanding sexual subjectivity means that we have to ask questions about the interior domain or the psyche and how it is shaped by cultural forces—in this case, the family system. How might the experience of being solicited by one's mother shape one's sexual subjectivity? Given the sexual landscape of Nevisan society, how do we understand the *experience* of sexual abuse in a cultural milieu in which sexual violence is the norm? Does this landscape minimize the trauma of such an experience? Is one permitted even to consider such a possibility?[13]

Judith Herman (1992), a psychologist specializing in trauma, documents that females who are raped, report crying out for their mothers in their moments of terror. They "spontaneously seek their first source of comfort and protection" (53) and feeling "utterly abandoned and utterly alone" (53) when their cries go unanswered. Nevisian girls who are betrayed by their mothers in instances where they are coerced into having sex with men are not likely to find comfort from their mothers. Herman would argue that such a profound disruption in a child's relationship with her mother potentially damages the child's ability to trust and develop emotional bonds. It is not difficult to imagine that given these circumstances, thereafter, some Nevisian girls may go through their adolescence and the rest of their lives, for that matter, with a deep sense of alienation and loneliness, coupled with an inability to fully trust and connect with the people around them.

Similar to what Bales reports among Thai girls, Nevisian girls who experience sexual abuse may begin to believe that they at fault. This, according to Herman, is not uncommon for abused children. They often justify the abusive situations, "When it is impossible to avoid the reality of the abuse." Herman (1992) writes: "the child must construct some system of meaning that justifies it. Inevitably the child concludes that her innate badness is the cause. The child clings to it tenaciously, for it enables her to preserve a sense of meaning, hope, and power. . . . Self-blame is congruent with the normal forms of thought of early childhood, in which the self is taken as the reference point for all events." (103)

The trauma produced by such sexual activity can lead, no doubt, to intense feelings of betrayal and loneliness, and when compounded by self-hatred, can radically affect the trajectory of a girl's sexual subjectivity—a subjectivity marked by violence, insecurity, shame, and guilt.

Furthermore, within the Nevisian context, we cannot ignore the immense gender disparities that impact these sexual relationships. When girls are forced into having sex by their mothers they have less power than other girls to insist that the men wear condoms, which puts them at a greater risk for pregnancy and sexually transmitted diseases. If a girl fails to comply with her mother's demands or with the men's demands, she also risks additional physical or emotional abuse.

While the traumatic effects of these circumstances cannot be overstated, we cannot not rule out the possibility that some girls, as a result of associating sex with access to goods and cash, however ambivalent, begin to desire the goods. We also cannot rule out the possibility that the attention the girls receive from their mothers and from the men, however exploitative, becomes significant in the girls' lives. Furthermore, like the children featured in Montgomery's study, some Nevisian girls might feel a sense of obligation to have sex with men in order to help their families financially. Indeed, some girls might feel entitled to the goods as a way of rationalizing the sexual encounters. And all of this is further complicated by the possibility that if a girl finds comfort or pleasure in the attention or goods she receives or if she begins to negotiate for goods and cash herself, in these instances, she may view this as evidence, or as Herman (1992) writes, "proof in her mind that she has instigated" (104) or provoked the abuse.

Given the conflicting possibilities and conditions, where do we locate sexual agency for Nevisian girls? Thus far, the stories woven together to describe Nevisian girls' sexualities suggests that it is not an either/or situation. In other words, we cannot characterize sexual agency as that which opposes systems of exploitation. Most observers would agree that the girls on Nevis have the capacity to make choices and to act in a deliberative manner, even those who are exploited, despite the difficulties associated with such choices. As Susan Hekman (1995) has suggested, "subjects find agency" (202). Kamala Kempadoo argues that even though sex workers, including girls who are prostituted, face extreme conditions of vulnerability and harm, to cast them as "exclusively 'victims'" denies a "respectful recognition of subjectivity and personal agency" (8). Kempadoo insists that we must not view sex workers as "objects" who can only be "violently manipulated and wrought into passivity" (9). The same can be said about the twelve-year-old or the fourteen-year-old Nevisian girls whose mothers arrange for them to have sex with men. They are, to borrow from Kempadoo, "both active subjects and subjects of domination" (9).

With this being the case, sexual agency is not absent among Nevisian girls; rather, it needs to be conceived of as relative or eroded.[14] Nevisian girls' sexual agency is contingent upon the options and opportunities that are made available to them within the limits of cultural and economic constraints within Nevisian society. For instance, recall how fifteen-year-old Sharmera negotiates the conditions of her life. She resists her mother's boyfriend's sexual advances, rather than submitting to all or *some* of his desires and she bears the consequences of this resistance in the form of beatings and harassment. Put simply, she could allow him to fondle her but she does not and fights back. She accepts the aid from her friend Grace and seeks additional assistance from the police. In other situations, Sharmera willingly leaves the schoolyard to join Leon, her new boyfriend. She has sex with him and enjoys what she considers lavish gifts. Grace describes Sharmera as actively seeking the attention of other men, too. When Sharmera describes herself, she lists being attractive and flirty as her attributes. These are examples of Sharmera's agency, her ability to act within the multiple discourses that provide spaces for girls like Sharmera to constitute her sexuality.

In these instances, Sharmera's sexual subjectivity is produced within the intersection of public health discourse, on the one hand, and consumer culture on the other hand. For example, that Sharmera reportedly seeks out and enjoys Leon's company, takes pleasure in the gifts he gives her, and fantasizes about future shopping trips to Saint Martin are suggestive of the effects of commodity erotics. Alternatively, the fact the Sharmera sought assistance from the police is suggestive of the way in which new public health scripts are attempting to subvert long-standing traditional structures of violence by providing options for girls like Sharmera. The idea that the police would offer assistance to a girl who was being sexual harassed was culturally inconceivable twenty years ago.

By highlighting the unintended consequences of the sexual-economic exchange system, I do not mean to disavow the pleasures, thrills, and multiple sites of enjoyment that are imbricated in the dominant Nevisian sexual culture. Together with discussions on sexual coercion, we need to attend to the ongoing and potentially pleasurable moments that operate simultaneously within and beside the structures of violence in Nevisian society. As well, the coexistence of pleasure and coercion pushes us to ask how they might be related. Chapter 7 will investigate what might be called the geography of pleasure on Nevis and how girls locate sexual delight and gratification in their lives.

CHAPTER 7

Theorizing Sexual Pleasure

EVERY DAY, while conducting fieldwork on Nevis, I encountered elements of eroticism, observed a multiplicity of sexual scenes, and experienced a seemingly incessant flow of sexual dialogues and images. The fact that Nevisian sexuality was my object of analysis may account for why the erotic domain so thoroughly permeated my encounters on the island. As an anthropologist looking for sex or, should I say, as an anthropologist on the lookout for signs and clues that would help me to understand more clearly and more fully the contours of Nevisian girls' sexuality, I often wondered whether—to paraphrase an American businessman I met while conducting fieldwork—Nevis is an unusually "lustful little island." Is Nevis an abundantly sexualized society or was I just obsessed with finding sex? I wondered how the vivid and highly sensual interactions in Nevisian society affected the everyday lives of Nevisian girls. But more importantly, I also wondered: What counts as pleasure for the girls? What counts as sex?

At times, Nevisian girls of all ages—and even some of the women I spent time with—seemed to enact a particularly uncodified and polymorphous sexuality. One day, after arriving at Gingerland Secondary School in the countryside just after morning assembly and climbing the concrete stairs to the main building, I noticed two girls in a doorway locked in a full embrace, their bodies pressed against each other's. Gently rocking back and forth with their cheeks touching, they impassively watched a group of boys nearby who were settling into their chairs for an outside lesson. The two girls wore jumpers, as opposed to pleated skirts and blouses, so I knew that they were either in First or Second Form. They were probably twelve or thirteen years old. Previously that morning, I had traveled to the countryside to conduct a focus group with sixteen- and seventeen-year-olds. As that group convened, I had also observed instances of bodily contact between girls. While the girls had gathered around a small wooden table, some of them propped their elbows up on the table and others sat sprawled out in their chairs with their legs spread open and their hands resting on their bellies. Some girls sat closely with their arms draped around each other. At one point I noticed one girl reach over and lazily stroke the inside of another girl's upper thigh. The gesture appeared as if it were done absentmindedly, and no one in the room reacted, including the girl whose thigh was caressed. This seemed precisely the sort of interaction that Jamaica Kincaid details in *Annie John* (1997): "No sooner were we back in our classrooms than the girls were in each other's laps, arms wrapped around necks (37)."

I witnessed the kind of physical contact between schoolgirls described by Kincaid every day while I was in the field. Walking through Charlestown it was quite common to see girls holding hands or walking arm in arm. In almost all cases, I seemed to be the only one who registered such displays of same-sex physical contact. I asked a number of girls and women on Nevis about this: "What," I queried, "Was the nature of this physical display of affection between girls?" Eleanor, one of the older women I spent time with, explained it this way: "Oh yeah, kissin' and touchin' [here she gestured to her breasts and then put her hands over her breasts, covering them] when you ten is what every girl do with other girls, but not when you sixteen, oh no." Eleanor's comment was substantiated by data from the focus groups I conducted with Nevisian girls. For example, it was more common for girls between the ages of twelve and thirteen to list kissing or touching other girls as a form of sexual practice than it was for the older groups to identify these behaviors as "sexual." However, Eleanor's arbitrary cutoff age for same-sex stimulation or pleasure did not match up to other stories I collected, nor does it coincide with my own observations of Nevisian girls. Interestingly, Eleanor's cutoff age of sixteen did not even match her own sexual history.

Once, while living on St. Kitts as a young woman, Eleanor watched as a female cousin masturbated in front of her for an extended period of time. The cousin had called her over to her house one afternoon under the auspices of needing to "show" Eleanor something. The cousin was alone in her house and when Eleanor arrived, she lifted up her dress and began to masturbate, instructing Eleanor to watch. I asked Eleanor the circumstances surrounding this event. "Was she teaching you how to masturbate; is that why she wanted you to watch? Or was it that she was getting off? Did your presence make her more excited? Did you like watching? Which was it?" I demanded Eleanor's insights—knowing full well that I was pushing her with my intense ethnographic curiosity. Glancing nervously at the tape recorder, Eleanor explained, "I no know Deb. She just tells me to watch her. So me did." Although in her recollection of girlhood, Eleanor accepts displays of same-sex affection, her nervousness in recounting her experience with her cousin not only points to her awareness that this incident was explicitly sexual, but also that she registers such interactions as socially prohibited.

Eleanor's ambivalent attitude toward same-sex encounters was evident in one particularly vivid encounter that she witnessed between me and Ruthie. After an early morning meeting at a local health clinic, I had stopped by the

4. Two schoolgirls walking back to school after lunch break.

laundromat to see Ruthie and Eleanor. Eleanor sat inside on the counter reading a romance novel while Ruthie and I hung out outside on the back steps. She stroked my hair as I stood with my back resting against her belly. Playfully, I turned to Ruthie and flexed my muscles, instructing her to feel my arm. Smiling, she reached down to touch the inside of my forearm. Just then

Eleanor appeared at the screen door, crying out in jest, "You two freaks! Ruthie you always touchin' and rubbin' up Debs." I made another attempt at a muscle and Eleanor bent over laughing.[1] While the whole scene evolved into a sort of slapstick routine, it was significant that Eleanor took notice of my interaction with Ruthie—that it registered with her. But still, a question lingered for me about the nature of Eleanor's laughter—whether it signaled discomfort, impossibility, or simply joy in sharing some sort of inside joke.

By contrast to Eleanor's inability to characterize the interaction with her cousin as sexual and her uncomfortable recognition of the potentially erotic interaction between myself and Ruthie, many of the younger women and girls who I interviewed seemed able to recognize same-sex erotic desires as such. During a conversation with sixteen-year-old Felicia, I learned a bit more about how teenage girls interpreted displays of affection between girls:

FELICIA: There are a lot of girls who just hold their friend's hand. Like I would coming down the roadside with one of me girlfriends. Nobody would suspect that we anything, because we just girls holding hands.

DEBRA: I see that more here than I do home in the states.

FELICIA: Yeah.

DEBRA: I see girls holding hands and braiding each other's hair and walking with their arms around each other.

FELICIA: Yeah, we do that.

DEBRA: At what age . . . how long does that continue?

FELICIA: Until you leave your friend, pretty much, because I have been holding me friends and hugging me friends since I was in preschool. Yeah, and I'm still doing it, because you know, it shows that we love each other, you know, but we're not lesbians. We just close.

DEBRA: Have you ever heard of a girl wanting another girl?

FELICIA: I guess so. I have a friend right now; me really think she bisexual.

DEBRA: How do you know?

FELICIA: Because she likes girls.

DEBRA: How do you know she likes girls?

FELICIA: And she likes guys. She see a girl, and she be like, "I love her breasts. I love her butt. She looks really, really nice." She goes on and on and on and on and on.

As Felicia's comments illustrate, certain same-sex practices are turning up with greater frequency on the collective Nevisian sexual landscape. That some of the youngest girls participating in the focus groups listed same-sex practices as something they regarded as "sexual," indicates the extent to which these behaviors are becoming codified.

This shift in cognition may represent a change in Nevisian culture brought about by the influx of American notions of sexual orientation. Unlike

Eleanor, Felicia has had a greater exposure to American culture during her coming-of-age process: she makes annual trips to New York to visit her maternal aunts in Brooklyn, she participates in a locally produced "reality show" sponsored by the AIDS education program, and she watches a great deal of American TV.

However, despite Felicia's easy recognition of the category "bisexual," it seems equally clear that on Nevis such codification of sexual pleasure is very much in flux. There seems to be a wide range of female bodily practices engaged in by Nevisian girls with other girls that are not regarded by the girls themselves as sexual. It may be that as the girls get older, they experience more pressure to follow an overt heteronormative trajectory. Thus, the majority of girls—and the older girls and women in particular—may circumvent defining some aspects of their behavior as sexual in order to avoid censorship. In doing so, Nevisian girls create multiple opportunities to explore their own bodies as well as the bodies of other girls without fear of social penalties. Thus, while these girls may not identify same-sex physical contact as "sexual," they might still experience pleasure in such contact. Whether or not Nevisian girls would themselves categorize such polymorphous experiences of pleasure as sexual or erotic—and none of my fieldwork experiences convinced me that there's a hard-and-fast line between what counts as sex and what does not among Nevisian girls—it is likely that this form of physical pleasure would inform a girl's sexual subjectivity.

While the variations on same-sex encounters captured my imagination, there are other equally pervasive and sexualized scenes that I observed on a daily basis. Having my young daughters with me on Nevis also made me intensely aware at the young age at which Nevisian girls are exposed to sexualized dialogue and imagery. One day, I was at the beach with the twins and with three local girls, Vanessa, Jasmine, and Shena, all of whom, as you recall, are cousins and live together in a small concrete house in a nearby village. Shena, the youngest, was six years old; Jasmine was fifteen; Vanessa, the oldest, and a mother herself, was twenty. While the three smaller children played in the water together, the two older girls and I lay on the beach sunning on towels and talking. Jasmine had lots of questions for me about whiteness, skin care, and personal hygiene issues. She unabashedly studied my body. At one point, in a manner that reminded me of my daughters, she asked, while staring at my breasts, "Why some part your titties white?" She was referring to my tan lines, which became visible as I shifted on my towel. A few minutes later Emma, Zoe, and Shena, emerged from the water. Shena was wearing a bright yellow one piece bathing suit, which clung to her small body. Jasmine leaned over, pointed to her younger cousin Shena, and said out loud, "She got a fat pussy; don't she?" Shena giggled. What seemed remarkable was that, while my twin daughters were oblivious to that use of slang, Shena, at six years old, was already aware of how this sexually explicit term is used to describe a female's pubic area that appears fleshy or plump, a feature that Nevisian men prefer, according to Jasmine and others with whom I talked.

Not only were my eyes wide open as an anthropologist, but also I was keenly aware of sexual imagery to which my small daughters were exposed. In the afternoons, after the hot sun had shifted in the sky, Emma, Zoe, and I took walks almost every day throughout the village to visit neighbors. The goats that grazed in the nearby pasture and often managed to find their way into our garden, charmed my daughters. On numerous occasions, the girls watched curiously as goats mated. These scenes often produced lots of snorting and grunting by the livestock. The display of male goats struggling for physical access to female goats, combined with the scene of the village donkey that seemed to have frequent erections, were daily episodes in the village. While commonplace, such scenes still incite curiosity in children, Nevisians and non-Nevisians alike. I once watched several primary school-aged girls from my village giggle and point as they passed a donkey with an erection while on their way to school. Children's fascination with donkeys' mating habits is so much a part of Caribbean culture that Oonya Kempadoo, in her fictional coming-of-age narrative *Buxton Spice* (1999), features a scene of giggling schoolgirls and a donkey with an erection.

Kempadoo's Caribbean narrative does a wonderful job of capturing the multiple influences on a girl's sexual development and the liminal stage between childhood and adolescence. *Buxton Spice* depicts precisely the sort of heterogeneous sexuality that I saw everyday on Nevis. The opening scene depicts four twelve-year-olds trying to persuade the "village idiot," a man in his thirties, that the old piano in the community center is actually Miss Annie, the woman of his dreams. The precocious girls convince him to expose himself and masturbate against the piano. In still another scene the inquisitive girls try to make sense of the images they see in *Man and Woman*, a book they discover in one girl's parents' collection of art and nature books. Later they engage in sex play where the girls experiment with batteries between their legs to stimulate their playmates. In other scenes in *Buxton Spice*, a gang of girls spy on teenage boys and girls having sex in sheds. They also listen outside opened windows of the small wooden houses in their villages to the sounds couples make while having sex. Kempadoo's Caribbean narrative characterizes West Indian childhood as filled with moments of free sexual exploration in the absence of procreative pressures and constraints.

Given the landscape of Nevis, including the arrangement of small houses in the villages, and the increasing availability of sexually explicit videos and DVDs as well as sexual information and scripts on the Internet and on TV, it is not difficult to imagine similar scenes incited by intense curiosity unfolding among the girls in the village where I lived or all over Nevis for that matter.

Disparate titillating images and dialogues permeate everyday life on the island compel me to ask: What happens to the polymorphous experiences of pleasure as children undergo the transition into adulthood? How do girls begin to recognize and make sense of these pleasures?

In this chapter, I map out the nature of sexual pleasure, the multiple forms it takes, and how it is constituted by and for Nevisian girls. In order to explore the nature of sexual pleasure as described by the girls themselves, I begin by exploring the culturally specific categories the girls use to understand sexual practices and desires. In the introduction I described how in focus groups, girls made lists of the sexual practices they thought other girls might engage in. These lists of practices may suggest the kinds of behaviors Nevisian girls consider pleasurable.

THE GEOGRAPHY OF SEX AND PLEASURE

Any attempt at studying sexual pleasure is not without its challenges. It remains unclear as to whether bodily sensations and pleasures can be accurately represented in language and consequently, in memory. Some sexuality specialists such as Paul Abramson and Steven Pinkerton (2002) assert that the porousness of sexual memories coupled with "the conceptual gulf that separates the experience of sexual pleasure and the cognitive structures employed to relate those experiences" (143–144) may prevent individuals from being able to accurately report sexual pleasures. Abramson and Pinkerton are treading on unexplored territory and admittedly acknowledge the paucity of research conducted on sexual pleasure. They tentatively assert that "it is not surprising to find that what people remember is how good sex felt at its peak (usually orgasm) rather than the duration of experience . . . (and that) . . . (a)lthough people are clearly capable of extracting and remembering the salient features of a pleasurable experience, it would seem that they are incapable of remembering the pleasure itself" (145). According to Abramson and Pinkerton, our linguistic constructs offer us labels, and we are able to recognize the sensations when reproduced, but we are unable to narrate the sensations.

If we take these assertions seriously, then evaluating the nature of pleasure for girls under any circumstances produces tenuous descriptions at best. Trying to reconstruct the nature of sexual pleasure from the lists the girls produced about sexual behaviors on Nevis also produces a series of narrative gaps. While the lists are richly suggestive of the sexual activities girls practice, they provide only a partial understanding of the nature of sexual pleasure. The lists are an excellent starting point from which to begin to map out the geography of the girls' pleasure, but they must be seen in the context of the stories the girls tell as well as the socioeconomic factors that impact the girls' sexual agency.

I would argue that not only might the frequency of items on these lists be interpreted in terms of their salience to informants, as Stephen Borgatti (1999) has suggested, but also that if the girls are claiming that this is what other girls are doing, then perhaps I can assume that this is what the girls as a group are doing themselves (122). Put simply, I would argue that what comes to mind more readily as the girls prepared their lists were activities in which the girls themselves might have engaged.

The cumulative list of sexual behaviors produced by girls in three different age groups is listed in their own words in table 1.

TABLE 1

List of Sexual Behaviors by Age Group

12–13-Year-Olds	14–15-Year-Olds	16–17-Year-Olds
Hugging	Fingering	Kissing body parts
Playing with hair	Sucking penis	Touching
Playing with ears	Backshot	Playing with hair
Grinding	Pumping boys	Saying I love you with no meaning
Kissing other girls	Allowing men to touch them	Lip kissing
Asking what color panties somebody wears	Leave school to go to boy's house to have sex	Looking into each other's eyes
Having me finger them	Drinking alcohol and smoking drugs	Discussing sex
Sitting on each other's lap	Lap dances	Back rubs
Rape	Oral sex	Whispering in ears
Oral sex	Petting	Nibbling on ears
French kissing	Sexual intercourse	They touch each other in private places
Sexual intercourse	Has sex with older men	Kiss and hold hands in dark areas
69	Hugging	They view each other naked
Backshot	Kissing	They would play orally with each other
Hold hands	Touching	They would heat up each other to get them horny
Suck tongue	Rubbing	Engage in having new views and activities on how they would make each other happy sexually
Touch each other	Snuggling	Be with men around the ages of 28–40 years old

(continued)

TABLE 1 *List of Sexual Behaviors by Age Group (continued)*

12–13-Year-Olds	14–15-Year-Olds	16–17-Year-Olds
Hug	Alone with each other privately	Be sexually active with more than one partner
Have sex	Having boys finger them	Leave school during class time to be with older partner and never return that day
Feel up bud	69	Liming
Sucking bud	Having oral sex	Different sex position
Sitting on boy's bud	Sitting on guys laps	Sex over the internet
Let boys feel up their breasts and pokey	Having guys touch them in private parts	Stripping
Ride for a ride	Anal sex	Writing love letters
Skinny dipping	Vaginal intercourse	Sex with condoms
Bisexual	Making out	Sex without condoms
Bull drop	Sucking of the penis	Screaming while having sex
Finger	Sucking of genital areas	Leaving home telling parents they are over at a friends and they go with a boy
Suck breast	Holding hands	Sneaking out at night and early morning to have sex while their parents are sleeping
Shine ball	Petting	Beating and getting beaten by boyfriend
Feel ups	heavy petting	
Touching private parts	group sex	
Wearing sexy clothing	Massaging	
Looking at each other in private	Dancing	
Prostitution	dirty dancing	
Sweet eye talk	they play with the boys' private parts	
Taking back shots	sex upside down	
Intimate touching		
Whoring		
Peer pressure		
Drugs		
Touching in parts where they're not supposed to		

(continued)

TABLE 1 *List of Sexual Behaviors by Age Group (continued)*

12–13-Year-Olds	14–15-Year-Olds	16–17-Year-Olds
Having boy friend older		
Leaving home		
Pregnant		
Touching one another in places some people don't want to be touched		
Have men feel up their private parts		
Get hickies on private parts and neck		
Kiss on cheek		
Lots of girls like to grind and dance (dance real close and dirty) with guys		
Giving blow jobs		
Being fingered		
Jerking off her boyfriend		
Sex with older men		
More than one partner		
Masturbating		
Holding hands and feeling up (as in touching all over each other's body even private areas)		
In the corner of the building on top of one another		
Kissing other girls		
Sex for money		

Scrutinizing these lists reveals differences as well as similarities across the age sets. For example, sex with older men is mentioned within all of the age sets, but it appears with greater frequency with girls over fifteen years of age. Anal sex is also listed by all three groups; however, it appears with greater frequency with the girls over fourteen years of age. Compared to the other practices, such as sucking tongue, sucking penis, or sexual intercourse, anal sex seems marginalized.

Not only frequency, but the order in which girls listed these sex acts is also significant. For example, while all of the age groups list kissing or sucking tongue, 73 percent of the youngest group of girls listed it as either the first or second item. Among the oldest group, only half of the girls listed kissing as first or second. I would argue that the younger group listed kissing first precisely because that is the sexual activity that most of them engaged in regularly. By contrast, the older girls were aware of and most likely practice a greater range of sexual activities and thus, kissing is not given such primacy in their lists. For example, sucking penis and the less transparent, non-gender specific phrase, oral sex, was listed by over 90 percent of the girls over 15, whereas less than half of the girls between twelve and thirteen years of age referenced oral sex.

The lists composed by the sixteen- and seventeen-year olds were, as to be expected, the most elaborate and descriptive. For example, the oldest girls' lists often provided detailed information about where sex occurs and with whom, providing such comments as "Sneaking out at night and early morning to have sex while their parents are sleeping" or "Leav[ing] school during class time to be with older partner and never return that day." In addition, the oldest group more frequently describes the emotional components of sexual practices, suggesting that while the youngest group may mention the same sex act as frequently as the older groups, the significance of the act may become more emotionally charged and hence more significant as the girls mature.

Only girls between twelve and thirteen listed sexual practices with other girls. Again, given the shift away from polymorphous pleasure to a more heteronormative model as the girls mature, this is not surprising. But the question remains open for me: Are these girls omitting same-sex activities because of societal pressure to conform to a heteronormative standard or because such activities actually decrease as the girls get older? I must keep my encounters with older Nevisians in mind when considering these lists. I am thinking specifically of Ruthie's revelations regarding her sexual encounters with other adult women and Eleanor's performative "disgust" for sexualized interactions between Ruthie and me. Such anecdotal evidence is compelling, and raises important questions about the extent to which these lists are able to capture the totality of the girls' sexual activity.

While the stories the girls and women tell certainly fill in some of the gaps left by the simple listing of activities, the lists themselves do not readily enable quantitative or qualitative observations about the girls' pleasure. It seems clear that the girls I surveyed are sexually active in a variety of ways that change over time, but it is crucial to ask this question: What do the girls themselves like to do? Because, in the absence of coercion (a subject to which I will turn shortly), and amid all of this kissing, rubbing, fingering, grinding, pumping, sucking, and caressing, there must be some degree of pleasure experienced by girls engaging in such practices. As evidenced by the variety of bodily practices just listed the potentiality for sexual pleasure clearly exists.

Moreover, if pleasure is conceived of as a gratifying experience, and if, even more importantly, pleasure indicates that the girls are making choices (at least in some circumstances), can we assert that pleasure is an index for sexual agency? This observation would not be unique to the girls coming of age on Nevis. Arjun Appadurai (1996) reminds us that "where there is pleasure there is agency" (7). Similarly, Vance (1984) asserts that theorizing pleasure forces us to recognize the "positive possibilities of sexuality—explorations of the body, curiosity, intimacy, sensuality, adventure, excitement, human connection" (1). While it is too simplistic to always conflate sexual pleasure with sexual agency, I would argue that understanding sexual pleasure helps to illuminate how girls produce their sexualities and thus helps us understand Nevisian girls as sexual actors. One of the most significant means of determining the extent of the girls' sexual agency is to look at the practices by which the girls come to recognize themselves as both the objects of desire and as desiring subjects. This is where the stories the girls tell become particularly helpful in filling in the gaps left by the lists.

In describing her first kiss, Yvonne, a fourteen-year-old girl, narrates just such a moment that suggests her own agency as a sexual actor as well as her ability to attract men: "Our church had a outin' near Mt. Lily. I was thirteen and he was seventeen. He came over to me to talk. He told me dat he really, really, really like me. All de time I see him and I really, really like him and now he standin' dere tellin' me dat he like me. He kiss me two weeks after at de Mr. Cool Show. We were in de back standin' up and den we went out back. We huggin' and den he kiss me. I never kiss nobody before. I seen people kissin' but me never kiss a boy like dat. After dat all I was thinkin' about was bein' close to him."

In acknowledging her own yearning in *relationship* to her young paramour's desires, Yvonne acknowledges a certain mutuality of desire that is a critical moment in subject formation. While girls like Yvonne may have experimented with boys and other girls when they were preadolescents, and while they might list "kissing" as a sexual activity at a very early age, there is something further that the listing of the activity does not fully capture. At some point in their narratives, the girls do not recognize such early forms of childhood exploration as sexual. Moreover, girls in Nevisian society are, from a very early age, objectified by male desire and are expected to be available for sex on demand. They are objects rather than subjects. In such a cultural milieu, it is not surprising to find that for many girls, like Yvonne, it is not simply any first kiss, but rather, the *first kiss that they willingly bestow*, which marks the emergence of their sexualities. This archetypal "first kiss" is important, at least in terms of the way girls spoke about it, not simply because it is pleasurable, but even more so because it is intentional.

There are, of course, complications to this scenario. Other girls told stories that are more complex than Yvonne's, stories that problematize the question of intentionality. Tamara's first sexual encounter, for example, is one in which sexual violence—or at least the threat of such violence—blurs the line between choice and coercion:

> My grandmother sent me down de street to a shop. I was fifteen years old. He was twenty-five years old. He was always callin' me and I would run. I didn't know what to do. I was young. One night he called me and I run and he caught me. He grabbed me. Dere was a moment when I was scared. [She smiles and closes her eyes.] Debbie, it was a moment I never forget. He was bigger dan me and strong and smelled all sweet. And de guy was doin' all dis shit to me and me feelin' so good. When he finish with me I went home and because he was wearin' a lot of cologne, I could smell it on me blouse, so I took me blouse off and slept with it. And I was inhalin' it all night and kept rememberin' what he did to me.

Tamara's intentionality is initially questionable: she was chased and caught, and acknowledges that she was fearful. However, the force exerted over her does not signal the absence of pleasure, but rather quite the opposite: Tamara was sexually aroused and excited by the encounter. "Doin' all dis shit to me," she later explained, meant that her lover fondled her breasts and put his hand up her skirt and touched her between her legs over her underpants. Her intense pleasure is indicated by the fact that she later took off her blouse and slept with it, inhaling her lover's scent while recalling the events. Indeed, that Tamara describes her encounter as an event that she will "never forget," and then reenacts her pleasure later, suggests an admission or an avowal of her sexuality. It is precisely this sort of acknowledgment that Foucault (1985) regards as key to forming one's subjectivity (4–5). However, despite the numerous indicators that this incident is a significant moment in the emergence of Tamara's sexual subjectivity, the specter of sexual coercion complicates the question of Tamara's agency. It is clearly not a straightforward trajectory from pleasure to agency.

Similarly, the extent to which Nevisian girls experience pain in their sexual encounters complicates any simplistic notion of establishing one's agency through sexual encounters. Indeed, pain was the dominant theme within the girls' sexual autobiographies and the subject of pain emerged during a variety of discussions with Nevisian girls, boys, men, and women alike. One day when I was visiting Gingerland Secondary School in the countryside, a group of boys who looked to be about fifteen and whose class had been conducted outside under the shade of a flamboyant tree, called me over. It was in between classes and the first bell had already rung. "Hey Professor, come talk to us," hollered one of the boys.[2] I had been on Nevis for over three months and it seemed like most of the students I met were aware that I had come to the island to write about girls. On this occasion, as I approached the boys under the tree, the second bell rang.

The more vocal boy, eager to engage and perhaps shock me, as well as to entertain his classmates, asked with a sheepish grin, "Why does it always hurt girls to
have sex?" At this point I was not surprised by the nature of the question. The
subject of pain during sexual intercourse came up frequently in conversations
with Nevisians.

Thomas, a British photographer and returning national in his thirties who
grew up in London, maintains that the average Nevisian girl has no idea the
extent of her individual potential for pleasure, nor of the relationship between
pleasure and pain. He attributes such lack of self-knowledge to inexperience.
Assuming the role of an outsider looking in, Thomas maintains: "It's not loving
sex or caressing sex. It's hard sex. The girls don't have the experience to draw
on. . . . When there's hard penetration and they say, 'oh me pussy sore' . . . they
thinking 'wow that was good.' Meanwhile, the man has had three orgasms
throughout the night and they haven't had any."

Similarly, Andrea Nisbett, the national AIDS coordinator who works
closely with girls and boys on Nevis, stressed that according to the girls with
whom she worked, "Good sex is hard penetration." She also pointed out that the
girls seem to "know" what they want: "The girls have a saying here, 'I want the
iron.' That's what they say. They say, 'I want the raw hard iron.' You know, they
have all these ways of describing what they want."

The references to sexual intercourse as painful for the girls were so pervasive
during my fieldwork that it forces me to take a close look at the relationship
between sex and pain.[3] There is a range of possible explanations for pain during
intercourse. Within the medical sciences this type of pain is commonly attributed
to lack of lubrication, irritants (e.g., condoms), vaginal or pelvic infections, or
physical trauma. The psychological explanations for pain during intercourse
include a fear of pregnancy, a past history of sexual violence, or increased anxiety
about the sexual encounter. It may very well be that one or more of these circumstances contributed to some of the girls' reports that sex was painful. However, the majority of girls with whom I spoke described sexual encounters in
which there were "lots of kisses" but a lack of what fifteen-year-old Jasmine
called "affectionate touchin'" of the genitals. From the narratives that the girls
themselves offer, it appears that pain during sex is mostly indicative of a traditional discourse in which female pleasure is so devalued that painful intercourse
is the norm. The desire of Nevisian girls for the "raw hard iron" and the girls'
repeated associations of hard penetration with "good" sex are most likely reflective of what Gayle Rubin (1984) calls a culturally specific valuation of sex. In this
case, the question is how pain has become equated with "good" sex among
Nevisian girls and the extent to which the subordinate status of Nevisian girls is
a determining factor in such sexual valuation of pain.

In terms of the hierarchy of sex on Nevis, female desires and pleasures have
traditionally been marginalized. During the entire duration of my fieldwork on

Nevis, I never once participated in a discussion where female desire and pleasure were described as "natural" or "healthy." I am not referring to the moments when my more mature informants, who were women over thirty and who already had children, talked privately and candidly about their sexual experiences and discoveries; rather, I am referring to the absence of public discussion of female sexual pleasure in discourses about sexual health, sexual needs, and the sexual desires of Nevisian females. As such, it is not surprising that I encountered numerous women and girls who told of inexperienced male partners. Some, like Ruthie, directly attributed the pain she experienced during sexual intercourse to her partner's lack of sexual skills: "We rubbin' up against each other, havin' a good time. He try to put it in before me ready. I mean, I sexy, but me not ready. Me own juices was not ready [laughs aloud]." Grace, a fifteen-year-old whose boyfriend was in his early twenties, told me this: "Most of the times, I mean, the younger guys there is just intercourse and that is it. They don't know—they don't know anything about kissing or—I mean, they'll be kissing—a guy and girl will be kissing and then—whatever will happen. And they will have sex with the girl, but there's nothing really—they won't be on [having intercourse] for a long time."

From the very youngest to the oldest informants, and by men and women alike, pain during intercourse was expressed as an accepted and normalized as part of the female sexual experience on Nevis. But, given the pervasive absence of public acknowledgment of female desire and pleasure, it is difficult to say whether this normalization occurs because women's desires have no ontological reality in Nevisian culture or because men are simply inattentive and somewhat aggressive as lovers because there is no cultural encouragement to be otherwise. Of course, until fairly recently, women themselves have enabled this normalization of pain in their sexual relations.

It is also likely that memory and imagination impact girls' experience of sex and exacerbate the normalization of painful sex. For example, although Ruthie may not have been lubricated enough to enjoy sexual intercourse, she certainly did experience other forms of bodily pleasure during that sexual encounter and others that followed. Indeed, several girls spoke of experiencing painful sexual intercourse during encounters about which they also reported feeling intense levels of excitement and arousal. A fifteen-year-old reflected on her first sexual experience and captured precisely this mixture of pain and pleasure: "I had been waiting for the right time. Our kisses were so passionate and was so full of sweetness. . . . I could feel his love for me, but when we did it, there was so much pain." As these comments suggest, pleasure for these women and girls is made up of experiences that sometimes seem contradictory— sweetness, passion, and pain commingle to produce a wide range of physical sensations. But moreover, over time, the lines between these seemingly disparate experiences may become more and more blurry. For instance, if a girl experiences pain during sexual intercourse, this does not preclude the possibility that she might come to attach erotic associations with the "painful" experience when she recalls that experience as she moves through her adolescence or adulthood. Thus, there is a distinction between the initial experience of pain and the way the body remembers, or perhaps forgets, such experiences. This perspective allows us to consider how past painful or pleasurable sexual encounters shape more immediate sexual encounters. It also speaks to the dynamic and ongoing integration of past sexual and non-sexual experiences with larger cultural discourses to form a girl's sexual subjectivity. The process of learning the social meaning of sex acts as well as learning the meaning of internal states is complex and continuous, particularly so in a society where sexual discourses and the sexual practices prescribed by those discourses are in such great flux.

POWER AND RESISTANCE: VARSHNIE'S STORY

While female sexuality has been traditionally marginalized in Nevisian culture, those cultural norms are shifting, in some cases dramatically. This is not to say that there has been anything like a wholesale "liberation" of female sexual desire and pleasure on the island, but rather that female pleasure and agency are beginning to surface more and more in both public and private settings. As this process unfolds, however, there remain numerous contradictions and constraints the girls must unravel and overcome when trying to establish themselves as sexual subjects. The story offered by Varshnie, a sixteen-year-old informant, is particularly indicative of this struggle. Caught between multiple discourses, Varshnie's sexual activities and her relationship with her husband capture precisely the type of change with which Nevisian girls and women are grappling as they produce their sexuality. When I interviewed Varshnie, she had been married for two weeks to a twenty-year-old fellow Guyanese immigrant, who, along with her mother and father, had been questioned and intimidated by the Nevisian police as to the circumstances of the marriage. Varshnie explained in great detail how she "fell in love" with a "nice man" and decided to run away with him. She had the support of her twenty-year-old-sister who, with Varshnie's encouragement, would secretly arrange meetings between Varshnie and her boyfriend. The following segment from my interview with Varshnie begins with her description of how she "ran away" with her boyfriend:

DEBRA: How did you leave your house? Tell me the whole story.
VARSHNIE: Okay. I left to go to school on Tuesday mornin', and I went over by him and he askin' me to go with him. My parents they keep lookin' for me after school because time had passed, and then it was after six, so my parents was lookin' for me. My parents come over by my sister's and saw

us and said to the guy in the driveway, "Okay, you love my daughter? My daughter like you? You goin' to marry her, if you agree."

That night, Varshnie and her boyfriend returned to her parents' house, and ten days later she was married. Even though he remained living at her parents' house for close to two weeks before they married, the couple, according to Varshnie, did not have sexual intercourse. Varshnie explains, "I tell him, 'No I'm goin' to wait till I'm married and den I'm goin' to have sex.'"

After Varshnie's mother and father signed the necessary legal documents that gave consent for their sixteen-year-old to marry, Varshnie's mother planned a traditional Guyanese wedding. Soon after the wedding, Varshnie dropped out of school and continued to live with her husband in her parents' house where her primary role was to tend to the household chores, that is, to cook and clean for her mother, father, younger sister, and her new husband. I interviewed Varshnie at length; we began with her sexual experience on her wedding night and continued with her sexual activity in general.

DEBRA: Tell me about your wedding night and about your first time having sex.

VARSHNIE: I was screamin', because it hurt; really hurt; remember I never had sex before, so it really hurt. He make it feel good afterward, but because I was a virgin, for de first time remember . . . he put a blanket in my mouth because I was screamin'. My momma was outside cleanin' up de place, pickin' up de glasses and. . . .

DEBRA: Do you think she could hear you?

VARSHNIE: Yeah, I think she did, and de next mornin', I ask her, "Did you hear me?" and she said, "Yes, I did, but don't tell your husband."

DEBRA: Did she talk to you the night before and tell you what to do?

VARSHNIE: Yeah, she tell me; she said, "Make sure he use some oil or Vaseline or somethin' on me, because it's goin' to pain, and she remember the first time when she had sex, and to make sure we use somethin' that I couldn't get pregnant or somethin'. She tell me, "Make sure you use some protection." I was screamin'; he said I have to behave myself, . . . we can't have people just outside kitchen hearing screamin', . . .

DEBRA: Did it ever feel good?

VARSHNIE: Yeah. After two or three times, den it did.

DEBRA: What's it like to be a married woman in your house?

VARSHNIE: Nice. It's nice to be married. You have somebody that loves you and shares your life with you. You have somebody to sleep with at night, hug you up when the place is cold. It's nice. My life is good, but you just have to know how to live it.

DEBRA: When do you want to have your first baby?

VARSHNIE: When I am over eighteen or maybe nineteen.

Debra: What do you have to do so that you won't get pregnant?

Varshnie: Use protection—tablets, injection, or a condom, or somethin'. . . . [but] my husband say he don't want me to use any tablet or any injection, or like that. He say some time when you are ready to get children, dose kind of things affect you from makin' egg fertilized.

Debra: Now, what has he used so far?

Varshnie: So far we have used nothin'. He keep usin' [a] condom, but I keep complainin' about it; I don't like it.

Debra: Okay, now tell me, you don't like condoms. So, what have you used in the last thirteen days?

Varshnie: Nothin'. Just, like that.

Debra: So, where does he cum?

Varshnie: Right inside of me.

Debra: But I thought you didn't want to have children now.

Varshnie: I don't. He say he's goin' to carry me next week to get a pregnancy test at the hospital to see if I am pregnant.

Debra: Why?

Varshnie: Because he is scared, because when they said they goin' to lock him up if I get pregnant in this early age.

Debra: But he still cums inside you?

Varshnie: Yes.

Debra: Have you had sex recently?

Varshnie: Yesterday, like four times a week. Every night he want to do it, but I like to control him and say "No . . . you can't make it a practice."

Debra: Why?

Varshnie: Sometime if I say [I have] "my menstruation" and . . . you can't have sex durin' them, [it] could cause cancer. . . .

Debra: Oh, you say, "Suppose when I get my menstruation, are you going to want to do it?" That's what you say. And what does he say?

Varshnie: He says, "I have to do it; I have to get it," and he is laughin'.

Debra: When you have sex, does he do anything else besides get on top of you? Does he kiss your breasts?

Varshnie: Yes.

Debra: Does he kiss between your legs?

Varshnie: Yes.

Debra: Like, he uses his mouth. . . .

Varshnie: Yes. He does.

Debra: And do you like that?

Varshnie: Yes.

Debra: Is this uncomfortable for you to talk about?

Varshnie: No, no.

Debra: Okay. Now, has he ever asked you to use your mouth on him?

VARSHNIE: Um–hmm.

DEBRA: Does he like that?

VARSHNIE: I never do it. He keep holdin' me down and I cannot. I am not goin' to do it. I never do it.

DEBRA: Why not?

VARSHNIE: I feel uncomfortable.

DEBRA: Why?

VARSHNIE: I don't know why; I just don't like doin' it.

DEBRA: What does he say to you? Does he say anything or does he just hold you down?

VARSHNIE: He asked me, I say "No." Then he try to hold me down, but he never puts it in my mouth. He holdin' me down, but he do not put it in my mouth.

DEBRA: Did you know about that?

VARSHNIE: Yes.

DEBRA: Where did you learn about it?

VARSHNIE: Once I hear my mother keep tellin' my dad, "Stop pushin' it in my mouth," but I never know what she meant, but then my sister used to talk to me about it.

DEBRA: Oh, so she told you?

VARSHNIE: Yes.

DEBRA: You just don't want to do it.

VARSHNIE: I just don't like to do it, no.

DEBRA: Has he ever wanted you to do anything else that you don't want to do?

VARSHNIE: No.

This interview fragment tells us a great deal about the production of Varshnie's sexuality and, I would argue, reveals a great deal about the shifting nature of female sexuality on Nevis—that is, the roles of women, what is expected of them, and what they can and should desire themselves. Like many of the girls I interviewed, Varshnie's situation is complex and she is subject to a variety of pressures and influences. On the one hand, Varshnie's family of origin plays a significant role in shaping her sexual practices as well as her ideas about sex. She learns about various aspects of sex from her sister and mother, as well as from having overheard her parents having sex when she was younger. Varshnie also learns about sex, of course, from her new husband and the emergence of her sexuality is intricately linked to her role as a wife and to her sense of obligation to her husband's needs. Varshnie's sexual subjectivity is influenced by traditional familial and by Guyanese norms and expectations.

However, as detailed in chapter 4, Varshnie also learns about sexuality by consuming imported pornographic videos with her husband's encouragement. Her exposure to mediated images of sexuality opens up the possibility for her sexuality to articulate with the commodifying influences of pornography and thus, for Varshnie to develop a more consumer-oriented subjectivity. While it appears, at least from this segment of the interview, that Varshnie's sexuality is constituted in a space in between her family and consumer culture, there are also moments that might suggest Varshnie's sexual agency as well. If agency is conceptualized as opportunities for deliberately practicing self-production (Hall 1996, 13) then certainly when Varshnie encouraged her sister to arrange meetings with her boyfriend, when she ran away and risked severe punishment by her parents, and when she encouraged her husband not to use condoms or insisted that they wait to have sex until they were married appear as moments of sexual agency. In addition, Varshnie's very perception of self-control and self-determination may also be viewed as part of her sexual subjectivity (Moore 2001, 264).

One might interpret Varnshie's choices and her motivations for such choices as anything but a sign of sexual agency, but rather as a sign of the complexity of the social structures shaping her life and sexuality. For instance, how much more independent will Varshnie become now that she has dropped out of school and terminated her future opportunities for education and training? What sort of agency might she assert now, when instead of submitting to her father, she must submit, in many ways, to her new husband? What about the combination of factors that have influenced Varshnie's decision not to use birth control? On the one hand, her husband tells her that injections or pills will interfere with her ability to conceive in the future and on the other hand, she herself does not like condoms because it impedes her pleasure; yet she does not want to have children for a few more years and her husband, fearing harassment from the local authorities, wants to make sure she has not conceived already.

While Varshnie appears to create her own destiny, her actions are clearly dependent upon social structures and myriad institutional constraints, such as her relationship with her parents and husband, and her position in Nevisian society as a Guyanese immigrant. Varshnie inhabits a society that is caught up in rapid social change where traditional social structures, such as family and male authority, compete with modern technologies and discourses that offer a new network of power relations. The interaction between changing social structures and sexual discourses is illustrated in the conflict between Varshnie and her new husband regarding the specific act of fellatio.

First, Varshnie talked at length about how she was trying to be a good wife and do what was expected of her. But in doing so, she also revealed the coercive environment in which she must carefully operate. For example, she told me of an instance when she disobeyed her husband by reading a love letter that his cousin had written to another girl. Her husband threatened to beat her if she did not do as she was told. One other time he kicked her repeatedly and forced her out of their bed for something she described as stupid. Varshnie alludes to this when she remarks, "My life is good, but you just have to know how to live it." Varshnie appeared to be eager to please her husband and to submit to his authority. Yet we see that perhaps as a result of ambiguous sexual scripts where the sexual rules and expectations—that is, what is sexually mandatory and what is off limits—do not appear to be clear-cut.

While this ambiguity creates a challenging terrain for Varshnie to negotiate her subjectivity, it should be noted that her life and expectations are not the only ones undergoing such changes. Varshnie's husband's authority is also being eroded. For example, Varshnie refused to comply with her husband's desire for fellatio; even when he held her down, she resisted. She explained that she was uncomfortable performing fellatio on her husband regardless of how insistent he was. This is an excellent example of Varshnie engaging in sexual self-determination.

THE EMERGENCE OF FEMALE SEXUAL ENTITLEMENT

Until recently, the cultural significance of heterosexual female pleasure on Nevis needed to be understood almost exclusively in relation to enduring traditional sexual discourse, which privileges male pleasure. Felicia, a sexually active sixteen-year-old informant, addresses the privileging of male sexuality and the concomitant invisibility of female sexual desire:

> I think that the majority of young girls in Nevis don't even understand that sex is supposed to be pleasurable for both people involved, so therefore girls probably just be doing it for the sake of doing it. In Nevis, we are kind of under the impression that it's all about the guy. Really young girls don't talk about sexual pleasure, period; because nobody wants anybody to know whether or not they are having sex. A girl wouldn't say to someone that she is having sex, because Nevis is still kind of stuck in the era where it is a sin to fornicate. I think that after a girl gets to realize that she's not the only one having sex then she starts to find friends that are doing the same thing that she is doing and then she is able to talk about sexual pleasures with her friends, but never with her parents or anyone older in society.

Felicia's comments demonstrate how the dominant traditional sexual discourse on pleasure is organized around male desires. Within the popular Nevisian imagination, men are thought of as having "uncontrollable" desires. The idea that men require sexual activity to maintain optimal health is popular among Nevisians as well. A strong sexual appetite is viewed as "natural" for a man and is socially expected, accepted, and rewarded. By contrast, girls are not supposed to be sexually active at all, according to the ideal moral discourse. This might explain why discourses on female pleasure were, until recently, all but mute.

As Varshnie's multifaceted narrative indicates, the sexual landscape of Nevis is changing dramatically; female pleasure is beginning to be recognized as a legitimate concern among sexually active Nevisians. Indeed, given the almost complete lack of public discourse on female sexuality, it might be said that female desire and pleasure are undergoing an ontological emergence in Nevisian culture. Clearly, this is due in part to the influx of global sexual discourses, many of which (as discussed in chapter 4) promote, market, or even "sell" images and accoutrements of active female sexuality. Nevisian girls are now drawing on outside influences like imported magazines, media images, and pornography to articulate sexual pleasures. Felicia explains the role that the magazine *Cosmopolitan* has played in the lives of older Nevisian girls:

> I know me and my friends talked about sex constantly and we used to read *Cosmopolitan* magazine when we about sixteen years old and it was like our bonding over the magazine. We used to read them and see what's new, and do the quizzes and stuff, and pretty much let *Cosmo* teach us everything from flirting with guys to keeping a man. I'm not sure where most girls get information about pleasure other than the television and magazines. I think girls learn what's supposed to feel good from the television and reading magazine[s]. For me, it was *Cosmo* magazine and my friends. We would talk about each others' experiences and sort of compare notes. I know definitely that it is not from a parent, even if a girl in Nevis is best friends with her mother, she will never tell her mother that she is not a virgin, and by extension, she can't discuss sexual matters with her mother.

Felicia describes how girls come together as friends, reading imported women's magazines, sharing sexual experiences and confidences, "comparing notes," and thus sanctioning and legitimating each others' ideas about sexual pleasure. When Felicia states that "girls learn what is supposed to feel good from the television and reading magazine[s]," it is in all likelihood that girls read about stylized sexual activities, and perhaps, given the nature of the items on the foregoing lists, they read about kissing, oral sex, sexual intercourse, dancing, and having boys fondle their breasts and genitals. Probably, given the nature of the magazines that are available to the girls, there is some discussion of the social situations in which these behaviors should occur—at night, in private, or in one's bed.

With the influx of sexual discourses that focus on female pleasures, there appears to be a growing sense of what can only be described as sexual entitlement expressed by both girls and women. This became especially apparent to me while working with older Nevisian women who had recently begun asking their partners to engage in particular sexual practices that had the potential to increase their sexual satisfaction, practices such as cunnilingus, which were not a part of the Nevisian sexual repertoire when these women were growing up.

Historically, at least from what I was able to learn from my informants, cunnilingus has been viewed very negatively among Nevisian men. Several of the girls informed me that this continues to be the case. Within popular discourse, the vagina is represented as dirty, offensive, and foul-smelling, and the typical male view is captured by a popular phrase, "salt-fish." However, a new song by Socrates, a Calypso musician, entitled *Go Down*, humorously draws attention to and reframes cunnilingus as a desirable activity for men. In the song, Socrates informs his audience that he is revealing a secret "recipe" for attracting and maintaining women. Socrates sings:

> Anytime you can't go up go down.
> A woman loves a man that don't tell her no when she asks,
> "Do you want to eat?"
> The cannibal lover is the giant in bed. . . .
> She takes a licking but she keeps on coming.
> Every woman needs a good tongue-lashing.

Of course, even though Socrates emphasizes female pleasure, he still promotes a type of dominant masculinity. Socrates declares in the song that a man who is willing to perform this particular sexual act is "in control" and thus will be more successful at keeping women satisfied and faithful. More than this, Socrates's assertion that "Every woman needs a good tongue-lashing," echoes the cultural acceptance of domestic violence as a way to maintain women's submissive cultural positions. Yet despite the repetition of several misogynist tropes, Socrates's song is also revolutionary in its way. While this might be interpreted as a generalization, Calypso as well as Jamaican dancehall music, which is widely consumed on Nevis, are known for being profoundly misogynist and homophobic. Indeed, cunnilingus and homosexuality were often paired as acts that signal submission and male demasculinization. Socrates's promotion of cunnilingus, even in such a limited manner, represents a sea change in West Indian popular culture.

Individual women's stories also highlighted the increased occurrence of cunnilingus in their own lives, even while acknowledging that it is not a practice universally accepted by Nevisian men. Ruthie, for example, notes the resistance of men to performing cunnilingus, but also clearly expresses her incredible delight in discovering its pleasures for herself:

> Nevisian men . . . don't like to blow women. Deir hair stand up and all. . . . I asked de father of my two older children to lick my pussy one night; he stood up, went to de mirror, laughin' and pointin' to his mouth, "See dis mouth, dis is for eatin' food, not lickin' pussy." The first time I got

my pussy licked, oh mon, it was licked too good! It Culturama week . . .
we went off to get freaky. . . . He went dere (pointing to her vagina) and
oh mon, I never forget it . . . he was a married man . . . me been lookin'
for him ever since. I tell you, me been lookin' for him ever since. [Ruthie
puts both her hands on her lower belly, sways her hips back and forth, and
rubs her lower belly lightly.]

Ruthie went on to explain that she "does everythin'" with the father of
her new baby, which presumably includes cunnilingus.

Clearly, the attitude toward cunnilingus, among both men and women, is
undergoing a shift. But it is not just this one sexual act. Indeed, the stories that
women and girls told me indicate that, on Nevis, entire sexual repertoires are
undergoing a rapid and noticeable shift. My sense is that among girls and
women, to borrow from John Gagnon and William Simon (1973), there is an
emerging indulgent sensuality (90) that reflects changes in sexual expectations as
the result of global flows colliding and interacting. This is the sense of sexual
entitlement that I mentioned earlier, and it clearly impacts the lives of individual Nevisians. But what seems to be most culturally significant is how the stories I heard reveal the way in which traditional sexual discourse on Nevis, which
privileged sexual acts such as heterosexual intercourse, now coexist with newer
discourses offering more diverse sexual activities, including anal sex, fellatio,
some same-sex relations and, of course, cunnilingus. It is important to keep in
mind that such changes are not merely a rearrangement of physical activities, but
rather that the *meaning* attached to the acts is itself changing so that such acts
appear possible. Again, as Gagnon and Simon observe, "the sequence of physical
activities is not the organizing factor in either sexual arousal or response, but it
is the meaning that is attributed to the activities themselves" (86). For Ruthie to
request that the father of her two children perform cunnilingus—an act, that at
least according to Ruthie, had never even occurred to her as an adolescent—the
meaning attributed to this particular activity has had to change dramatically
even if the father of her child refused her.

Amid these large-scale social shifts where there appear to be more cultural
venues for exploring and consuming sex, I found that older women in their
thirties and forties were able to narrate their erotic subjectivity and sexual histories with clarity, assurance, and conviction. For example, one thirty-five-year-
old mother of three small children talked about the power of her desires: "Sex is
powerful Debra. You know that? . . . I no want more children. I got three. But
when me boyfriend and me—you know when we together and we gettin' into
it, me not thinkin' about gettin' pregnant. Ya know what I mean? Den, later,
minutes later me thinkin', 'Oh my God, me not want to get pregnant.' Some
days at work me thinkin' how hard it is to raise three kids alone and dat night, I
mean dat very same night . . . me be foolin' around and me not thinkin'".

That the older women's sexual narratives are audacious and unrestrained doesn't surprise me. With maturity, many women gain confidence or lose inhibitions. Furthermore, the dynamics of my conversations with older women were different. Compared to my discussions with younger girls, my interviews with older women were more informal, perhaps because the age difference between us was less pronounced than it was with the girls. Older women may also perceive that there is less at stake in sharing their stories since they already have children, which unmistakably reveals that they have been sexually active. The fact that these women are more economically independent and have a great many more life experiences to draw upon, including sexual experiences, no doubt also figures into the dynamics of our interactions. When I spoke with women about their sexual histories and their notions of pleasure, I could hear in their stories a greater sense of entitlement to sexual gratification. The women, and particularly Eleanor and Ruthie, with whom I spent so much time, were eager to discuss how they actively and boldly look for and desire sexual pleasure.

For example, after Ruthie had vividly described her first and ongoing experiences with cunnilingus, Eleanor was desperate for her turn to talk. In her inimitable way, however, Eleanor changed the subject. She immediately began telling us about the first time her current boyfriend, the father of her youngest child, asked if he could "fuck her in the ass." Eleanor laughed, "I said mon what you crazy?" But despite acknowledging her own resistance, Eleanor proceeded to describe her first experience with anal sex in great detail. She stressed that she allowed her boyfriend to try this only after he put on a "greased" condom. "De secret," Eleanor insists, "is slow at first and you have to go poop before. Try to go two times dat day if you know you're goin' do it." She was looking at me earnestly and offering advice. But then she went right back to telling me how good it felt, saying, "I can feel it all de way, de way up here," and grabbing her belly. Eleanor lowered her voice as a tourist walked through the yard. We stopped talking for a moment, impatiently waiting for the tourist to disappear. As soon as the tourist was out of sight, Ruthie wasted no time in taking back the floor, telling us about her friend who likes to have orgasms but prefers not to have sexual intercourse: "She tell me dat she just has him grab her nipples and den she squeeze her legs together, just squeezin.'" Ruthie puts her hands on her breasts and crosses her legs and bends a bit at the waist. "You ever heard of dat, Debra?"

These type of conversations with older women indicate the extent to which sexual repertoires on Nevis are very much in flux: as women come in contact with new sexual activities, they experiment and explore. It is important to note that this ability to explore and more importantly, choose, a variety of sexual behaviors, differs a great deal not only from these women's individual coming-of-age experiences, but also from the overall Nevisian discourse about female sexuality. It is equally important to note that while some behaviors seem to have encountered a fuller acceptance in Nevisian culture, others are still marginalized.

Weeks later I was sitting with Ruthie and Eleanor under the shade of a breadfruit tree and Ruthie announced quite abruptly, "Let me tell you about de first time I was with a woman." Ruthie had our undivided attention. She began again after reading our faces, "Yeah, let me tell you." But before she could continue, Eleanor interjected, "Me never got to do dat." Eleanor's reaction was particularly interesting. At other times, she had displayed a great deal of discomfort in discussing her own same-sex experiences, and had disparaged my homoerotic interactions with Ruthie. But at this particular moment, Eleanor seemed downright disappointed that she had never had sex with another woman. Both Ruthie and I registered the reaction, and then Ruthie continued:

> She mixed girl from de states. She husband work at de Four Seasons. She me friend and she really friendly see. One night we at Eddy's dancin' and she real drunk and holdin' on me. She wearin' a tight skirt and heels, big heels. We leavin' and she gots to pee, so she just pull up she skirt and squat in de road. Den she take my hand and pull it to her pussy. Me thinkin', "What freak?" She drive a nice jeep and had two kids. Dis is before me had my man. So we go back to my house. Yeah dis is two years ago, yeah dat right. She so drunk, she pull off she skirt and she not wearin' panties. Den she take off she shirt. Oh she have sweet pussy. Real sweet and clean. She lickin' my pussy and my titties and oh my God, me thinkin', "Is dis really happenin'?" She do most of de work. Me do little. Next day I wake up and think, "Did dat really happen?" When she leave de island, she leave me a soft sexy robe and when me wear it, me think of she, oh so sweet.

Ruthie's story must be seen in context. Like Eleanor, when I first met Ruthie she was disparaging about same-sex relations. Months before she told me this story, I had asked her to share with me her opinions about homosexuality. At that point she wrinkled her nose in disdain, murmuring something about "freaks." Soon after that initial conversation about same-sex relations, however, I observed Ruthie looking over and admiring a neighbor of mine, a Swedish woman in her thirties. Unabashedly, Ruthie summoned me and while peering out the window and smiling she asked, "Who's that? She real sexy."

Just as interesting was what occurred a few days later while I was chatting with two rather trendy white Dutch female tourists who also happened to be Emmy award-winning producers for children's television in Holland. I was not surprised to learn that they had been harassed in St. Lucia by an elderly woman who mistook them for lesbians. When I spotted them in town earlier that day, I too assumed that they were partners. Ruthie was eavesdropping on the conversation by positioning herself near an open window. After the tourists left, Ruthie approached me with a smile and surmised, "The one with the long hair has a fat pussy." Pressing her lips together tightly Ruthie let out a low and deep but instantly recognizable sound of approval, "Hmmmm." I couldn't help but laugh, asking, "What do you mean? Does it mean she likes sex?" Eleanor and Ruthie attempted to respond to my query. Eleanor raised her voice and said, "No, Deb it means she has a fat pussy." I asked again, "What does it mean?" Evading my question, Eleanor responded, "I've always wanted a fat pussy."

I was confused by all of this, mostly because I had been sitting close to the Dutch tourist and never noticed anything particularly unusual about her physical appearance. Finally, Ruthie, a bit exasperated by my repeated requests, explained, "It's the kind of pussy men like; it's the kind of pussy you can grab." Ruthie inferred that the Dutch tourist had a "fat pussy" because of her apparent sex appeal and attractiveness. It was only months later, when I was reflecting on this set of stories, that it occurred to me that Ruthie's keen interest in my Swedish friend and then her later interest in the female Dutch tourist might have signaled her interest in them as potential erotic partners.[4]

The significance of Ruthie's same-sex desires and practices remain unclear to me, despite the significant amount of time I spent with her and Eleanor. It might be that, while same-sex eroticism has begun to be recognized as an activity that is not limited to preadolescent girls, such activities are yet to be fully accepted in Nevisian culture. The attitudes toward same-sex relations that I found among the girls bear this out, indicating the same sort of ambivalence toward same-sex relations as that expressed by the older women. At one point, when I asked a group of fifteen to sixteen-year-olds about the significance of same-sex practices, an outspoken girl explained: "In this school a girl might touch your breasts, but you don't think she's a lesbian. She might touch your behind or say, 'What's up sexy?' But it's *how much* they do it and how they look at you."

Such comments suggest that while all cultural groups mark off sexual practices as acceptable or unacceptable, thus influencing how people engage in sex, the rules are not always inflexible, particularly in a society that is undergoing a great deal of social change. Moreover, while sexual rules are socially learned and shared to some extent, there is not always a direct link between collective sexual rules and individual preferences and sexual styles. For example, some girls might experience sexual pleasure when, for instance, another female classmate inquires, "What's up sexy?" and touches her behind, while still another barely registers the interaction.

The detailed narratives of Ruthie and Eleanor clearly indicate the extent to which sexual repertoires are changing on Nevis. Many new sexual activities have been introduced to the culture and, not surprisingly, some have taken hold more tenaciously than others. Layered on top of these multifarious cultural shifts, Ruthie and Eleanor's stories also demonstrate how subjective notions of desire and pleasure are also fluid and changeable throughout an individual lifetime. As Vance (1984) writes: "The notion of sexual transformation and change occurring within an individual lifetime is a crucial one, because it forces us to give up the static picture of an unchanging sexual order" (14). Unfortunately, given the nature of this study, I am unable to explore with the girls who are now coming-of-age the changes in their own sexualities over time. But some girls anticipated such changes, like sixteen-year-old Felicia, who told me that "I really don't think that sex starts to feel good until you've been doing it for a while."

But this is yet another reason why the narratives of the older women were particularly valuable. Their recollections of changing sexual repertoires contributed valuable insight not only into their own experiences, but also provided a long-term glance at Nevisian cultural shifts. While sexual cultures are changing throughout the world, what's so unique about Nevis is how rapidly and radically change is occurring and how comprehensive those changes are, transforming Nevisian society, its sexual order, and Nevisians themselves.

CONSUMER SEXUAL SUBJECTIVITIES: IS PLEASURE AGENCY?

Older Nevisians assume that girls who consume too much American TV are bound to be promiscuous, given the liberal attitudes and norms that American TV supposedly sanctions. Moreover, girls who engage in sex with older men for money or commodities are considered immoral, and are held up by the older generation as examples of the moral decline of Nevisian society. Some girls, however, quite specifically and consciously, choose to resist these traditional discourses. One way that they do so, as I argued in chapter 6, is by actively engaging in commodity erotics, that is, they willingly exchange sex for access to desirable commodities and services. Girls who do so may be seen as immoral by traditional Nevisians, but they resist traditional discourse because those discourses do not serve their interest. In exchanging sex for consumer goods, girls experience pleasure by having their sexual and consumer desires satisfied.

As discussed previously, the image of an ideal Nevisian girl is of a girl who is academically successful, chaste, and churchgoing. By contrast, the potentially dangerous girl, with an unruly sexuality, is embedded in social scripts and gender ideology and is best expressed in a poem, entitled "Girl," by Jamaica Kincaid who writes at length about coming-of-age in the West Indies. Kincaid (1983) writes: "On Sunday try to walk like a lady and not like the slut you are so bent on becoming" (3). Many girls with whom I engaged would not retreat at this sentiment; rather, they might circulate their own gender ideology about sexually inactive girls.

In my attempt to uncover the changing sexual ideology on Nevis, I asked the girls in the focus group the following question: "Are there any Nevisian girls who turn eighteen and are virgins?" By asking this I was trying to get a sense of the social expectations and value of virginity. In answering, my informants were adamant and usually shouted out their responses. According to them, if there were girls on Nevis who had not had sexual intercourse by the time they turned eighteen, then it could be accounted for by one of the following explanations: 1) they could not get a boyfriend; 2) something was wrong with them; or 3) they were in "lockdown," or under strong parental supervision. The girls making such statements assume a lot about the nature of their peers who appear to be more sexually reserved. More interesting, however, is that when taken together, these statements suggest a type of sexual self-determination and sexual autonomy that is characteristic of consumer-oriented sexual subjectivities.

The globalized Nevisian consumer culture relies on the commodification of lifestyles, which promotes the idea of self-cultivation and sexual lifestyles—all of which implies sexual choice. As Anthony Giddens explains (1991), within consumer culture "freedom of individual choice becomes the enveloping framework of individual self-expression" (197). In this case, consumer culture and the structures of feeling that it generates has become so much a part of how Nevisian girls produce their sexual subjectivities and recognize themselves that it mediates how they view sexuality in general. The Nevisian girls have bought into the idea of individual freedom to the extent that they do not acknowledge the cultural constraints shaping the choices they make. The explanations for why a girl might still be a virgin at the age of eighteen imply that the sexually reticent peer is missing out on something. The girls assume that there has to be "something wrong with her." According to these girls, if there was not something wrong with a sexually inactive peer, then, given the opportunity, she would pursue or submit to sexual encounters, thus experiencing the pleasure on which she is missing out.

The girls' explanations as to why the eighteen-year-old is still a virgin are predicated on aspects of their own pleasure-seeking behavior, their sense of sexual entitlement and, to some extent, their belief that they are autonomous agents. The girls' belief that they can craft their own sexuality, completely independent from a larger cultural and economic context, is an expression of their new consumerist sexual subjectivities. By stressing this, I am not dismissing such formulations as false consciousness on behalf of the girls. I recognize that the girls' beliefs that they are in control of their lives are an indication of the effects of a growing consumer culture; however, there *are* moments when the girls do craft their own lives. The question here is *not* whether one can distinguish between the moments when the girls are agents crafting their own lives from the moments when they are subjects of a growing consumer culture. My point is that these disparate moments are indistinguishable because subjectivity is a fusion of the effects of both discursive regulation and practices of self-constitution. The reason for this open-ended and complex construction of sexual subjectivity is that when we talk about the regulating effects of discourse, we must understand that discursive formations are not closed systems (Foucault 1980). To illustrate this point, I want to come back to Loida, a fourteen-year-old girl who was rumored to have worn black thong panties for the busman and was roundly chastised by her peers for being so sexually aggressive.

Through extended interviews, I was able to assemble fragments of Loida's life. The first time I met with Loida she kept me waiting in the car in Charlestown while she went looking for a boy from Lynn Jeffers, the private secondary school on Nevis. Later, as I sat with Loida at a restaurant, she told me how she lived with her Nevisian father and stepmother and that her mother, who was from the Dominican Republic, abandoned her when she was two years old. Loida's mother now lives in Miami with her two of her children whom Loida has never met. While Loida reportedly has never had sexual intercourse, she seemed to have a lot of interactions, some that were of a sexual nature with older men. A week or two before we met, a man from her village, with whom she spent a great deal of time, had purchased a cell phone for her use, which she hid from her father. The day before we met, she watched an adult film with a twenty-seven-year-old man from her village. Loida explained that she visited this man, whom she considered her friend, in the basement of his mother's house. Together they watched pornography. She said she had a hard time watching the movie because her male friend continuously shouted throughout the movie explicit instructions to the male actor, such as "Fuck her; fuck her; don't be a one-minute man!" In the past, she has snuck out of her house on a school night to meet this same, older friend, while her father was in the states, to go out dancing and drinking at Sanddollars, a popular beach bar.

I asked Loida if she was in love with this man, to which she responded, "No. He has like two other girlfriends." I asked if she thought he was in love with her and she replied, "He says so all the time . . . and says dat when I'm ready he be de one." Later that day Loida asked if I would drop her off in town because she was hoping, again, to find the boy from the private school. As we approached the bus stop, we both noticed a group of teenage boys leaning against a building. The boy she hoped to see was not among them. I carefully watched Loida as she got out of my car. She never took her eyes off the group of boys. What impressed me was the way she stared fiercely at them, almost seductively, casting a strong and steady gaze in their direction, never wavering.

When provocatively dressed Nevisian girls, like Loida, aggressively seek out boys and men, as I often witnessed, they may be subverting existing religious discourses and traditional social structures, thus carving out a space for new subjectivities. Certainly, when Loida hides her newly acquired cell phone from her father, visits her male friend in his basement, and sneaks out of her house at night to go out dancing with him at a beach bar while risking being seen by adults who know her, she is acting in a deliberative manner. Nevertheless, I would argue that Loida and girls like her are not fully conscious of the social constraints that have determined the manner in which she constitutes her sexuality.

Despite the apparent agency of girls like Loida, their attempts at self-constitution are mired in, and determined, by intersecting discursive fields, including imported consumer culture and enduring local discourses. Jasmine, for example, a fifteen-year-old who took particular pride in dressing in the latest fashions, sported a tattoo that read "Baby" across her lower back, enjoyed dancing at the beach bars, had at least two boyfriends when I met her, carried a cell phone, and cultivated what Lila Abu-Lughod (1990) refers to as a "sexualized femininity associated with the world of consumerism" (50). Jasmine, Loida, and girls like them may be resisting the dominant Nevisian moral code, but they continue to be subject to traditional sexual discourses as well as subject to new and more global forms of subjection. Locating the girls' pleasures and agency in circumstances that appear exploitative and coercive is a challenging endeavor. Such examples reveal both the activities of self-constitution and experimentation in which Nevisian girls engage as well as the constraints of a larger, dynamic cultural system. What the girls' lives make clear is that to emphasize one without the other misses the point entirely.

PRODUCING SEXUAL SUBJECTIVITIES, PRODUCING EROTIC ENCOUNTERS

Before closing, it seems important to address what, if any, are the implications of conducting research on sexualities while simultaneously producing sexuality. Embedded in this question is the assumption that sexuality, both on the collective and individual level, is produced by and through myriad engagements, encounters, and processes.

One way to interpret this is to ask: How might the research process itself affect the production of girls' sexualities on Nevis? Throughout this chapter, as well as the ones preceding it, I have tried to stress the dynamic aspects of the production of sexualities, particularly the ways in which sexual discourses and the social and economic structures in which they are enacted are never static. My presence in the field undoubtedly influenced aspects of sexual discourse on Nevis. I view my presence in the field when I encouraged girls to reflect upon and articulate their desires, and to narrate their sexual histories, as no less influential as the mixed girl from the states with whom Ruthie had a sexual encounter. For example, by asking detailed questions about sexual histories and by getting girls to name their pleasures, I potentially influenced the way girls recognized, organized, or made sense of their sexualities. Merely asking questions encouraged the expression and articulation of some practices and desires, while possibly discouraging others. The in-depth interview process that the girls took part in was just one site throughout my research project that may have produced sexualities. Girls participating in focus groups, for instance, listened to their peers describe sexual acts in great detail. I cannot rule out the multiple ways that the focus groups might have sanctioned certain practices, incited desires, and influenced some girls to engage in new sexual acts, thus contributing to the production of girls' sexual subjectivities.

Additionally, the question of what it means to conduct research on sex while simultaneously producing sex suggests that there is an erotic potential that requires consideration. How does the erotic equation (Newton 1993) figure into ethnography? What sort of work did my erotic subjectivity do (Kulick 1995, 5)? And what does it mean to produce an ethnography that has the potential to produce erotic effects?

The erotic, like any other bodily, affective, or intellectual state, has the potential to condition how one conducts fieldwork. Does conducting research on sexuality increase the significance of the erotic domain in the field? In "Snatches of Conversation," Jane Gallop (1988), a feminist critical theorist, asserts that conducting research on sexuality always increases the significance of the erotic. Gallop insists: "[i]t is only the white-coat fantasy that allows us to imagine that either sexual activity or discourse about sexuality could ever be purified of subjective content. It is the same white-coat fantasy that subtends the belief that there can be a discourse about sexuality that is not sexual talk, a scientific discourse that is not vulgar but clean and sterile" (78).

Gallop makes her argument on the grounds that sexuality is "always bound up in emotional situations (and) intersubjectivity" (78). While there is merit in Gallop's assertion about the way sexuality is linked to intersubjectivity, her assumption that discourse about sexuality is always "sexual talk" is overstated. For example, during the in-depth interview process, when I talked to girls about sexual practices, it cannot be assumed that these instances were always sexual or erotic. In other words, while talking about sex may produce sex (Foucault 1978), such encounters are not *always, already sexual or erotic.* "Sexual excitation requires . . . a script that defines the setting . . . and the actors as potentially erotic" (Strong and Devault 1982, 134). With that said, Nevisian sexual culture is in flux and new erotic connotations are continually being produced; therefore, I cannot dismiss the possibility that throughout the course of my fieldwork, during varied engagements and encounters, including the ones with girls, there may have been erotically charged moments. Take, for example, my relationship with Ruthie. I often wondered if Ruthie's affection and her interest in our relationship stemmed from an erotic attraction or her desire and hope that our relationship might provide her with a greater access to goods and services, given my perceived status as a wealthy American. Of course, given the nature of commodity erotics, we cannot rule out the possibility that it was both, simultaneously. Yet, to assert as Jane Gallop (1988) does that modern sexology can never be "above the sexual register, or else it would lose its validity as a contact with the truth of sex" (87) would be to contradict a basic foundational tenet of this project, namely, the sheer contingency of the nature of sexualities. In other words, there is no "truth of sex" that Gallop insists upon. The irony here is that the primary purpose of "Snatches of Conversation" is to resist modern sexology's efforts to codify women's sexual desires and to assume a more polymorphous understanding of female sexual pleasures. But in the end, by arguing that all sex talk is sexual, Gallop evokes the same transcendent truth about sex that Foucault so eloquently disrupted.

I must admit that that does not rule out the possibility that the erotic domain has the potential to affect and did affect my research practices in certain instances. The difference between my argument and Gallop's (1988) is that, while there may be an erotic dimension to fieldwork, to assume that "talk about sex is [always] sexy" (86) misses the point about the discursive nature of sexualities and how sexuality is contingent upon social scripts.

It seems clear to me how my own erotic subjectivity figured into the ethnographic process. For instance, Ruthie displayed a sort of sexual candidness that I find attractive in individuals. But more than that, Ruthie's willingness to reflect upon and talk about her sexual history and feelings were intellectually productive as well. In terms of my own erotic subjectivity, this relationship produced a sort of intellectual satisfaction that is not always easily separated from my notion of the erotic.

In what other ways did my erotic subjectivity affect my work? Was I able to use my erotic subjectivity in an epistemologically productive way (Kulick 1995, 20)? Most anthropologists recognize the importance of establishing rapport in the field. My ability to establish rapport and to elicit sexual stories from Eleanor and Ruthie, for example, reflects my erotic subjectivity. The varying questions I raised, the way I organized questions and the tone in which they were asked, and my reactions to my informants' stories, for example, are all embedded in who I am as a person. In these instances, my erotic subjectivity in the field was productive. In other instances, that same subjectivity might have turned people off. What comes to mind here are the numerous comments I received about my appearance while conducting fieldwork.

Throughout my fieldwork, informants, friends, and strangers, commented on and offered unsolicited advice about my sense of fashion. My informants thought I needed a makeover. The local women with whom I worked closely teased me about not shaving my armpits even though they themselves sported hairy legs. Once, while visiting with Ruthie, I kicked off my shoes and she admonished me for not keeping up an old pedicure. On another occasion, a woman reportedly asked one of my informants, "How can she write about sex . . . what could she possible know about sex? She's so frumpy."

Lornette, a woman with whom I was friendly, confessed that before we got to know each other, she and another woman who worked at the restaurant where I ate everyday would make bets on what I'd be wearing. Lornette explained, "We wondered, Debra, if you'd be wearing your black or purple sundress. And then we made bets." This confession amused Lornette. The black and purple sundresses were part of my standard uniform. I had them made when I arrived in the tropics after I realized early on that I was overheating in my tan slacks and long-sleeved white blouse purchased at Banana Republic. These snippets of stories suggest that while the erotic equation needs to be factored into the dynamics of fieldwork, my own erotic subjectivity had the potential to be quite productive.

Inserting my own subjectivity into this ethnography points to a related question: What does it mean to craft an ethnography that has the potential to produce erotic effects? Ethnographies like this one, containing sexualized images and narratives, have the potential to produce or incite desires. Is this an erotic ethnography? If so, are there ethical considerations in producing such a document? For instance, would a potentially erotic ethnography be more likely to produce stereotypes about the individuals or culture portrayed? If the sexual narratives appear to be gratuitous to some, could it be that it is because they incite desires? If the narratives were less sexually descriptive would they convey the same meaning? The relevance of an ethnography on sexuality is its ability to convey the micro-scale processes of sexual lives, including erotic pleasures and sexual practices. A less sexually descriptive ethnography could not accomplish this and simultaneously translate dynamic and changing Nevisian sexualities. If ethnography is framed as an intersubjective process, which I believe it is, then, as my colleague and friend, Edgar Rivera Colon says, "It is always about fractious friendships that trade in various pleasures," including erotic pleasures. I share Colon's comment because it is a useful way to think about the possible erotic aspects of this ethnography as well as the possibilities for the erotic to condition fieldwork. It suggests that the relationships between the ethnographer and her subjects as well as those between the ethnographer and her readers have the potential to be unpredictable and unruly, but no less productive. The pedagogical value of such an erotic ethnography is that it forces readers to consider how they, like Nevisian girls, may be influenced—may come to embody—dimensions of sexual discourses.

Finally, concerning the data I have collected on Nevisian girls' sexualities that included the array of descriptions of sexual practices scrawled on scraps of paper from focus groups, detailed first love accounts, and confessions by girls about their consumption of pornography videos as well as the wide range of physical affection publicly displayed, I can say this, paraphrasing Vance (1984): none of it is the straightforward report about girls' sexual realities that I sometimes imagined that I had collected (11). Relying on sexual autobiographies and data collected through participant observation to understand subjective notions of pleasure and sexual realities has its drawbacks. Admittedly, even I, who spent a great deal of time with my informants, cannot read these as straightforward reports about girls' sexual realities or experiences.

These are examples of public presentations of sexual lives (Vance 1984, 10) which reveal a considerable amount about Nevisian sexual culture. I view the narratives as part of a self-fashioning process. As such, the narratives do not stand alone as transparent data on girls' sexualities. Sexual subjectivities are enacted in the narrative, through the process of crafting, telling, and revealing. In the production process, girls constitute their sexual subjectivities just as they would if they were pulling together a provocative outfit, adorning their hair with extensions, writing love letters to their boyfriends, flirting, or making out in the backseat of a Toyota. This is not to say that their stories are not "real"—that the details of their first accounts of sexual intercourse did not happen. Rather, the stories represent a sexual mosaic, fragments of their intimate desires and experiences which, when placed together alongside other girls' stories, translate into public discourses of pleasure.

CHAPTER 8

Conclusion

THIS EXAMINATION of sexual subjectivity to which my field-work on Nevis was dedicated has exposed (1) the complicated relationship between discourse and sexual agency, (2) the fluidity and malleability of sexuality within a culture and throughout a subject's life, and, perhaps most importantly, (3) sexuality as a site of multiple contradictions. But there is another aspect of sexuality that represents in many ways a subtext of this project, a subtext that will serve as a springboard for these final comments.

SEXUALITIES BEYOND THE NARRATIVE

Eight months after I had returned to New England, I received a lengthy correspondence from a woman named Helena, an expatriate living on Nevis. Helena's children had attended the same preschool as my twin daughters. In her letter, Helena describes how she had hired a friend's daughter, Cecilia, a thirteen-year-old girl from Charlestown, whom she had known since the girl was in primary school, to baby-sit for her two small children. Each time Helena tried to call home over the course of several hours to check in on her children, the phone line was busy. After awhile she gave up, assuming that one of her children had left the phone off the hook as they often did when they played with it. Later that night, when Helena returned home, young Cecilia, in response to Helena's queries, explained that she had been on the Internet most of the night. The next day, Helena noticed that a number of porn sites had been downloaded. About three weeks after the incident Helena read in the nation's newspaper, the *Observer*, that a thirteen-year-old girl was raped by a thirty-year-old neighbor, a man with whom the girl reportedly spent time. Although the girl's name was left out of the report, Helena learned from Cecilia's best friend that Cecilia was the girl about whom the article was written. In her letter to me, Helena reiterated how close she was to the girl and to the girl's mother, and then writes, "(they) never mentioned a thing to me, and I wouldn't mention it to them. They were at my house two days after the incident happened and acted completely the same as always, laughing and joking." Later, during that same visit, according to Helena, Cecilia asked if she could use the computer. Helena made up an excuse to discourage Cecilia from using the computer because she did not want to give Cecilia "access to more porn."[1]

I found Helena's story intriguing because it reminded me of the many times I learned about aspects of girls' sexualities "secondhand"—girls whose confidences I thought I had gained. Fifteen-year-old Sharmera, for example, told me in great detail how she sneaked around with her boyfriend and often left school to be alone with him at his house or on some secluded beach, but it was only from one of Sharmera's closest friends that I learned that Sharmera's mother's boyfriend had been molesting her, that he beat her on more than one occasion, and that police assistance had been sought. Similarly, fifteen-year-old Jasmine's cousin told me that Jasmine was "gang-raped" by several men one night at a beach bar. Just as Helena was taken aback by the mother and daughter's omission, I was surprised by what Jasmine and Sharmera had "left out" of their stories, especially given that both girls appeared to be candid about their sexual relationships with men. The girls' reticence in revealing certain events is every bit as significant as what they did, in fact, reveal. This is what I refer to as "sexuality beyond the narrative," or what Foucault calls, "the thing one declines to say, or is forbidden to name" (1978, 27).

The contents of Helena's correspondence suggest the edges of our social knowledge about sex. In other words, there are dimensions of sexuality that are hidden and unknowable not only to the anthropologist but to subjects as well. I am not suggesting that sex is not public or social, for it is eminently both. Nor am I suggesting that sex represents our deepest truth and that it requires interpretation (Foucault 1978). Rather, I am referring to the clandestine nature of sexualities, to the fact that there remain aspects of sexualities that are not always accessible. There are several possible reasons for this, and the first is quite obvious. For the most part, sex acts occur in "private" sites that are off-limits to anthropologists. Less obvious, perhaps, is that aspects of sexuality remain inaccessible because subjects may be unable, or unwilling, to narrate their sexual desires, erotic preferences, and sexual histories. To what do we attribute these silences or gaps?

To be certain, there are cultural silences around sex on Nevis that determine what is spoken about and what is not. For instance, sexual coercion or nonconsensual sex has only recently become a part of the Nevisian discourse of sexuality. This affects not only girls' experiences, but also their willingness to talk about those experiences. Furthermore, as the result of cultural taboos, embarrassment, and shame, it is conceivable that some girls did not reveal certain desires and practices. It is also quite possible that girls may have forgotten fragments of their sexual histories. And finally, girls may not be able to recognize the basis of their desires, thus hindering their own ability to narrate their erotic subjectivities.

These moments of silence, whether they represent collective or individual omissions, "function alongside the things said" (Foucault 1978, 27) and are equally as constitutive of sexual subjectivities as the sexual acts and erotic moments to which we have access. As Foucault writes, "there is no binary division to be made between what one says and what one does not say; we must try to determine the different ways of not saying such things. There is not one but many silences, and they are an integral part of the strategies that underlie and permeate discourses" (27). Whether it is the result of cultural omissions, that which is unobservable to the anthropologist, or the subject's own unwillingness or inability to narrate her subjectivity, there are, as Foucault reminds us, many silences—multiple acts, erotic moments, and sexual desires—that make up Nevisian girls' sexualities. Cecilia's secretive consumption of Internet porn, and her unacknowledged and unfortunate encounter with her thirty-year-old male neighbor are both integral to the constitution of her sexuality, however pleasurable or disturbing these instances may have been.

It is somewhat ironic that my closing remarks focus on the ways in which sexualities are concealed, particularly in the light of the fact that the focus of this project, namely, the social and economic determinants that shape the coming-of-age process on Nevis among adolescent girls, spotlights the exteriority of sexualities. This ethnography has attempted to demonstrate that sex "is not outside the boundaries of culture and society" (Weeks 1986, 33); however, when researching sexuality, there are aspects of sexuality that are difficult to access.

This point is effectively illustrated when one considers the subject of commodity erotics. I have argued that sexuality is compelled by, and compels, economics by theorizing that girls conflate commodity desire with sexual desire. Consequently, teasing apart commodity desire and sexual desire remains a challenge. I am reminded of a TV commercial in which a young man driving a new car pulls up to a curb in an urban setting. Seated at an outdoor café are three women, who look desirously at both the car and the driver, a man in his thirties. When he gets out of the car and enters the café, the women are still focused on the car. In the driver's facial expression there is an acknowledgment that the women desire the car rather than him. One would think the women just want a luxurious car, but their looks definitely appear to be indicative of sexual desire—indicated by their partially open mouths and by the way they move their tongues to the front of their teeth and/or clench their teeth.

This is a perfect example of commodity erotics, the collapsing of sexual desire with commodity desire or conflating sexual pleasure with pleasure received from commodities. Not only do commodity erotics illustrate the inaccessible aspects of sexuality, in the sense that both the anthropologist and the subject cannot always determine the source of desire or pleasure, but commodity erotics also complicates our understanding of the discursive production of sexual subjectivity by blurring the distinction between discourse and sexual agency. Sexual desire seems to be a conscious act, that is, the "conscious self" seems to be the source of desire (Lancaster 1996, 614), giving the appearance of agency. However, as I have argued, sexual desire does not always signal agency and is not always a willful or voluntary act. More to the point, commodity erotics discourages the automatic inference of agency when desire is in evidence. All of this leads me to ask: When the source of desire is ambiguous, do we grow suspicious of agency? The question itself assumes that if a girl understands or recognizes the basis for her desire, then she exerts greater control or greater capacity for agency, but this may not necessarily be the case. In terms of commodity erotics, whether commodity desire compels sexual desire or conversely, whether sexual desire, shaped by sexual scripts and discourses, compels commodity desire, we still need to attend to the social and economic determinants shaping the practices. Within the context of the growing Nevisian consumer culture, commodity desire and consumption do not signal "freedom" any more than sexual desire does.

BLURRING THE LINES: DISCOURSE AND AGENCY

So where do we locate "sexual freedom" among Nevisian girls? To return to a question posed in the introduction, are Nevisian girls ever "free" to act out their sexualities. Put simply, yes, as long as "freedom" is not conceptualized as the lack of social influences and constraints. The production of sexuality is paradoxical. While discourses constitute girls' sexualities, this does not prevent them from acting intentionally or to borrow from Ortner (2006, 144), acting on their own behalf to influence the course of events in their lives or in the lives of other individuals. [2] To illustrate this point, recall how sixteen-year-old Felicia was exposed to new sexual scripts on Black Entertainment Television, (BET) music videos. She described in detail how she learned "to be sexy." Her exposure to new bodies and new postures, as well as her exposure to the notion that if a man finds a girl desirable then this is more preferable than not, have shaped the production of Felicia's sexuality. Surely this is an instance in which her sexuality is shaped by sexual discourses. However, Felicia later explained that, in her estimation, the extent of her dependency on men's attention and affection waned in her adolescence. Is Felicia undoing the effect of the social norms that constituted her early teen years? Similarly, recall the shift in Nevisian sexual scripts in which cunnilingus appears to be a more acceptable practice. If, and when, a Nevisian girl expects and desires cunnilingus from her partner, do we interpret this as a sign of agency? Or is this an instance in which pleasure is used to control girls? At this point I want to stress, as Judith Butler does (1997), that we need to reframe the issue so that agency and discourse are not antithetical. To do this, I want to revisit a favorite Nevisian cultural pastime for adolescent girls, posing for pictures, which

provides a closure to this ethnography not only because it captures so precisely
aspects of the coming-of-age process among Nevisian girls but also it is a cultural practice that resists the dichotomy between discourse and agency.

As described in chapter 6, a favorite pastime among Nevisian girls is to
have their pictures taken by a photographer or to go to the photo lab in Nevis,
and then to compile the photos in albums and distribute the photographs to
their boyfriends or men whom they seek to attract. The most sought after
photographer was Dwight, a Nevisian man in his early thirties. Dwight was
well-known throughout Nevis for his artistic abilities and accomplishments.
He lived in a large house, owned at least two cars, and had won several awards
for men's pageants. Dwight was the most popular photographer for girls who
needed publicity photographs for various talent shows and pageants, including
the annual Miss Culturama. I was told by at least two women, one of whom
was competing for the title of Miss Culturama 2003, that Dwight was seen as
an "image maker." Ellen explained, "He's the man you go to when you need
your best self."

On a number of occasions, girls proudly showed me their albums. Many
of the images and poses were strikingly similar. Girls often had photos of
themselves smartly dressed in the latest fashions, shots of themselves dressed in
sport jerseys and shorts, as well as photographs of themselves in swimsuits.
When I met sixteen- year-old Tamara, she described how she had been posing
for photographs since she was thirteen years old. Leafing through her photos,
I recall being taken aback by an image of Tamara at fourteen wearing a skimpy
string bikini. She was lying on the beach, close to the water's edge. Her pose
was similar to an image that might be found in the *Sports Illustrated* swimsuit
edition. She was rolled over on her side with her right hip supporting most of
her weight. Her left knee was bent and with her elbow propped up, her head
rested in her right hand. Her other hand was positioned on her hip. Her
mouth was parted slightly, her chin tilted downward, and her eyes peered up
at the camera. Tamara had several photographs of this pose or slight variations
of it that she had given to her boyfriend. Tamara claimed that the image of her
on her stomach, lying in the sand, was "definitely the sexiest photograph." She
described herself as "hot." Tamara was proud of her photographs. I was struck
by the way she studied the images as if seeing them for the first time. Holding
a photograph of herself in which she was dressed wearing a Lakers' sports jersey and matching purple and gold ribbons in her hair she explained, "I give a
copy of dis one to a boy in my class. Me knows he showed it around. His
cousin is me friend; she tell me so. Me look good. I look good in the Lakers
colors. Nobody else would find purple and gold ribbon like dis. . . . I try on
lots of fashions before I pick dis one. Me look real good in dis one."

Later that day I asked Ruthie to tell me more about this pastime among
the girls. She explained: "When I was sixteen years old, me had no kids. So

when me get me paycheck me run to have me picture taken and give it to me boyfriend even if he don't want it. Me still give it to he. I was just like de silly girls, into clothes and picture-takin.' Waste me money. De girls today, dey just like me. Dey figure dey love de man and he loves dem. Dey figure he wants de picture, so dey waste dere money. When dey young, dey stupid. Dey spend dere money on pictures, but den dey give de man a picture and he throw it out or tear it up, because he got so many dam women."

However, not all the girls I met who engaged in this pastime did so with the intent of sharing the photographs with their boyfriends. Felicia enjoyed getting her pictures taken and was proud of her extensive photograph collection. She was also very much involved in modeling. Here she describes her interest in "picture-taking":

> Most of the pictures that I have posed for in my life were usually taken by my family and friends. . . . I love picture-taking. . . . I've always had extraordinarily high self-esteem so people would always find me posing naturally. My first "caught on film pose" was when I was two years old. . . . [M]y first modeling experience was when I was five years old. I modeled with the Miss Culture Queen. . . . For the most part, when I take pictures they are taken for family albums or to put in albums for my girlfriends. I've never taken a picture with the intention of giving it to a boyfriend because I've always been really cautious about that sort of stuff. I always think that if I take a picture for guy he can do something horrible to it . . . with technology or something like that . . . or he'd want to put it on a wall to celebrate his conquests. So I just don't do it. I have a lot of pictures of myself ranging from when I was in diapers to now. Every time I look at the pictures of when I was younger, I always say to myself "You think you're hot stuff," because I always used to pose like I was some kind of model and even when I continued modeling as I got older, when I was on stage I was always posing even if someone tried to catch me off guard with a camera it still came out like I was posing for it. Nevis girls tend to take a lot of pictures at photo labs for the purpose of giving them to boyfriends. I guess they just feel like when they take pictures they are kind of living a celebrity type life, I guess, since that's where a lot of influence comes from. I don't think that many older women do this too. There are a few that behave like they are still in high school but not too many . . . even younger girls in Primary school get dressed up and go to the photo lab to take pictures.

Clearly Felicia's comments point to her own pleasure and self-confidence. Felicia's self-reflexive remarks also serve as an example of the differences among the girls who engage in this practice. Unlike Tamara, Felicia does not use photographs of herself to lure men. However, it is apparent from Felicia's comments that she is invested in looking good and performing. This perform-ance, which is at the center of the picture-taking pastime among Nevisian girls, is an expression of the coming-of age process, a subject I will return to shortly.

In late May, I went to Dwight's home, accompanying a Swedish woman with whom I had become friendly. She wanted Dwight to take pictures of her so that she could give one to her husband and one to her Nevisian lover. She had come prepared with an image torn out of the women's magazine that she wanted Dwight to use as inspiration. When my friend introduced me to Dwight, he said, "You must be the white woman talking to the girls about sex." When I asked him how he had heard of me, he explained that several schoolgirls whom he had known had mentioned that they had met me and were "taking part in my book about Nevis." While my friend posed for her pictures, I waited in his study where there were two Dell computers. The screen savers on both computers changed every sixty seconds or so, and the images were very similar to a pictorial spread that might be found in *Penthouse* magazine. All of the images were frontal nudes of young women. I surveyed the images wondering if I might spot one of the schoolgirls I had known. I learned from Dwight that many of the images I had seen were downloaded from the Internet; others he had taken of girls on the island. Later that day, I visited Ruthie and Eleanor. When I told them that I had come from Dwight's home, Ruthie proclaimed, "What a freak!" Without explaining what she meant by this comment, she proceeded to tell me that "he well-hung." When I asked her how she knew this, she casually explained how when she sees him in town or on the street, she sometimes "rubs he dick over he pants." Upon hearing this, I exclaimed in disbelief, "You do what?" A little exasperated and as if I were hard of hearing, Ruthie looked at me with disdain, wrinkled up her nose, and said loudly, "He my buddy." As she says this, she raised one arm off to the side and began making circular motions in the air, demonstrating how she caressed his groin area. "He like dat," Ruthie assured me. While Ruthie was talking, I noticed Eleanor studying my display of disbelief. When Ruthie finished, Eleanor, commented, "Deb, no say me so, but it all about sex here on Nevis."[3]

Why close this ethnography with a story about schoolgirls, picture-taking, a photographer's proclivity for female nudes, and a thirty-something woman's display of what I would describe as excessive sociability? First, Ruthie's admission that she caresses Dwight in public is a playful flirtation that may or may not obligate Dwight in some way to Ruthie. But more impor-tantly, it represents a type of sexuality that is acceptable within Nevisian soci-ety and one that is not hidden from girls of all ages. This story of schoolgirls and picture-taking also speaks to a number of issues related to the production of sexualities. I tell the story about the schoolgirls and their picture-taking pastime because it serves as an example of a deliberate display of one's persona and perhaps is an opportunity to craft one's sexuality. Getting dressed up in an array of outfits, including skimpy bikinis, may not be an overt sexual act; nevertheless, one is producing a certain subjectivity that articulates with sexuality.

Part of what is happening when girls get their pictures taken and then paste them in albums or give them to their boyfriends or girlfriends, is that they are, in a Foucauldian sense, recognizing themselves as subjects, as desiring subjects. However, the pastime also exposes the paradoxical nature of the formation of sexual subjectivity. When a girl poses for a photographer like Dwight, who has a penchant for a certain type of female sexuality, she is attempting to project a certain image, perform a type of sexuality and/or femininity, and experiment with various personas. I would argue that, among Nevisian girls, picture-taking is linked to the production of subjectivity and it is both, to borrow from Henrietta Moore (2001) "performative and structured, conforming and innovative" (265). In other words, it is suggestive of both cultural control and self-determination. A girl thinks that she has control over what the camera is going to see or more to the point, the type of persona that will be captured and projected, but the persona she attempts to don remains scripted as an enactment of social norms or what it means to be a girl on Nevis. Picture-taking and the pastime of compiling photos in an album and/or sharing them with friends and paramours also suggests that one wants to be noticed and observed. As one local photographer said, "It is like asking the world to relate to you or to observe you, and then believing that you have a certain amount of control over that projection." The photographer's insight hints at how picture-taking is symbolic of the coming-of-age process on Nevis in that it involves the "production of self as an object in the world" (Hall 1996, 13).

How else does picture-taking as a pastime among schoolgirls on Nevis encapsulate aspects of the coming-of-age process? As just emphasized; the pastime is an expression of self-fashioning and experimentation within the constraints of a larger dynamic cultural system. The girls are not "free" to don any persona, just as they are not completely "free" to produce their own sexualities as adolescent girls. In addition, there is a "theatrical bent" to this practice, in the sense that it is an exaggeration of the presentation of the self. Girls want to project their "best selves," and they wear different outfits as if they are trying out different personas. In the process, like the coming-of-age process itself, the girls attempt to "invent" themselves. The paradox here is that as innovative as the process appears to be in terms of the girls' experiences, the girls are still reproducing social scripts. These photographs emphasize sexuality; girls are not donning conservative evening wear nor are they wearing their Sunday best. It is clear that the photographs function to display the body in order to increase desirability, and thus marketability. Within a system of sexual-economic exchange, picture-taking makes perfect sense. When girls take pictures of their "best selves," they make themselves appear more valuable—they increase their capital, so to speak. But what do the girls gain by posing for a photographer, compiling pictures, and then giving them to their boyfriends or prospective boyfriends?

When girls come-of-age on Nevis, they enter a cultural milieu in which "twelve is lunchtime." Recall that this is a cultural expression identifying the social category in which girls find themselves viewed as sexual objects. In a system of sexual-economic exchange where girls are sexualized and men are encouraged to have multiple partners, a girl's currency is her subordinate sexual status. Might the opportunity to make herself appear more valuable present her with the opportunities for greater social and economic rewards, perhaps even the potential to mitigate her subordinate status?[4] So often, the practice of trading sex for access to goods and services is seen as a demeaning act, as a self-destructive act, but on Nevis, in the context of a growing consumer society, when girls exchange sex for access to goods and services, is it possible that the girls are doing more than just reiterating the conditions of their subordination?

How do we reconcile the apparent contradictions embedded in these concluding remarks? At the beginning of this conclusion, I argued that effects of commodity erotics might diminish the capacity for agency, in the sense that girls are not conscious of the source of their desires. Now I am suggesting that the acquisition of agency and power result from agreeing to subordination; in other words, if girls play by the cultural rules, they may increase their opportunity to attain social and economic capital. So, do commodity erotics erode agency or do they help shape it? Moore (2001) helps to reconcile the two possibilities: "Subjectivity is itself a linking term, a borderland product, the result of individual intention and agency in contact with social, economic, and political discourses, practices and institutions. The nature of the contact varies: critical self-reflection, embodied performativity, outright resistance, easy compliance, impassioned engagement. All individuals are capable of all these forms of 'contact,' simultaneously and serially, consciously, subconsciously, and unconsciously (264)."

In my own work with Nevisian women and girls, it is clear that their sexual subjectivities are as open and multifarious as the discourses in which they are embedded. Partially hegemonic, partially liberating, the production of Nevisian female sexualities is always shifting and changing, ambivalent and expansive.

Notes

Chapter 1   Introduction

1. See Becker (1995); Burbank, Whiting, and Whiting (1988); Dietrich (1998); Herdt (1987); Herdt and Boxer (1996); Schensul (1998); Herdt and Leavitt (1998); Malinowski [1929] 1987; Mead [1928] 1967; Moffat (1989); and Nichter (2000) for their important works on adolescent sexuality.
2. For an understanding of sex and sexuality as socially constructed see Herdt (1987); Foucault (1978); Vance (1989); and Weeks (1977).
3. I borrow this line of questioning from Hall (1971) who reminds us that we can also inquire into how subjective meanings and intentions, under certain determining conditions, come to generate and shape the structures of the sexual lives of Nevisian girls. Conversely, we need to question how structures of sexual life shape the interior spaces of girls' consciousness as they articulate with sexual practices and desires producing girls' sexual subjectivities (98 cited in Grossberg 1997, 211).
4. Furthermore, as Moore (2001) argues, theorizing the production of subjectivity requires a conceptual relationship of "agency, motivation, and intentions to hegemonic discourses, distributions of discursive power, and institutionalization" (263). Moore's position, like Hall's, offers a way to theorize sexual subjectivity that avoids the trap of reinstituting the humanist subject, which is premised on the notion of a self-autonomous individual, while at the same time avoiding a radical structural interpretation that would disavow the subject and subjectivity almost entirely (cf. Althusser 1970, 1971).
5. For additional discussions on the relationship between culture and the individual or ideas related to the formation of subjectivity see Giddens (1979), Ortner ([1984] 1994, 2006), and Sahlins (1981). Bandura (1977), a leading social psychologist, has been writing about the relationship between "free-will" and "determination" since the 1970s. Judith Butler's performativity theory offers a variation on this theme as well (1990, 1993, 1997).
6. My understanding of sexual subjectivity draws on Foucault's (1978, 1980, 1985, 1988) notion of subject formation. Foucault offers a discursive understanding of the subject—namely, he suggests that social discourses produce subjectivity. For Foucault, discourse constitutes the subject as much as the subject's understanding of self-reflexivity, that is, the means by which the subject comes to recognize herself (1982, 212). The emphasis in his work is on the *process* of recognition. In terms of sexual subjectivity, Foucault's work allows me to ask questions such as these about the nature of sexuality: What are the global/local discourses shaping Nevisian girls' desires and practices? What are the discourses that define Nevisian girls' notions of pleasure? Asking such questions is critical because it provides an understanding of subject formation as a dynamic process.
7. My understanding of sexuality has also been informed by Gagnon and Simon's (1973) notion of sexual scripts.

8. World Bank (2006). St Kitts and Nevis, in *ICT at a Glance Tables*.
9. Douglas (Address, Board of Governors, Annual meetings, Washington, DC, 2005).
10. See in particular Farmer (1992); De Zalduondo and Bernard (1995); and Lancaster and Di Leonardo (1997).
11. For an in-depth study on Caribbean life and consumption see Miller's (1994) *Modernity*.
12. I should reiterate that in terms of my purposes, the GDP is not a measure of economic freedom; rather it is used to stress the increasing role of consumption in the daily lives of Nevisians.
13. See especially Morris (1994); and Parker (1991).
14. See Brennan (2004); Clarke (1997); Jackson (1997); Kelsky (1996); Manderson and Jolly (1997); Mankekar and Schein (2004); Morris (1994); Puar (2001); Povinelli and Chauncey (1999); Schein (1999); and Wilson (1988).
15. *Thinking Sexuality Transnationally*, for example, is a collection of essays in the *Journal of Lesbian and Gay Studies* that spotlights the impact of globalization on sexuality. In the opening essay the anthropologist Povinelli and the historian Chauncey (1999) stress that while the world has always been interconnected, "the scale, intensity, and density" (440) in today's world have qualitatively altered cultural production. They draw on Harvey's (1989) notion of "space-time compression" to conceptualize the "spatiotemporaral effects" of modernity and its technologies and to critique earlier studies of sexuality and of globalization that do not consider the relationship of globalization to sexualities. Povinelli and Chauncey assert that, in the past, ethnographers situated sexuality in a given cultural context and that the typical focus on the external social forms influencing sexualities was overly regional (444). Povinelli and Chauncey maintain that early globalization studies were similarly limited: they "often proceed[ed] as if tracking and mapping the facticity of economic, population, and population flows, circuits, and linkages were sufficient to account for current cultural forms and subjective interiorities"(445).
16. See especially Mankekar and Schein (2004) for a lengthy treatment of the subject of media and sexuality.
17. For some, the focus on commodity consumption might be interpreted as deploying a liberal understanding of economics or capitalism. By that I mean, an understanding of capitalism that privileges the role of the individual and views the market as a site of liberation, freedom, or individual choice. This ethnography refuses to celebrate the market just as it refuses to demonize it. Rather, the focus remains on the contradictory effects of consumer culture, more precisely, how this complicates our understanding of "individual freedom."
18. This line of inquiry is inspired by a question posed by Lancaster (1995) in which he asks whether one could "distinguish, rigorously and a priori, between Eros and economics, desire and consumption, love and political economy?" (144).
19. There are many important works, that explore the complicated relationship between sexuality and economics (cf. Brennan 2004; de Zalduondo and Bernard 1995; Farmer 1992; Kulick 1998; and Lancaster and Di Leonardo 1997). Brennan (2004) offers a richly crafted ethnography on the intimate lives of Dominican and Haitian women who work in the sex tourism industry in the Dominican Republic. This work is of significance because of the way in which it challenges conventional notions of sex workers as powerless victims. Instead, it raises important questions about the nature of sexual exploitation and individual agency.

    Lancaster's *Life Is Hard* (1992) is one of the best full-length ethnographic examples of how sexuality (practices and desires) can be conceived of as a matter intricately connected to political economy. Lancaster's reinterpretation of Marx shows how sexuality, colorism, and machismo are irreducible to either the base or superstructure and that they have both symbolic and material consequences (287) which structure social inequalities.

Kulick's *Travesti* (1998) by far the most engaging ethnography on sexuality, examines the lives of Brazilian men who live as women and exchange sex for money. While many ethnographies purport to be about sexuality, they are really about gender. Kulick's ethnography, however, is about both. Among its strengths, it offers a vibrant analysis of the pleasures of sexual-economic exchange.

In their work on Haiti, de Zalduondo and Bernard (1995) also posit sex as a "resource with both symbolic and material value" (157). In Haiti, as elsewhere in the Caribbean, conjugal unions are based on economic exchange: an exchange of male economic input for female household labor and sexual access (166). While men and women may also look to each other for affection, according to de Zalduondo and Bernard, this "does not detract from the salience of sexual-economic exchange as the organizing metaphor for normative sexual relations" (167). The researchers also assert that much of the literature on sex and economics focuses almost exclusively on survival sex, which turns attention away from the myriad economic conditions affecting sexual practices across a population (159).

20. See Schein (1999) and Mankekar (2004) for the original use of the phrase "commodity erotics."

21. This appears to resemble Freud's notion of sexual fetish. The difference, however, is that Mankekar's formulation includes a more diffused notion of erotic significance. Recall that, according to Freud, sexual arousal is tied to a particular object.

22. With the exception of public officials and government employees, including school teachers all of the names used in this study are pseudonyms.

23. See Chambers and Chevannes (1991); E. Clarke (1957); Freeman (1997, 2000); Mintz (1974, 1985); Safa (1995); Senior (1991); Slater (1977); Smith (1956, 1971, 1988).

24. The idea that women's sexuality might be influenced by desires and the erotic is hinted at by Chambers and Chevannes (1991) who suggest that many women will maintain outside relationships not only to help offset economic needs but also to meet "sexual needs" that might be neglected in the primary relationship. There are also other studies that engage Caribbean sexualities, focusing mainly on heteronormative constructions of sexuality linked to gender, kinship, the state and tourism (Alexander 1991, 1994; Austin-Broos 1984; Chevannes 1993; Cohen 1995; Cohen and Mascia-Lees 1993; Davenport 1961; MacCormack and Draper 1987; Smith 1995). There is a valuable collection of essays on tourism and sex work in the Caribbean (Kempadoo 1999). There is, however, an uneven silence surrounding the subject of same-sex practices in Caribbean anthropology, reflecting not only the anthropology's general legacy of silence (Weston 1998) but also the negativity about same-sex relations that reportedly dominates the region (Behar 1994; Chevannes 1993; E. Clarke 1957; Slater 1977). Murray's (1995) dissertation on Martinique society, the first of its kind, offers rich ethnographic data on the courtship practices of gay men and a unique discussion of how race figures into homosexual narratives of desire. Puar (2001) offers fresh insight into transnational sexualities in her study on the Trinidadian circuits of globalization and how they may affect what it means to be gay and lesbian in Trinidad.

25. See Kempadoo (2004) for her analysis of twentieth-century studies of Caribbean family life. Kempadoo writes that there is a tendency to characterize sexuality in such a way that men's sexuality is linked to "pleasure, identity, and power" while women's sexuality is linked to "procreation, money, and status" (19).

26. See Brennan's ethnography, *What's Love Got to Do With it?* (2004) for a discussion on how sexual-economic exchange can be formulated as an advancement strategy.

27. My focus on both violence and pleasure is influenced by a key debate in feminist scholarship. *Pleasure and Danger* (1984) and *The Powers of Desire* (1983) represent an important shift in the feminist literature on sex. More than twenty years ago when

these two volumes were published they represented a radical attempt to disrupt the more conservative feminist scholarship on rape, pornography, and the "sex as violence" narrative that characterized much of the 1970s literature on sex, particularly the major works of Dworkin. Vance (1984) argues in her introduction to *Pleasure and Danger* that the anti-pornography movement fed into the dominant gender ideology of male as aggressor and female as passive—one that denies female desire or renders it suspect. Rubin's (1984) "Thinking Sex" article, appearing in the collection, is considered to be a watershed piece. Rubin takes a radical stand, arguing that there are limits to feminist analysis, particularly in its inability to theorize sex. Like Vance, Rubin maintains that feminists have reproduced the sex negative tradition, which has hindered our understanding of sexual diversity. Moreover, the feminist view of "sexuality as a derivation of gender" (308) or reducible to gender, fails to distinguish between sexual practice, gender and desire.

28. See Gilman (1985) for a historical reading of black sexuality.

29. It is important to stress that the latter two groups of scholars are not directly opposed to one another, but for the purposes of discussion I juxtapose them to expose the tensions and complications of analyzing postcolonial girls' sexual subjectivities.

30. I was fairly consistent in the manner in which I introduced myself. Upon meeting new people, I explained, "I am an American anthropologist and I have traveled to Nevis to study girls, how girls come-of-age, and how the recent influence of consumer culture is changing Nevisian society." I also explained that I was affiliated with Rutgers University. Depending on the background of the individual, I offered more or less of an explanation relative to research protocol. For example, if I was speaking with a local doctor or a representative from the Department of Education, I explained in great detail how I had gained permission to conduct research from the Hon. Earl Martin, Minister of Health and Environment. I also offered a brief explanation of human subjects protocol. Regardless of with whom I was speaking, I always explained that I would be living on Nevis for close to seven months and that I had brought with me my two daughters who would be attending a local preschool. Finally, I made it clear that I hoped to have the opportunity to interview and work with a variety of people and that whatever I wrote in the future would be shared with members of the community. After I had spent time with people, whether in their homes, on the streets, at social events, or in the schools, if they appeared interested I would try to explain how my research findings might benefit people living on Nevis and what role my research played in terms of my own career objectives. Many times, the girls with whom I engaged had a difficult time understanding why I would want to study Nevisian girls and why, if I were going to write a book, Americans would want to read about girls from Nevis. This usually involved a lengthy discussion about the nature and scope of anthropology that I imagine many, if not all of my colleagues, have had at one time or another while conducting fieldwork.

31. This beauty contest takes place during Culturama week. This is an annual festival on Nevis comprised of many events, including pageants, Calypso competitions, parades, concerts, and dances. It is held in celebration of Emancipation Day in August.

32. "Beach boys" are local men who associate informally with tourists. Often the men will meet female tourists at a beach bar and establish a short-term sexual relationship and in exchange the female tourist might pay for meals, drinks, hotel accommodations, and transportation.

33. See Dell's (2005) interesting discussion of sexuality and national identity in postcolonial India. She offers an important insight into what she calls the perception of "newness" of sexual practices. In postcolonial India oral sex and anal sex are now associated with "English" sex or foreigners as the result of the influx and consumption of imported films. Dell writes, "oral and anal sex are not new in India, such 'newness' is an invented absence" (188) that reflects the nation's desire to strengthen

its identity using sexual practices as indicators of true national identity in India. Dell draws on a rich tradition of paintings, books, and temple sculptures to craft her argument, stating that these sexual practices have been depicted for centuries in India. My point here is not to draw the same set of conclusions about Nevisian society. On the contrary, I remain convinced that there is something new happening on Nevis regarding the introduction of new sexual practices over the past ten years. Again, this is not to say that Nevisians did not engage in oral or anal sex prior to the availability of HBO or the great influx of media images and pornography, but that rather these practices were not dominant and generally accepted among Nevisians, nor were there multiple cultural references made about oral and anal sex circulating on television, in music videos, in public health programs, within pornography, or in woman's magazines.

34. There are multiple shifts in the theoretical approaches used throughout this book. Some might note a disjuncture in the ethnography produced by a shift from a more poststructuralist approach to one that is less so. I am the first to admit that I have always been a bit theoretically promiscuous. I learned from reading Hall that we do not need to be card-carrying Marxists or utter Foucauldian devotees. Conceptualizing sexuality on multiple analytic levels—from global flows to intimate sexual practices requires that we use a variety of theoretical approaches. Depending on the phenomenon being described or explained, particular theoretical perspectives may generate greater or sharper focus and hence more insight. With that said, focus groups are not typically used by anthropologists adopting a more traditional poststructuralist approach. In light of Foucault's understanding of the teacher-student relationships, focus groups would be regarded as "knowledge relationships" or as mechanisms of power, ways to extract the "truth of sex." I view focus groups or small group interviews as an acceptable method for working with adolescents. Bringing teens together in small groups proved to be a productive method for establishing rapport, and for getting the girls to open up and discuss sensitive matters. These small groups also served as a useful way to build contacts with other girls.

35. I used a survey to gather data from approximately 153 Nevisian girls ranging in age from twelve to seventeen. The guidance counselors gave me access to their health classes and home economics classes. All fifteen girls attending Lynn Jeffers completed the survey. The questionnaire was designed to collect data on age, education, sexual knowledge, attitudes and practices, contraceptive experience, religiosity, media/TV consumption, TV viewing habits and patterns, and family life. The surveys were administered anonymously in the school setting. With the exception of the students at Lynn Jeffers, I presented it to each age group separately and generally had success at getting girls in all schools and age groups to fill out the survey in the allotted time.

36. That I engaged in a form of sexual-economic exchange with the girls, namely providing the girls who participated in the study with rides and meals, will be taken up in chapter 7.

CHAPTER 2   GLOBALIZING NEVIS

1. In recent years globalization theories (Featherstone 1990; Hannerz 1996; and Harvey 1989) have been critiqued because of how the "global" and "local" have been conceptualized—with local cultures formulated as separate and distinct from the global. Critics of these models have argued that there needs to be more of a focus on the way societies are mutually constitutive, focusing instead on linkages and flows and how global flows affect the daily lives of people. My own representation of Nevis might be similarly critiqued because of the way it reproduces the global/local divide that Caribbeanists such as Basch, Glick-Schiller, and Szanton-Blanc (1994) and

Freeman (2001) have challenged. This chapter might be interpreted in simplistic terms as a story about the impact of globalization on Nevis, particularly in light of how it focuses on recent changes within Nevisian society. The fact is, Nevis has been a global society since the 1600s. To limit the scope of this ethnography and to emphasize the extent of the recent radical changes I have elected to focus on the last twenty years, intentionally stressing the changes in technology, infrastructure, and educational reforms, as well as the social and economic changes brought about by the rise in consumer culture. Anytime an anthropologist offers what appears to be a "before and after picture" he or she runs the risk that others might interpret the story as a modernization story. The invocation of change in this ethnography does not assume a "fixed past" nor is it suggestive of a specific trajectory.

2. By using the phrase "subsistence living," I do not mean to imply that Nevisians were completely disengaged from local, regional, or international markets. As we shall see, prior to the 1980s, migration was prevalent, which not only meant that some Nevisians were employed as wage laborers within the Caribbean, as well as in the United States and England, but that commercial goods and cash were often sent from overseas to Nevisians who remained at home. I am using the phrase "subsistence living" to connote the fact that, prior to the 1980s, Nevisians relied heavily on cultivating small gardens and tending to goats, chickens, and pigs as part of their subsistence pattern as opposed to being tied to, and dependent upon, consumer goods as they are now.

3. See Olwig (1993) for a lengthy discussion of the economic conditions of Nevis from the 1840s, following Emancipation, to the 1980s.

4. See Richardson (1983) for discussion on Nevisian migration patterns. He maintains that from early on, Nevisians migrated throughout the region to other islands to work in various industries. At the turn of the century, the Panama Canal and the Bermuda naval docks attracted large numbers of both Kittician and Nevisian men and women. From the 1900 to the 1930s, with American capital and interests, Cuba and the Dominican Republic modernized their sugar industry, drawing labor from all over the Caribbean including the smaller Leeward Islands. In the 1930s economic depression reduced U.S. investment in the Caribbean, having a huge impact on the region by reducing employment opportunities. By the beginning of World War II, the U.S. military bases in British Guiana, Antigua, and Chaguaramas employed a large number of West Indians from around the region. By the 1950s, there was a massive migration throughout the Caribbean to the United Kingdom. It is estimated that over a ten year period, from 1951 to 1961, close to 280,000 people moved to the UK. In the 1960s, Caribbean migrants flowed north to the east coast of the United States and Canada, and for the past forty years, with an increase in foreign capital investment in the tourist industry, particularly in the U.S. Virgin Islands, West Indian migration patterns have become more regionalized (Richardson 1983, 20–23). The history of migration patterns, as well as contemporary ones, illustrates that Nevis has continuously been influenced by regional and global political and economic events. Migration has not only served as a "mobile livelihood system" (1983, 6), economically sustaining migrants, but it also sustained families and individuals who remained on Nevis. There are, of course, paradoxical effects of migration. On the one hand, migration offers a legitimate way to sustain families that remain behind and whose livelihoods depend on remittances. On the other hand, given that for the most part, young, educated, and perhaps the more enterprising individuals migrate (Weisburd 1984, 34), it depletes the island of laborers, manpower, and locally based entrepreneurial activities.

5. Most of the early schools were built by local churches, such as the Charlestown Methodist Church. In 1916 the Nevisian government took over administering the schools. The Charlestown Secondary School was built with government funds in 1950 and constructed out of reinforced concrete. The first teacher on the island to

offer secondary education and training that would prepare students to earn the Cambridge School certificate was Miss Helen Bridgewater, the daughter of a Methodist minister (Robinson 2000).

6. These relationships might be considered "romance tourism" in that the emphasis is placed on "courtship rather than the exchange of money and sex" (Pruitt and LaFont 1995, 423). Recent studies of sex work in the Caribbean (c.f. Brennan 2004; Kempadoo 2001; and Pruitt and LaFont 1995) have focused on the meanings and the experiences of these relationships as defined by the participants. Pruitt and LaFont write, "the term romance tourism is used to distinguish these relationships from those of sex tourism . . . (T)he fact that it is women rather than men traveling in pursuit of relationships is central in their nature. Gender is constitutive of the relationship, not ancillary to it" (423); as such, "these relationships are constructed through a discourse of romance . . . an emotional involvement usually not present in sex tourism" (423). With that said, it is important to stress that while romance is the lens with which the relationships are constructed, these relationships nevertheless represent one form of sexual-economic exchange that are not dissimilar to what takes place among Nevisian girls and older men.

7. It should be noted that skin color on Nevis is a shifting signifier in the sense that it lacks a clear and fixed meaning. In some instances, it is apparent that skin color is performative and predicated on social interactions (Segal 1993, 90). For instance, one dark-skinned woman gained social prestige from her association with a wealthy "white" American expatriate. In another instance, members of the community looked favorably upon a "white" American woman for her ability to mix well with "real Nevisians" and for her ability to speak like a Nevisian.

Chapter 3   Competing Discourses and Moralities at Play

1. Very few contemporary anthropologists use the concept "traditional" to discuss cultural practices. This is because, for many, it evokes reference to an "authentic culture" that is fixed, static, or unchanging. It suggests that a society or culture is distinct and separate from others, a kind of bounded entity (Clifford 1986). As pointed out in the introduction and in chapter 2, in terms of Nevisian society, this could not be further from reality. Caribbean societies, including Nevisian society, have always been interconnected regionally and globally to other places in the world. In fact, to understand the history of the rise of capitalism in Europe, one has to consider fully the history of the Caribbean. I use concepts such as "traditional" to orient the reader, to point out that there are, indeed, enduring cultural patterns in which people engage—patterns that are at once lasting and resilient. Without such a notion, it would be virtually impossible for anthropologists to convey the constraining nature of culture. With that said it is important to keep in mind that traditions are invented (Hobsbawn and Ranger 1983) and embedded in cultural politics. In the case of Nevis, as we shall see, traditional sexual discourses are rooted in colonial practices.

2. See Olwig (1993) for a historical analysis of the Methodist society and its affects on Nevisian social life.

3. For a discussion on the literature on Caribbean post-emancipation societies see Austin-Broos (1997); and Smith (1987).

4. See for example, Kelsky (1996); Manderson and Jolly (1997); Morris (1994); Parker (1991); Povinelli and Chauncey (1999); and Schein (1999).

Chapter 4   Consuming Global Scripts

1. For a discussion on the globalization of sexuality, see Povinelli and Chauncey (1999) for the way they encourage an examination of global linkages, such as web sites and

cable networks, to explore how mediated forms of sexuality and desire insinuate into local cultures and reconfigure notions of embodiment and intimate spaces and behaviors (439–450).

2. The proliferation of commodity desires surrounding the scripts and images consumed through television ads, network programs, and music will be investigated more fully in chapter 6.

3. For a more in-depth analysis on television and culture see Abu-Lughod (1997); Ang (1996); Fiske (1987); Kottak (1990); Mankekar (1999); Miller (1992); and Silverstone (1994).

4. See especially Collins (2004); Rose (1994); and Stephens and Phillips (2003).

5. For an analysis of how the contemporary representations of black female sexuality as depicted in hip-hop are linked to historical, colonial representations of black sexuality see Collins (2004, 119–122) and Stephens and Phillips (2003, 4–49).

6. Here I am indebted to Bandura's (1977) theory of observational learning.

7. Again, as discussed in the introduction, my understanding of this theoretical issue, namely the dynamic relationship between culture and the individual is informed by Bandura (1977); Bourdieu (1978); Bulter (1993); Giddens (1979); Ortner ([1984]; 1994, 2006); and Sahlins (1981). What I take away from their work is the idea that norms precede individual actions, such that individual actors like Felicia have options and choices, but that these are limited and shaped by larger cultural processes.

8. My point of departure is to understand pornography as polysemic. More specifically, the old anti-porn argument that views pornography as monolithic and as a vehicle for the production of violence and exploitation against women is no longer useful for understanding forms of mediated sexualities that are produced in a multitude of genres and formats. As a result, I cannot assume that on Nevis the recent consumption of porn 1) produces sexual scripts that sexualize female submissiveness or 2) exacerbates the prevalence of violence against girls on Nevis. Nor can I assume that it does not. The connection between the exposure to, and consumption of, pornography and a girl's subjectivity is complicated, to say the least. While pornography offers representations of elaborate sexual scripts, it is difficult to determine how it might change a girl's sexual practices. Whether girls like Varshnie and Tamara engage in new practices or not as a result of their consumption of pornography is a function of a number of variables, including their past sexual practices, their past and future exposure to mediated sexual images, the changing Nevisian societal codes, and other aspects of their sexualities, such as erotic preferences. Put simply, as long as pornography continues to be consumed by Nevisian girls there will be a great variability in their sexual scripts. What is offered in this book are mere sketches of the possibilities of how pornography, as a global influence, is reshaping the Nevisian sexual landscape. My views on pornography were inspired by Barr Snitow (1983); Gagnon and Simon (1973); Rubin (1984); and Snitow, Stansell, and Thompson (1983).

9. I am using the phrase "coded discourse" to refer to a codified knowledge of female pleasure. When we think of pleasure it is hard to imagine that pleasure is coded, but this is exactly the point I am trying to make, namely, that sensations and bodily experiences are systematically arranged by a set of rules—rules that may appear as technical erotic knowledge circulating in imported pornography, the lyrics and images in hip-hop videos, or the narratives of romance novels. Chapter 7 is centrally concerned with the subject of sexual pleasure.

10. Tolman (2002), for example, maintains that romance scripts support a female sexuality that limits pleasures (81) and rewards females who are submissive and docile. Differing from Tolman's perspective, *Loving with a Vengeance*, by Modleski (1982) offers a psychoanalytic interpretation of Harlequin romances that asserts that romance fantasies might be about the longing for power and revenge and that "the reader of romances, contrary to the arguments of many popular literary critics, is

engaged in an intensely active psychological process" (58). This is particularly plausible if romances are read simultaneously as both forms of protest and as endorsements of women's experiences.

Radway (1984) too, offers an innovative approach to ethnographies of reading. In *Reading the Romance*, she explores her readers' habits, pays attention to the rewards of romance fiction, and understands consumption as complex and contradictory. On the one hand, Radway views romance reading as a pleasurable escape, but on the other hand, she argues that it also is an indication of profound discontentment with heterosexuality. Women who read romance novels return again and again to find pleasure in novels where the heroine's desires and fantasies, unlike their own, are fulfilled. Romance readers are seeking resolution for their own discontentment, according to Radway. Similarly, Snitow (1983) reminds us that romance novels are not just an escape from the mundane; if interpreted as a form of pornography, romance novels offer a form of sexual release.

11. Personal conversation, February 24, 2003.

Chapter 5 The State and Sexualities

1. I am fully aware that this might be interpreted as theoretically retro, in light of Foucault's insights around biopower, modern economies, and governance.
2. While the participants of this forum are not all public health experts, it is comprised of community leaders who are in positions of power and thus capable of authorizing ideas about the nation's health and welfare.
3. While latex allergies exist, they apparently are rare. I took this as a sign of resistance among men or a strategy to avoid using condoms.
4. Gregor (1985) writes at length about sexual coercion and rape among the Mehinaku Indians of Brazil. He describes in detail how women submit to sex rather than resist, which would put them at risk for increased physical violence.
5. Recall that corporal punishment was viewed on Nevis as an acceptable form of punishment and was also permitted in schools.
6. See Das and Kleiman's (2000) discussion of how collective memories of violence become embodied by members of the community, including kin.
7. One exception to this general tendency was a case in 1999, in which a twelve-year-old girl was raped and murdered on her way to school. A local man, who was considered deranged and troubled, attacked her while she was walking on a footpath that led to the main road. This incited Nevisians almost to the point of a riot when officials moved the man from the local jail to board a ferry to Saint Kitts. According to a number of youth workers, this incident later mobilized members of the community to look more seriously at issues related to sexual violence. However, I would assert that the case gained notoriety because the child was not only raped but also murdered.
8. See Bourgois's (1995) ethnography, *In Search of Respect* in which he explores this issue among Puerto Rican men in East Harlem.

Chapter 6 Rethinking Sexual-Economic Exchange

1. While I was working on this project I had numerous interactions with people about what it means for Nevisian girls to trade sex for access to goods and money. I teach at a small Catholic college in New England and a number of my students and colleagues, although not all, expressed outrage at the idea of sexual-economic exchange. For many, it represents a form of prostitution and signals moral depravity. Kempadoo (1998) offers a critique of the popular understanding that sex without love or intimacy is immoral. She argues that the "conflation of sex with the highest form of intimacy presupposes

a universal meaning of sex, and ignores changing perceptions and values as well as the variety of meanings men and women hold about their sexual lives" (5). While I defend Kempadoo's perspective, neither she nor I would dismiss the very real social and economic forces that influence people's lives and their decisions or willingness to engage in commercial sex. It is also worth emphasizing the fact that sexual-economic exchange has been organizing relationships between men and women throughout history in many different ways. Peiss's (1986) study, *Cheap Amusements*, is a wonderful example of this. Peiss examines the dance hall culture and heterosexuality from 1880 to 1920. Given their low wages and limited finances, working-class women were "treated" by men with drinks, gifts, and meals, and in exchange they offered "flirtatious companionship" and varying degrees of sexual intimacy.

2. With the exception of Olwig's (1993), Richardson's (1983), and Weisburd's (1984) works, there is little research on the social life of Nevisians, and none of the research addresses the cultural production of sexualities or family systems. There are a number of important works on this subject of West Indian family systems including Alexander (1977); Allman (1985); Austin-Broos (1997); E. Clarke (1957); De Zalduondo and Bernard (1995), Lazarus-Black (1994); Rodman (1963); Slater (1977); Smith (1987); and Sobo (1993). It cannot be overstated that Nevisian family forms, as in the case in many societies throughout the Caribbean, are polymorphous. For instance, of the twelve girls with whom I conducted in-depth interviews, four lived with both of their parents. Of those four, one girl lived with her American parents, the other with her American mother and British father, and the remaining two with their Guyanese parents. Of all the girls who were born to West Indian parents (parents who were born and raised on Nevis or neighboring islands), of which there were eight out of the twelve, none of the girls lived with both their fathers and mothers. Additionally, of the fifteen women with whom I conducted informal interviews, whose ages range from twenty-one to forty-five, only two were legally married. Twelve of the fifteen women had children and ten were raising them in a household where the father was absent. Of the two who are married legally, one was married in Guyana and the other was married in Canada and later returned to Nevis with her Nevisian husband.

3. As such, malnutrition was prevalent. A considerable share of the average Nevisian's diet came from imported and very costly foods, such as wheat, frozen chicken parts, pasta, white potatoes, and evaporated milk. Given the expense of the items, most people, especially women, children, and the elderly were considered undernourished; more than likely, this, combined with poor state-run health-care facilities, contributed to an infant mortality rate of 45.7/1,000 live births (Weisburd 1984).

4. The fact that Nevisians distances themselves from women from the Dominican Republic, predominately women of Spanish ancestry, represents a twist in the European discourse that sexualizes women of color. Conflating "race" with sexuality is nothing new. Historically, emerging out of colonial relations, Europeans produced images of black sexuality as insatiable and promiscuous. Dark-skinned colonial subjects were seen by their white counterparts as lacking in European moral sensibility, thus legitimizing the European sense of superiority (Gilman 1985). What emerged was a colonial racial hierarchy in which whiteness was positioned as superior and blackness as inferior, with the middle ground constituted by the mulatto figure. The image of the mulatto or the brown-skinned girl came to represent an exotic sexuality. She is not quite white, yet not quite black either. She was different, but not too different to render her undesirable. Interestingly, Nevisians may be reordering the colonial racial hierarchy when, for example, contemporary Nevisians of African descent distance themselves from the Dominican brown-skinned women. Among Nevisians sexual "otherness" appears as foreign. Recall how white women supposedly introduced oral sex to the island; in the mind of some Nevisians, brown-skinned Spanish women introduced prostitution, thus representing the "true whore." See Brennan

(2004); Fusco (1998); and Kempadoo (1999) for discussions on the legacy of colonial discourses on sex, race, and nationality in the Caribbean.

5. See Freeman's (2000) ethnography on the impact of globalization on Barbados in which she explores transnationalized labor and consumption in the everyday lives of Barbadian women.

6. While the phrase "sexual-economic exchange" does not circulate within the popular discourse among Nevisians, the practice of girls exchanging sex for money or goods is a topic that is widely debated within Nevisian society among health care workers, the intelligentsia, community leaders, and the girls themselves. In December 2002, the *Observer*, the nation's most widely circulated newspaper, published an article that covered a radio call-in show, *Let's Talk*, in which a panel comprised of community leaders and the nation's public heath officer, Dr. Patrick Dias, debated with callers about the nature and extent of "prostitution" on Nevis. The article was entitled, "Foreign Women Blamed for Prostitution in Nevis, Panelist Says." Interestingly, the majority of callers and two of the panelists argued that the sex workers on Nevis were foreigners and that "no Nevisian women and girls are involved in trading their bodies for money" (7). Dr. Dias was cited as stating that "local girls get favors from men, such as tickets to go to St. Kitts or shoes and clothes" in exchange for sex. Following this comment, one caller argued that girls exchanging sex for favors led to prostitution. Referring to the rewards girls gain from sex, the caller suggested that "[g]irls have petty sex for a reward. It starts small and then they get intoxicated." Wallace, who, as you will recall, has worked for the Nevisian government for over two decades, maintained that sex workers on Nevis are not just foreign women, as many Nevisians would like to believe. "There are prostitutes in every social stratum," he says. Wallace maintains that Nevisians attribute the increase in commercial sex to women from the Dominican Republic as a way to stigmatize the growing "Spanish population" on Nevis.

7. This is taken from an interview with Wilbekin, former editor of *Vibe* magazine (*New York Times*, May 20, 2003).

8. That clothes and fashion play an important role in the lives of girls on Nevis is evident when one walks through Charlestown after school or attends any number of community events. Fashion-conscious girls on Nevis wear the latest styles, including tight-fitted low-riding jeans, short skirts, peasant blouses, and platform shoes. Hair extensions and braids are also popular. See Freeman's (2000) discussion of the fashion frenzy on Barbados. She writes: "The fashion frenzy is represented in the vast continuum encompassing informal imports as well as small, home-based independent needleworkers who make everything from school uniforms to corporate-looking suits. . . . Networks of family and friends abroad, as well as the global media, provide important sources of style and material goods. Young women's and young men's desire for brand-name clothes and shoes and the latest 'exotic hairdos' and 'dance hall fashions' is often satisfied through 'barrels' sent by parents and relatives overseas . . . The escalating preoccupation with fashion was even noted in a recent sermon of a Pentecostal preacher who bemoaned the trend for young people today to come to the house of God merely to 'check a style'" (225).

9. In 2007, my colleague, Art Frankel and I, with the help of a few students, conducted an experiment that revealed how status affects perceptions of physical attractiveness. College students participating in our study were shown photographs of men and women dressed in business attire. Participants were asked to judge how good-looking the individuals were. We manipulated a traditional aspect of status, namely, the salary ostensibly earned by men and women who appeared to be in their midtwenties ($30,000, $47,500, and $65,000). All of the images were associated with all of the salaries. For example, one group of participants were led to believe that one individual earned $30,000 and other groups of participants were led to believe that this same person earned either $47,500 or $65,000. We found that men and

women were considered better looking when they earned more money (Frankel et al. 2008). Interestingly, recent research shows that wine tastes better and affects people's brains differently when they think it is expensive (Plassman et al. 2008). What fascinates me about these two studies is how status shapes perception. It would not be out of the question to assume that if people actually perceive others to be better looking when they are associated with wealth and that wine tastes better when it is associated with a higher price, then maybe sex feels better when it is associated with more prized goods and services.

10. In 2006, three years after I completed my fieldwork, another article focusing on this exact topic was published in the *Observer*, entitled, "Sexual Predation-The Best Kept Secret in the Federation." Similar to the Girl-Child series, the article spotlighted the practice of parents soliciting men to have sex with their daughters and, it too, focused on cases in which parents, having learned that their daughters had been molested or raped by men in the community, accepted "hush money" from the men involved to keep them from pressing charges. These articles in the nation's most widely read newspaper represents a cultural shift in terms of the society's willingness to look at the areas of sexual violence and exploitation among girls.

11. See especially Bales (2003); Mayorga and Velasquez (1999); Montgomery (1998); and Sobo (1993).

12. See Kempadoo and Doezema's valuable collection entitled *Global Sex Worker* (1998). It is important to point out that this is not a new form of sexual solicitation by any means. Within the historical record, for instance, Gailey (1987) reports how young girls' sexuality was controlled by older relatives among the Tongan, people who lived on the Tongan Islands in Polynesia, located south of Somoa. Relying on European written accounts, including Captain Cook's ship logs, Gailey describes how relatives of low-ranking young women would often barter with the crew members and Cook himself in their effort to exchange young women's sexual services for cloth, nails, or other iron goods. "Older and higher-ranking relatives, including chiefly people in the region, would benefit materially from the adventures of their lower-ranking kin." Furthermore, Gailey asserts, "The sailors provided one means for unmarried, nonchiefly women to acquire highly desirable iron tools and exotic cloth that they would not otherwise have been able to obtain. They would present the goods to higher-ranking relatives and thereby gain prestige not generally accorded women of their age and status" (156). Gailey notes that as a result of the young girls' sexual encounters with the Europeans, the girls were not stigmatized nor were their reputations or the expectation that they would marry tarnished or diminished in anyway. There are obvious differences between what Gailey is describing and what occurs within many contemporary societies. The most obvious difference has to do with the highly variable and culturally specific meanings of sex and sexual practices.

13. Scheper-Hughes (1998) takes on the complicated issues of "a universal definition of child sex abuse" by analyzing the problems of broad definitions such as adult-to-child sexual contact "for the purposes of adult sexual gratification or economic gain" (299). Given that the norms for physical contact between children and adults vary and are cultural constructed and thus culturally specific, what is required instead, are "important distinctions between cultural norms and individual pathology . . . between survival strategies and malicious intent" (300–301).

14. See Farmer et al. (1996, 202–203) discussion on the dangers of overestimating poor women and girls' agency.

Chapter 7   Theorizing Sexual Pleasure

1. Eleanor's use of the term *freak* has similar connotations to its usage in hip-hop culture where it signifies "kinky" sexuality, as discussed in chapter 3. See Collins' (2004,

120–122) reading of the freak concept in popular culture. It was originally invoked by Rick James in his hit *Superfreak* and later used by Missy Elliot to represent sexual practices outside the norm.

2. Although I had explained to the individuals within the Ministries of Health and Education that I was a graduate student conducting research for my dissertation, members of the community, including the teenagers who learned about my work secondhand, often referred to me as the "professor who was writing a book about Nevis and sex."

3. It is crucial to distinguish here between the pervasive female experience of pain during heterosexual sex on Nevis and the concept of pain as defined by sex theorists in relations to sadomasochism. Sadomasochism; according to contemporary sex theorists, by definition includes only consensual activities. If consent is not a part of the activity, most practitioners and theorists would not consider such activity to be sadomasochism but rather to be abuse. By contrast, I would argue that despite the argument I am making about agency, the women and girls' ability to give full consent to the experience of pain in the Nevisian cultural context, which so profoundly devalues female sexual pleasure, is severely limited. Thus, my critique of the connection between sex and pain on Nevis hinges on the coercive environment in which sexual relations between men and women are established and negotiated. See Kulick's *Travesti* (1998) on the subject of coercion and early sexual experiences. The narratives in Kulick's ethnography and the analyses that follow are exceptional in the way they capture the conflicting feelings of desire and fear experienced in early sexual encounters.

4. I first heard the term *fat pussy* when I was with Jasmine and her cousins. When Jasmine used it to describe her six-year-old cousin's body, I was taken aback, because to me, while the child's bathing suit clung to her small frame, her appearance was not remarkable. Later when Ruthie used the phrase to describe the Dutch tourist, I experienced similar confusion, given the fact that the tourist was fully clothed and not wearing anything that would reveal her anatomy, such as a bathing suit. It was only later I surmised that it represents sexual attractiveness.

CHAPTER 8   CONCLUSION

1. It is important to emphasize that I am not inferring a causal relationship between Cecilia's consumption of pornography and the incident involving Cecilia and her neighbor.

2. See Ortner's (2006) recent discussion of agency. Butler's (1997) understanding of the formation of the subject is also helpful. For Butler "(s)ubjection consists precisely in the fundamental dependency on a discourse we never chose but that, paradoxically, initiates and sustains our agency. . . . Subjection signifies the process of becoming subordinated by power as well as the process of becoming a subject" (2).

3. "No say me so" is a common Nevisian expression which means, "Don't tell anyone I said this, but. . . ." Eleanor said this in response to a face I made at Ruthie when she explained that in her estimation, Dwight likes it when she rubs his groin area. It is not that I did not trust Ruthie's assessment of Dwight's pleasure, but her honesty, which I always appreciated, sometimes took me by surprise.

4. While I separate this type of sexual-economic exchange from sex work, it is important to point out that a similar argument has been made extensively in relation to sex work. See specifically Kempadoo and Doezema (1998).

Bibliography

Abramson, P. and S. Pinkerton. 2002. *With Pleasure: Thoughts on the Nature of Human Sexuality.* New York: Oxford University Press.

Abu-Lughod, L. 1990. "The Romance of Resistance: Tracing Transformations of Power through Bedouin Women." *American Ethnologist* 17(1):41–55.

———. 1997. "The Interpretation of Culture(s) After Television." *Representations.* 59:109–34.

Adams, V. and S. Leigh Pigg. 2005. "Introduction." In Vincanne Adams and Stacey Leigh Pigg, eds., *Sex in Development: Science, Sexuality, and Morality in Global Perspective*, pp. 1–38. Durham, NC: Duke University Press.

Alexander, J. 1977. "The Culture of Race in Middle-Class Kingston, Jamaica." *American Ethnologist* 4:413–435.

Alexander, J. 1991. "Redrafting Morality and the Sexual Offenses Bill of Trinidad and Tobago: The Postcolonial State and Sexual Offenses Bill of Trinidad and Tobago." In Jacqui Alexander and Chandre Talpade, eds., *Third World Women and the Politics of Feminism*, pp. 143–152. Bloomington: Indiana University Press.

———. 1994. "Not Just (Any) Body Can Be a Citizen: The Politics of Law, Sexuality and Postcoloniality in Trinidad and Tobago and the Bahamas." *Feminist Review* 48:6–23.

———. 1996. "Erotic Autonomy as a Politics of Decolonization: An Anatomy of Feminist and State Practice in the Bahamas Tourist Economy." In Jacqui Alexander and Chandre Talpade, eds., *Feminist Genealogies, Colonial Legacies, and Democratic Futures*, pp. 63–100. New York: Routledge.

Allman, J. 1985. Conjugal Unions in Rural and Urban Haiti. *Social and Economic Studies* 34(1): 27–57.

Althusser, L. 1970. *For Marx.* Translated by Ben Brewster. New York: Vintage.

———. 1971. Ideology and Ideological State Apparatuses (Notes Toward an Investigation). In *Lenin and Philosophy and Other Essays*, pp. 121–173. New York: Monthly Review Press.

Altman, D. 2002. *Global Sex.* Chicago: University of Chicago Press.

Ang, I. 1996. *Living Room Wars: Rethinking Media Audiences for a Postmodern World.* London: Routledge.

Appadurai, A. 1996. *The Social Life of Things: Commodities in Cultural Perspective.* Cambridge: Cambridge University Press.

———. 1996. *Modernity at Large.* Minneapolis: University of Minnesota Press.

Apter, E. 1993. "Introduction." In Emily Apter and William Pietz, eds., *Fetishism as a Cultural Discourse*, pp.1–12. Ithaca: Cornell University Press.

Austin-Broos, D. 1984. *Urban Life in Kingston, Jamaica: The Culture and Class Ideology of Two Neighborhoods.* New York: Gordon and Breach.

———. 1997. *Jamaica Genesis.* Chicago: University of Chicago Press.

Bales, K. 2003. "Because She Looks like a Child." In Barbara Ehrenreich and Arlie Russel Hochschild, eds., *Global Woman*, pp. 207–229. New York: Metropolitan Books.

Bandura, A. 1977. *Social Learning Theory*. Englewood Cliffs, NJ: Prentice-Hall.

Barr Snitow, A. 1983. "Mass Market Romance: Pornography for Women Is Different." In Ann Barr Snitow, Christine Stansell, and Sharon Thompson, eds., *Powers of Desire: The Politics of Sexuality*, pp. 245–263. New York: Monthly Review Press.

Basch, L., N. Glick-Shiller, and C. Szanton-Blanc. 1994. *Nations Unbounded: Transnational Projects, Postcolonial Predicaments, and Deterritorialized Nation-States*. Langhorn, PA: Gordon and Breach.

Becker, A. 1995. *Body, Self, and Society: The View from Fiji*. Philadelphia: University of Pennsylvania Press.

Beckles, H. 1996. "Black Masculinities in Caribbean Slavery." Presented at the University of the West Indies Centre for Gender and Development Studies (St. Augustine) Conference on *The Construction of Caribbean Masculinity: Towards a Research Agenda*. January 11–13, 1996.

Behar, R. 1994. "Queer Times in Cuba." *Michigan Quarterly Review*. Summer-Fall.

Belk, R., G. Guliz, and S. Askegaard. 2003. "The Fire of Desire: A Multisited Inquiry into Consumer Passion." *Journal of Consumer Research* 30:326–351.

Bernard, R. 2000. *Social Research Methods: Qualitative and Quantitative Approaches*. Thousand Oaks, CA: Sage Publications.

Borgatti, S. 1999. "Elicitation Techniques for Cultural Domain Analysis." In Jean J. Schensul, Margaret Diane LeCompte, Bonnie K. Nastasi, and Stephen P. Borgatti, eds., *Enhanced Ethnographic Methods*, pp. 115–150. Walnut Creek, CA: AltaMira Press.

Bork, R. 1997. *Slouching Towards Gomorrah: Modern Liberalism and American Decline*. New York: Harper Collins.

Bourdieu, P. 1978. *Outline of a Theory of Practice*. Translated by Richard Nice. Cambridge: Cambridge University Press.

Bourgois, P. 1995. *In Search of Respect: Selling Crack in El Barrio*. Cambridge: Cambridge University Press.

Brennan, D. 2004. *What's Love Got to Do With It?* Durham, NC: Duke University Press.

Burbank, V. K., J. W. M. Whiting, and B. Blyth Whiting. 1988. *Aboriginal Adolescence: Maidenhood in an Australian Community*. New Brunswick: Rutgers University Press.

Butler, J. 1990. *Gender Trouble: Feminism and the Subversion of Identity*. New York: Routledge.

———. 1993. *Bodies that Matter*. New York: Routledge.

———. 1997. The Psychic Life of Power: Theories of Subjection. Stanford: Stanford University Press.

CFR Consulting. 2000. Report: Situation and Analysis National AIDS Program Saint Kitts and Nevis. Trinidad: Maraval.

Carey, B. 2004. "Long after Kinsey, Only the Brave Study Sex." *New York Times*, November 4, section F. P. 1.

Chambers, C. and B. Chevannes. 1991. *Report on Focus Groups: Sexual Decision Making Project*. Kingston: Institute of Social and Economic Research, University of the West Indies.

Chevannes, B. 1993. "Sexual Behavior of Jamaicans: A Literature Review." *Social Economic Studies* 42(1):1–45.

Clarke, E. 1957. *My Mother Who Fathered Me*. London: George Allen and Unwin.

Clarke, J. 1997. "State of Desire: Transformations in Huli Sexuality." In Lenore Manderson and Margaret Jolly, eds., *Sites of Desire, Economies of Pleasure: Sexualities in Asia and the Pacific*, pp. 191–211. Chicago: University of Chicago Press.

Clarke, R. 1998. *Violence against Women in the Caribbean: State and Non-state Responses*. New York: United States Development Fund for Women.

Clifford, J. 1986. *The Predicament of Culture*. Cambridge: Harvard University Press.

Cohen, C. B. 1995. "Marketing Paradise, Making Nation." *Annals of Tourism Research*. 22(2): 404–421.

Cohen, C. B. and F. E. Mascia-Lees. 1993. "The British Virgin Islands as Nation and Desti-Nation: Representing and Siting Identity in a Post-colonial Caribbean." *Social Analysis* 33:130–151.

Collins, P. H. 2004. *Black Sexual Politics*. New York: Routledge.

Comaroff, J. and J. Comaroff. 1993. *Modernity and Its Malcontents*. Chicago: University of Chicago Press.

Curtis, D. 2002. *Globalization and Sexuality in the West Indies*. Dissertation Proposal. Rutgers University.

Curtis, D. 2004. "Commodities and Sexual Subjectivities: A Look at Capitalism and Its Desires." *Cultural Anthropology* 19(1):95–121.

Danticat, E. 1998. *Breath, Eyes, and Memory*. New York: Vintage.

Das, V. and A. Kleinman. 2000. "Introduction." In Veena Das, Arthur Kleinman, Mamphela Ramphele, and Pamela Reynolds, eds., *Violence and Subjectivity*, pp. 1–18. Berkeley: University of California Press.

Davenport, W. 1961. "The Family System of Jamaica." In Sydney W. Mintz and W. Davenport, eds., Working Papers in Caribbean Social Organization, pp. 420–454. *Special edition of Social and Economic Studies 10*.

Delany, S. 2001. *Times Sqare Red, Times Sqare Blue*. New York: New York University Press.

de Zalduondo, B. and J. M. Bernard. 1995. "Meaning and Consequence of Sexual Economic Exchange: Gender, Poverty, and Sexual Risk Behavior in Urban Haiti." In Richard Parker and John Gagnon, eds., *Conceiving Sexuality*, pp. 157–180. New York: Routledge.

Dell, H. 2005. "Ordinary Sex, Prostitutes, and Middle-Class Wives: Liberalization and National Identity in India." In Vincanne Adams and Stacy Leigh Pigg, eds., *Sex in Development: Science, Sexuality, and Morality in Global Perspective*, pp. 187–206. Durham, NC: Duke University Press.

Dietrich, L. 1998. *Chicana Adolescents: Bitches, 'Ho's and Schoolgirls*. Westport, CT: Praeger Publishers.

Douglas, D. 2005. Address by the Honourable Denzil Douglas, Governor of the Bank for St. Kitts and Nevis, on Behalf of the Joint Caribbean Group and the Joint Annual Discussion, Broad of Governers, Annual meetings, Washington, DC.

Fanon, Franz. 1967. *Black Skin, White Masks*. New York: Grove Weindenfeld.

Farmer, P. 1992. *AIDS and Accusation: Haiti and the Geography of Blame*. Berkeley: University of California Press.

Farmer, P. 1996. "Women, Poverty, and AIDS." In Paul Farmer, Margaret Connors, and Janie Simmons, eds. *Women, Poverty, and AIDS*, pp. 3–38. Maine: Common Courage Press.

Farmer, P., M. Connors, K. Fox, and J. Furin. 1996. "Rereading Social Science." In *Women and Poverty*, pp. 147–208. Maine: Common Courage Press.

Featherstone, M. 1990. *Global Culture: Nationalism, Globalization, and Modernity*. London: Sage.

Fine, M. 1988. "Sexuality, Schooling and Adolescent Females: The Missing Discourse of Desire." *Harvard Educational Review* 58(1):29–53.

Fiske, J. 1987. *Television Culture*. London: Routledge.

Foucault, M. 1978. *The History of Sexuality*. New York: Random House.

————. 1980. *Power/Knowledge: Selected Interviews and Other Writings, 1972–1977.* Colin Gordon, ed. New York: Pantheon Books.

————. 1982. "The Subject and Power." In *Michel Foucault: Beyond Structuralism and Hermeneutics.* Translated by H. Dreyfus and P. Rabinow. Chicago: University of Chicago Press.

————. 1985. *The Use of Pleasure.* New York: Vintage Press.

————. 1988. *The Care of the Self.* New York: Random House.

————. 1988. *Politics, Philosophy, Culture: Interviews and Other Writings, 1977–1984.* Edited by Lawrence Kritzman. New York: Routledge.

Francis, D. A. 2004. "Silences Too Horrific to Disturb: Writing Sexual Histories in Edwidge Danticat's Breath, Eyes, Memory." *Research in African Literatures* 35(2): 75–90.

Frankel, A., M. Fitzpatrick, K. McAuley, and D. Curtis. 2008. Money Becomes You: How Good Looking You Are May Depend on How Much You Earn. Poster presented at Eastern Psychological Association Meetings, Boston.

Freeman, C. 1997 "Reinventing Higglering across Transnational Zones." In Consuel Lopez Springfield, ed., *Daughters of Caliban: Caribbean Women in the Twentieth Century,* pp. 68–95. Bloomington: Indiana University Press.

————. 2000. *High Tech and High Heels in the Global Economy.* Durham, NC: Duke University Press.

————. 2001. "Is Local: Global as Feminine: Masculine? Rethinking the Gender of Gobalization." *Signs* 26:1007–1037.

Freud, S. 2000. *Three Essays in the Theory of Sexuality.* New York: Basic Books.

Fusco, C. 1998. "Hustling for Dollars: Jineterismo in Cuba." In Kamala Kempadoo and Jo Doezema, eds., pp. 151–166. *Global Sex Workers: Rights, Resistance, and Redefinition.* New York: Routledge.

Fuss, D. 1994. "Interior Colonies: Franz Fanon and the Politics of Identification." *Diacritics* 24/20–42.

Gagnon, J. and W. Simon. 1973. *Sexual Conduct: The Social Sources of Human Sexuality.* Chicago: Aldine Publishing Company.

Gailey, C. W. 1987. *Kinship and Kingship.* Austin: University of Texas.

Gallop, J. 1988. *Thinking through the Body.* New York: Columbia University Press.

Giddens, A. 1979. *Central Problems in Social Theory: Action, Structure, and Contradiction in Social Analysis.* Cambridge: Cambridge University Press.

————. 1991. *Modernity and Self-Identity: Self and Society in the Late Modern Age.* London: Polity Press.

Gilman, S. 1985. *Difference and Pathology of Sexuality, Race, and Madness.* Ithaca: Cornell Press.

Goffman, E. 1959. *The Presentation of Self in Everyday Life.* New York: Doubleday.

Gordon, J. 1998. *Nevis: Queen of the Caribees.* London: MacMillan Education.

Gregor, T. 1985. *Anxious Pleasures: The Sexual Lives of an Amazonian People.* Chicago: University of Chicago Press.

Grossberg, L. 1997. *Bringing It All Back Home.* Durham, NC: Duke University Press.

Grosz, E. 1993. "Lesbian Fetishism." In Emily Apter and William Pietz, eds., *Fetishism as a Cultural Discourse,* pp. 101–118. Ithaca: Cornell University Press.

Hall, S. 1971. "Response to People and Culture." *Working Papers in Cultural Studies* (6): 97–102.

————. 1996. "Introduction: Who Needs "Identity?" In Stuart Hall and Paul du Gay, eds., *Questions of Cultural Identity,* pp. 1–17. London: Sage Publications.

Hammonds, E. M. 1997. "Toward a Genealogy of Black Female Sexuality: The Problematic of Silence." In Jacqui Alexander and Chandre Talpade, eds., *Feminist Geneologies, Colonial Legacies, and Democratic Futures*, pp. 170–182. New York: Routledge.

Hannerz, U. 1996. *Transnational Connections: Culture, People, Places.* New York: Routledge.

Harvey, D. 1989. *The Conditions of Postmodernity.* Oxford: Basil Blackwell.

Haug, W. F. 1996. *Critique of Commodity Aesthetics: Appearance, Sexuality, and Advertising in Capitalist Society.* Translated by Robert Bock. Minneapolis: University of Minnesota Press.

Hekman, S. 1995. "Subjects and Agents: The Question for Feminism." In *Provoking Agents: Gender and Agency in Theory and Practice*, pp. 194–207. Urbana: University of Illinois Press.

Henry-Lee, A. 2000. "Conflict, Gender Relations and the Health of Women in Two Low Income Communities in Jamaica." CICRED Seminar Social and Economic Patterning of Health Among Women. Paper presented at Tunis.

Herdt, G. 1987. "The Sambia: Ritual and Gender." In *New Guinea*. New York: Holt, Rinehart and Winston.

———. 1999. *Migration and Sexuality in the Era of AIDS.* Oxford: Clarendon Press.

Herdt, G. and Boxer, A. 1996. *Children of Horizons: How Gay and Lesbian Teens Are Leading a New Way Out of the Closet.* Boston: Beacon Press.

Herdt, G. and S. Leavitt, 1998. *Adolescence in Pacific Island Societies.* Pittsburgh: University of Pittsburgh Press.

Herman, J. 1992. *Trauma and Recovery: The Aftermath of Violence—from Domestic Abuse to Political Terror.* New York: Basic Books.

Higman, B. 1984. *Salve Populations of the British Caribbean. 1807–1834.* Baltimore: Johns Hopkins University Press.

Hobsbawn, E. and T. Ranger. 1983. *The Invention of Tradition.* Cambridge: Cambridge University Press.

Hubbard, V. 2002. *Swords, Ships and Sugar: History of Nevis.* Corvallis, OR: Premiere Editions International Press.

Jackson, P. 1997. "Kathoey < Gay < Man: The Historical Emergence of Gay Male Identity in Thailand." In Lenore Manderson and Margaret Jolly, eds., *Sites of Desire, Economies of Pleasure: Sexualities in Asia and the Pacific*, pp. 191–211. Chicago: University of Chicago Press.

Julien, I. 1993. "Confessions of a Snow Queen: Notes on the Making of the Attendant." *Critical Quarterly* 36(1):120–126.

Kairi. 2001. *Poverty Assesment Report. Saint Kitts and Nevis.* Kairi Consultants. Trinidad and Tobago, West Indies.

Kelsky, K. 1996. "Flirting with the Foreign: Interracial Sex in Japan's "International" Age." In Rob Wilson and Wiimal Dissanyake, eds., *Global/Local: Cultural Production and the Transnational Imaginary*, pp. 173–192. Durham, NC: Duke University Press.

Kemp, K. M. 2003. "25 Ways to Have Your Best Orgasm Ever." *Marie Clarie*, p. 235.

Kempadoo, K. 1999. *Sun, Sex, and Gold: Tourism and Sex Work in the Caribbean.* New York: Rowman and Littlefield Publishers.

———. 2001. "Freelancers, Temporary Wives, and Beach-boys: Researching Sex Work in the Caribbean." *Feminist Review* 67(1) pp. 39–62.

———. 2004. *Sexing the Caribbean: Gender, Race, and Sexual Labor.* New York: Routledge.

Kempadoo, K. and J. Doezema. 1998. *Global Sex Worker: Rights, Resistance, and Redefinition.* New York: Routledge.

Kempadoo, O. 1999. *Buxton Spice*. New York: Dutton.

Kincaid, J. 1983. "Girl." In *At the Bottom of the River*, pp. 3–5. New York: Farrar, Straus, and Giroux.

———. 1997. *Annie John*. New York: Farrar, Straus, Giroux.

Kleinman, A., V. Das, and M. Lock. "Introduction." In Arthur Kleinman, Veena Das and Margaret Lock, eds. *Social Suffering*. pp. 1–24. Berkeley: University of California Press. pp. ix–xxvii.

Kleinman, A. and J. Kleiman. 1997. "The Appeal of Experience; The Dismay of Images: Cultural Suffering in Our Times." In Arthur Kleinman, Veena Das, and Margaret Lock, eds., *Social Suffering*, pp. 1–24. Berkeley: University of California Press.

Kottak, C. P. 1990. Prime Time Society: An Anthropological Analysis of Television and Culture. Belmont, CA: Wadsworth Publishing Co.

Kulick, D. 1995. "Introduction." In Don Kulick and Margaret Wilson, eds., *Taboo: Sex, Identity and Erotic Subjectivity in Anthropological Fieldwork*, pp. 1–27. New York: Routledge.

———. 1998. *Travesti: Sex, Gender, and Culture among Brazilian Transgendered Prostitutes.* Chicago: University of Chicago Press.

Lancaster, R. 1992. *Life Is Hard: Machismo, Danger, and the Intimacy of Power in Nicaragua.* Berkeley: University of California Press.

———. 1995. "That We Should All Turn Queer." Homosexual Stigma and the Making of Manhood and the Breaking of the Revolution in Nicaragua." In Richard Parker and John Gagnon, eds., *Conceiving Sexuality*, pp. 135–156. New York: Routledge.

———. 1996. "Coming-Out Stories: Recent Videos on Gay and Lesbian Themes." *American Anthropologist* 98(3): 604–616.

Lancaster, R. and M. di Leonardo. 1997. "Introduction." In Roger Lancaster and Micaela di Leonardo, eds., *The Gender/Sexuality Reader*, pp. 1–8. New York: Routledge.

Lauman, E. and J. Gagnon. 1995. "A Sociological Perspective on Sexual Action." In Richard Parker and John Gagnon, eds., *Conceiving Sexuality: Approaches to Sex Research in a Postmodern World*, pp. 183–214. New York: Routledge.

Lazarus-Black, M. 1994. *Legitimate Acts and Illegitimate Encounters*. Washington, D.C.: Smithsonian.

Leiner, M. 1994. *Sexual Relations in Cuba*. New York: Westview Press.

MacCormack, C. and A. Draper. 1987. Social and Cognitive Aspects of Female Sexuality in Jamaica. In Pat Caplan, ed., *The Cultural Construction of Sexuality*, pp. 143–165. New York: Routledge.

Manderson, L. and M. Jolly. 1997. *Sites of Desire, Economies of Pleasure: Sexualities in Asia and the Pacific*. Lenore Manderson and Margaret Jolly, eds., Chicago: University of Chicago Press.

Mankekar, P. 1999. *Screening Culture, Viewing Politics: An Ethnography of Television, Womanhood, and Nation Postcolonial India*. Durham, NC: Duke University Press.

———. 2004. "Dangerous Desire: Television and Desire in Late Twentieth Century India." *Journal of Asian Studies* 63(2): 403–431.

Mankekar, P. and L. Schein. 2004. "Introduction: Mediated Transnationalism and Social Erotics." *Journal of Asian Studies* 63(2): 357–365.

Martin, S. 2001. Health Information Unit. Ministry of Health, Nevis.

Martinez-Alier, V. 1974. *Marriage, Class, and Colour in 19th Century Cuba: A Study of Racial Attitudes and Sexual Values in a Slave Society*. London: Cambridge University Press.

Malinowski, B. 1922. *Argonauts of the Western Pacific*. Long Grove, IL: Waveland Press.

————. 1927. *Sex and Repression in Savage Society*. New York: Meridiam.

————. 1987. *The Sexual Life of the Savages*. Boston: Beacon Press.

Mayorga, L. and P. Velasquez. 1999. "Bleak Pasts, Bleak Futures: Life Paths of Thirteen Young Prostitutes in Cartagena, Columbia" In Kamala Kempadoo, ed., *Sun, Sex, and Gold: Tourism and Sex Work in the Caribbean*, pp. 157–182. Maryland: Rowman and Littlefield Publishers.

Mead, M. [1928] 1967. *Coming of Age in Samoa*. New York: Morrow Quill Paperbacks.

————. 1975. *Male and Female*. New York: Perennial.

Miller, D. 1992. "The Young and Restless in Trinidad: A Case of the Local and the Global in Mass Consumption." In Roger Silverstone and E. Hirsch, eds., *Consuming Technologies*, pp. 163–182. London: Routledge.

————. 1994. Modernity an Ethnographic Approach: Dualism and Mass Consumption in Trinidad. Oxford: Berg Press.

Mintz. S. 1974. *Caribbean Transformations*. New York: Columbia University Press.

————. 1985. *Sweetness and Power: The Place of Sugar in Modern History*. New York: Viking.

Mills, M. B. 1999. *Thai Women in the Global Labor Force*. New Brunswick: Rutgers University Press.

Modleski, T. 1982. *Loving with Vengeance: Mass-Produced Fantasies for Women*. New York: Routledge.

Moffat, M. 1989. *Coming of Age in New Jersey*. New Brunswick: Rutgers University Press.

Montgomery, H. 1998. "Children, Prostitution, and Identity: A Case Study from a Tourist Resort in Thailand." In Kamala Kempadoo and Jo Deozema, eds., *Global Sex Workers*, pp. 139–150. New York: Routledge.

Moore, H. 2001. "Afterword: A 'Masterclass' in Subjectivity." In Gail Currie and Celia Rothenberg, eds., *Feminist (Re)vision of the Subject: Landscapes, Ethnoscapes, and Theoryscapes*, pp. 261–265. Lanham, MD: Rowman and Littlefield Publishers.

Morris, R. 1994. "Three Sexes and Four Sexualities: Redressing the Discourse on Gender and Sexuality in Contemporary Thailand." *Positions* 2 (1):15–43.

Murray, D. 1995. "Martiniquais: The Construction and Contestation of Cultural Identity." PhD diss., University of Virginia.

Nevis Co-Operative Credit Union Limited. 1999, 2003. Breakdown of Loans Approved.

Newton, E. 1993. "My Best Informant's Dress: The Erotic Equation in Fieldwork." *Cultural Anthropology*. 8:3–23.

Nichter, M. 2000. *Fat Talk: What Girls and Their Parents Say About Dieting*. Cambridge: Harvard University Press.

Olwig, K. 1993. *Global Culture, Island Identity: Continuity and Change in the Afro-Caribbean Community of Nevis*. Victoria: Harwood Academic Publishers.

Ortner, S. 1994 [1984]. "Theory in Anthropology Since the Sixties." In Geoff Eley, Nicholas B. Dirks, and Sherry B. Ortner, eds., *Culture/Power/History: A Reader in Contemporary Social Theory*, pp. 372–411. Princeton: Princeton University Press.

————. 2006. *Anthropology and Social Theory: Culture, Power, and the Acting Subject*. Durham, NC: Duke University Press.

Parker, K. 2002a. "The Girl Child: How Statutory Rape Feeds the Cycle of Poverty for Women." *Observer*, August 9–15.

————. 2002b. "The Girl Child: Domestic Abuse, Sexual Abuse and Deconstruction of the Family Unit." *Observer*, August 16–22.

————. 2002c. "The Girl Child: One Young Man's Journey." *Observer*, September 27-October 3.

Parker, R. 1991. *Bodies, Pleasures and Passions*. Boston: Beacon Press.

Parker, R. and J. Gagnon. 1995. *Conceiving Sexuality*. New York: Routledge.

Patterson, O. 1967. *The Sociology of Slavery: An Analysis of the Origins, Development and Structure of Negro Slave Society in Jamaica*. Rutherford: Fairleigh Dickinson University.

Peiss, K. 1986. *Cheap Amusements*. Philadelphia: Temple University Press.

Pietz, W. 1985. "The Problem of the Fetish 1." *Res 9* (Spring): pp. 5–17.

———. 1993. "Fetishism and Materialism: The Limits of Theory in Marx." In Emily Apter and William Pietz, eds., *Fetishism as a Cultural Discourse*, pp. 119–151. Ithaca: Cornell University Press.

Plassman, H., J. O'Doherty, B. Shiv, and A. Rangel. 2008. Marketing Actions Can Modulate Neural Representations of Experienced Pleasantness. *Proceedings of the National Academy of Sciences* 105 (2), 1050–1054.

Povinelli, E. and G. Chauncey. 1999. "Thinking Sexuality Transnationally." *Journal of Lesbian and Gay Studies* 5(4):439–450.

Pruitt, D. and S. LaFont. 1995. "For Love and Money: Romance Tourism in Jamaica." *Annals of Tourism Research* 22(2): 422–440.

Puar, J. K. 2001. "Global Circuits: Transnational Sexualities and Trinidad." *Signs* 26: 1039–1066.

Radway, J. 1984. *Reading the Romance: Women, Patriarchy, Popular Literature*. Chapel Hill: University of North Carolina Press.

Richardson, B. 1983. *Caribbean Migrants*. Knoxville: University Of Tennessee Press.

Robinson, J. 2000. *Nevis: The Last 100 Years. 1900–1999*. Charlestown, Nevis: Nevis Historical and Conservation Society.

Rodman, H. 1963. "The Lower-Class Value Stretch." *Social Forces* 42:205–215.

Rose, T. 1994. *Black Noise*. Hanover: Wesleyan University Press.

Rubin, G. 1984. "Thinking Sex: Notes for a Radical Theory of the Politics of Sexuality." In Carol Vance, ed., *Pleasure and Danger Exploring Female Sexuality*, pp. 267–319. Boston: Routledge and Kegan Paul.

Safa, H. 1995. *The Myth of the Male Breadwinner: Women and Industrialization in the Caribbean*. Boulder, CO: Westview Press.

Sahlins, M. 1981. *Historical Metaphors and Mythical Realities: Structure in the Early History of the Sandwich Island Kingdom*. Ann Arbor: University of Michigan Press.

Scarry, E. 1985. The *Body in Pain: The Making and Unmaking of the World*. New York: Oxford University Press.

Schein, L. 1999. "Of Cargo and Satellites: Imagined Cosmopolitanism." *Postcolonial Studies* 2(3): 345–375.

———. 2003. "The Body of the Hmong Transnational Suitor." Manuscript.

———. 2004. "Homeland Beauty: Transnational Longing and Hmong American Video." *Journal of Asian Studies* 63(2): 433–464.

Schensul, J. 1998. "Learning about Sexual Decision-making from Urban Adolescents." *International Quarterly of Community Health Education*, special issue on Cross Cultural Perspectives of Women's Sexual Decision Making: Implications for Sexual Health Protection at the Community Level, edited by M. I. Torres and M. Weeks, Vol. 18(1):29–48.

Scheper-Hughes, N. 1998. "Institutionalized Sex Abuse and the Catholic Church." In *Small Wars*, 295–317. Berkeley: University of California Press.

Schwartz, B., E. Wasserman and S. Robbins. 2002. *Psychology of Learning and Behavior*. New York: Norton.

Segal, D. 1993. "'Race' and 'Colour' in Pre-Independence Trinidad and Tobago." In Kevein Yelvington, ed., *Trinidad Ethnicity*, pp. 82–115. London: Macmillan.

Senior, O. 1991. *Working Miracles: Women's Lives in the English-Speaking Caribbean.* Bloomington: Indiana Press.

"Seven Ways to Please a Man." 2003. *Cosmopolitan*, pp. 176–179.

Silverstone, R. 1994. *Television and Everyday Life.* New York: Routledge.

Simon, W. and J. H. Gagnon. 1986. "Sexual Scripts: Permanence and Change." *Archives of Sexual Behavior* 15(2):97–120.

Slater, M. 1977. *The Caribbean Family: Legitimacy in Martinique.* New York: St. Martin's Press.

Smith, R. T. 1956. *The Negro Family in British Guiana.* London: Routledge.

———. 1971. "Culture and Social Structure in the Caribbean: Some Recent Work on Family and Kinship Studies." In Michael Horowitz, ed., *Peoples and Cultures of the Caribbean*, pp. 448–475. New York: Natural History Press.

———. 1987. "Hierarchy and the Dual Marriage System in West Indian Society." In Jane Fishburne Collier and Sylvia Junko Yanagisako, eds., *Gender and Kinship: Essays Toward a Unified Analysis*, pp 163–196. Stanford: Stanford University Press.

———. 1988. *Kinship and Class in the West Indies: A Genealogical Study of Jamaica and Guyana.* Cambridge: Cambridge University Press.

———. 1995. *The Matrifocal Family.* New York: Routledge.

Snitnow, A. B., C. Stansell, and S. Thompson. 1983. "Introduction." In Ann Barr Snitow, Christine Stansell, and Sharon Thompson, eds., *Powers of Desire: The Politics of Sexuality*, pp. 9–47. New York: Monthly Review Press.

Sobo, E. 1993. *One Blood: The Jamaican Body.* Albany: State University of New York Press.

Spivak, C. G. 1990. *The Post-Colonial Critic: Interviews, Strategies, Dialogues.* London: Routledge.

Statistical Report. 2001. Health Information Unit. Ministry of Health, Nevis.

Stephens, D. and L. Phillips. 2003. "Freaks, Gold Diggers, Divas, and Dykes: The Sociohistorical Development of Adolescent African American Women's Sexual Scripts." *Sexuality and Culture*, pp. 3–49.

Strong, B., and C. DeVault. *Understanding Our Sexuality.* Saint Paul: West Publishing Company.

Sutton, J. W. 1987. *A Testimony of Triumph: A Narrative of the Life of James Sutton and Family in Nevis and St Kitts, 1920–1940.* Ontario: Edans Publishers.

Taussig, M. 1980. *The Devil and the Commodity Fetishism in South America.* Chapel Hill: University of North Carolina Press.

Tolman, D. 2002. *Dilemmas of Desire: Teenage Girls Talk about Sexuality.* Cambridge: Harvard University Press.

Trebay, G. 2003. "Taking Hip-hop Seriously." *New York Times*, May 20.

Vance, C. 1984. "Introduction." In Carole Vance, ed., *Pleasure and Danger: Exploring Female Sexuality*, pp. 1–27. Boston: Routledge and Kegan Paul.

———. 1989. "Social Construction Theory: Problems in this History of Sexuality." In A. van Kooten Nierkerk and T. Van Der Meer, eds., *Homosexuality, Which Homosexuality?* pp. 13–34. Amsterdam: An Dekker,

Weeks, J. 1977. *Coming Out: Homosexual Politics in Britain from the Nineteenth Century to the Present.* London: Quartet.

———. 1986. *Sexuality.* New York: Routledge.

Weisburd, C. 1984. "Household Food Production Systems Nevis, West Indies." (Master's thesis, Cornell University).

Wekker, G. 2006. *The Politics of Passion*. New York: Columbia University.

Weston, K. 1993. "Lesbian/Gay Studies in the House of Anthropology." *Annual Review of Anthropology* 23:339–367.

———. 1998. *Long Slow Burn: Sexuality and the Social Sciences*. New York: Routledge.

Wilkes, S. 2000. "A Survey: Reproductive Health and Teenage Pregnancy on Nevis." Manuscript.

Williams, R. 1977. *Marxism and Literature*. Oxford: Oxford University Press.

Wilson, A. 1988. "American Catalogues of Asian Brides." In Johnetta Cole, ed., *Anthropology for the Nineties*, pp. 114–125. New York: Free Press.

Wilson, M. 1994. *Crossing the Boundary: Black Women Survive Incest*. New York: Avalon Publishing.

World Bank. 2006. St Kitts and Nevis, in *ICT at a Glance Tables*. Retrieved April 11, 2007, from http://web.worldbank.org/WBSITE/EXTERNAL/ DATASTATISTICS/0,,contentMDK:20459133~menuPK:1192714~pagePK: 64133150~piPK:64133175~theSitePK:2

Index

Italicized page numbers refer to illustrations and tables.

About the Author

Debra Curtis teaches anthropology at Salve Regina University in Newport, RI. She is the mother of twin daughters who accompanied her to Nevis in 2003. She is married to Steve Butler and lives in Portsmouth, RI.

Breinigsville, PA USA
29 December 2010

252378BV00001B/56/P

9 780813 544304